Film Stars' Television Projects

ALSO BY RICHARD IRVIN

*George Burns Television Productions:
The Series and Pilots, 1950–1981* (McFarland, 2014)

Film Stars' Television Projects

Pilots and Series of 50+ Movie Greats, 1948–1985

RICHARD IRVIN

McFarland & Company, Inc., Publishers
Jefferson, North Carolina

ISBN (print) 978-1-4766-6916-8 ♾
ISBN (ebook) 978-1-4766-2843-1

LIBRARY OF CONGRESS CATALOGUING DATA ARE AVAILABLE

BRITISH LIBRARY CATALOGUING DATA ARE AVAILABLE

© 2017 Richard Irvin. All rights reserved

No part of this book may be reproduced or transmitted in any form or by any means, electronic or mechanical, including photocopying or recording, or by any information storage and retrieval system, without permission in writing from the publisher.

Front cover: Joan Crawford as a journalist in a scene from *The World and I* (author's collection)

Printed in the United States of America

*McFarland & Company, Inc., Publishers
Box 611, Jefferson, North Carolina 28640
www.mcfarlandpub.com*

Acknowledgments

I would like to thank the following individuals for their contributions to this work: Peter Bonerz, Douglas Cramer, John Fink, Paul Gregory, Tom Hallick, Bill Hayes, Stephany Hurkos, Peter Key, Christopher Knopf, Norman Lear, Andrew Lewis, Barry Oringer, Gail Parent, John Pasquin, Austin Pendleton, Roger Perry, Bill Persky, Robert Pierce, Steve Pritzker, Nancy Randle, Garry Settimi, Davey Davison Silverman, Steve Stevens, Gay Talese, Joan Van Ark, Susan Watson, William Wellman, Jr., and Carole Wells.

I am also extremely grateful to the following institutions for permitting access to their archives: UCLA Library Special Collections for access to the Ann Morrison Chapin Papers (1922–1980s), Mort Fine Papers (1950–1968), Larry Gelbart Papers, Shirley Jones Papers (1942–1980), Herbert Leonard Papers (1957–1977), Norman Lessing Papers (1943–1982), Daniel Mainwaring Papers (1930–1970) and Steve Pritzker Papers (1967–1986); UCLA Television Archives; University of Michigan Special Collections Library for access to the Orson Welles–Oja Kodar Papers (1910–1998); Academy of Motion Pictures Arts and Sciences, Margaret Herrick Library, for access to material in the Bert Granet, Buster Keaton and Mae West collections; Harry Ransom Humanities Research Center, the University of Texas at Austin, for information from the Gloria Swanson Papers; the University of Texas at Austin for access to the James Pinckney Miller Papers (1939–1999); Wisconsin Center for Film and Theater Research, Wisconsin Historical Society, for information from the Sidney Sheldon Papers and the William Spier and June Havoc Papers (1931–1963); American Heritage Center at the University of Wyoming for material from the William Dozier, Jane Powell and Harry Ackerman collections; Dartmouth College for material from the Harry Ackerman collection; Popular Culture Library, Bowling Green State University, for copies of various television scripts; Library of Congress, Motion Picture and TV Reading Room; Syracuse University Libraries for information from the Ted Key Papers; Thousand Oaks Library for information from the Broadcasting Collection, the American Radio Archives Collection; the Billy Rose Theatre Division of the New York Public Library; and the University of Illinois, Urbana-Champaign Script Collection, for copies of various television pilot scripts.

Table of Contents

Acknowledgments v
Preface 1
Introduction 3

Fred Astaire and Ginger Rogers	7	Alan Ladd	95
Joan Blondell	15	Hedy Lamarr	101
Stephen Boyd	22	Janet Leigh	105
Claudette Colbert	25	Peter Lorre	110
Gary Cooper	28	Myrna Loy	114
Joan Crawford	30	Chico, Groucho and Harpo Marx	118
Bette Davis	35	Roddy McDowall	128
Irene Dunne	45	Ethel Merman	134
Nelson Eddy and Jeanette MacDonald	48	Pat O'Brien	137
Douglas Fairbanks, Jr.	51	Maureen O'Hara	141
Jose Ferrer	57	Anthony Perkins	145
Geraldine Fitzgerald	61	Walter Pidgeon	147
Joan Fontaine	64	Jane Powell	150
Janet Gaynor	68	Basil Rathbone	153
Stewart Granger	70	Edward G. Robinson	155
Kathryn Grayson	73	Jane Russell	157
Susan Hayward	76	George Sanders	160
Betty Hutton	79	Randolph Scott	162
Van Johnson	84	Zachary Scott	164
Buster Keaton	91	Ann Sheridan	166
		Alexis Smith	170

Barbara Stanwyck	173	Mae West	200
Gloria Swanson	182	Esther Williams	208
Shirley Temple	187	Shelley Winters	210
Orson Welles	189		

Chapter Notes 215

Bibliography 222

Index 223

Preface

Often overlooked in the biographies of movie stars from the 1920s, '30s, '40s and '50s are their attempts at television stardom. Many film stars from the "Golden Age of Hollywood" tried to get their own TV series after their movie careers slowed or became virtually nonexistent. This work looks at the "forgotten" TV pilots and the (mostly) short-lived television series of more than 50 movie stars. Fred Astaire as a horse breeder and trainer, Bette Davis as an Eurasian archvillain, the Marx Brothers as angels, Mae West dishing out advice to help people with their personal problems—these are just some of the TV projects involving motion picture stars described in this book.

While the list of movie stars described is somewhat arbitrary, they all have in common at least one attempt at starring in a TV pilot that did not result in a series. Golden Age stars like Cary Grant, Katharine Hepburn and Clark Gable avoided television series work altogether. As Grant once remarked, "I have refused to do TV because I feel I am a part of the motion picture industry and I can't see any reason for helping a competitor—and in my opinion TV is a competitor."[1] Gable, somewhat echoing Grant, once said, "TV is a wonderful medium for sports, and a fine showcase for young talent. A lot of people, some of them friends of mine, are on TV and have given fine performances. But TV has hurt the picture business, and I don't want to be a contributing factor by being on it. I don't want to get in it; you're too limited in story and scope."[2] Actor Gregory Peck noted, "I would never do a series. Once the characterization is set, the actor has to play the same part every week—which to me has no appeal."[3]

On the other hand, several feature film stars enjoyed as much, if not more, success on television as they had in films. Robert Montgomery, Lucille Ball, Dick Powell and Loretta Young ventured into the TV industry in its early days and were not only popular but also became wealthy in the process. Robert Montgomery was one of the first movie stars to enter television on a full scale, hosting and producing his own anthology series on NBC beginning in 1950, and his initial goal was to build a relationship between movies and television by gaining the rights to various movie properties and turning them into episodes of his series. He bought rights to such features as *The Letter, Kitty*

Foyle and *Our Town* and had stars like Madeleine Carroll and himself as the leads in the TV versions.

The story of Lucille Ball and her then-husband Desi Arnaz is a legendary tale about how both actors came to star on the hit situation comedy *I Love Lucy* and form their own production company, Desilu, to make their series (and others). Loretta Young followed somewhat the same model with her self-titled anthology show she produced with her spouse. Dick Powell initially signed with Official Films in 1952 to be one of the rotating hosts of *Four Star Playhouse*. (Originally the other hosts were to be Charles Boyer, Rosalind Russell and Joel McCrea, but the latter two declined to appear and were replaced by David Niven and Ida Lupino. Powell, Boyer, and Niven formed their own television production company, Four Star Productions, to produce numerous series in the 1950s and '60s.)

The television attempts of the motion picture stars profiled in this book fall somewhere between the two extremes of those who avoided television altogether and those who flourished in the new medium. As will be seen, many of these stars had ambivalent feelings about having their own series, but they all tried with varying degrees of success.

Introduction

During the second half of the twentieth century, many movie stars from earlier decades attempted their own television series. This book details the endeavors of more than 50 such stars. As feature film stars from the '20s, '30s, '40s and '50s were aging and the television industry was having an impact on movies with fewer films being produced, several big screen stars ventured into television. Most wanted to continue their fame in the new medium as well as make money in a venture that could be very lucrative, particularly if a series lasted for a few seasons and could be rerun. Some stars wanted to repeat the successes of Lucille Ball and Desi Arnaz or of Dick Powell and his partners David Niven and Charles Boyer in forming a production company to make their own series and thus have some control over their careers.

The television series careers of the film stars described in this book took one of four basic trajectories. Most (for example, Joan Crawford, Hedy Lamarr, Myrna Loy and Edward G. Robinson) made one or more pilots but were never able to get their own series. Bette Davis, Joan Blondell and Van Johnson made several pilots that didn't sell but finally prevailed with a project that was picked up (but proved to be short-lived). Still others, like Groucho Marx and Shirley Temple, had some success early in their TV careers but were never able to repeat that success. Finally, actors like Douglas Fairbanks, Jr., Orson Welles and Alan Ladd wanted to become television producers *à la* Powell, Lucy and Desi, but failed in their attempts.

Because appearing on a weekly television series was hard work (making 39 episodes in a typical season in the industry's early days), not every movie actor was cut out for starring in his or her own TV show. Also, the pace of making a television show was much quicker than moviemaking, and some film stars had difficulty adapting to the faster pace. One way many motion picture stars found to avoid appearing as a continuing character on their own series was to host and occasionally act on an anthology series that featured a "story of the week" with a different cast of characters. Filming introductions and closings for a number of installments of this type of series was comparatively easy and portraying different characters on some of the episodes did not pin the star down to the same character each week. The first attempts at TV fame for many of the motion picture stars profiled in this work were as hosts of a potential anthology series.

Rather than hosting a TV anthology, other movie stars endeavored to become television personalities on a variety or a game show and essentially bring their silver screen persona to TV. Some actors and actresses took their big screen persona one step further by playing a version of their movie star image as a continuing character on a proposed television comedy or drama. A few even attempted to turn one of their iconic movie characters into a main character on a television series.

First radio and then television gave rise to two different types of series "packagers": the producer-packager and the talent-agent-packager. The former developed his own idea for a series, recruited talent to star in the project, sold it to a sponsor or network, and then produced each show. The agent-packager sold his or others' ideas for a series along with the talent for the show and recruited a production company to make the series. The demarcations between these two types of packagers were not always clear with producer-packagers often using talent agents to sell their series ideas and with agent-packagers becoming *de facto* producers. The Screen Actors Guild had a policy that prohibited talent agencies from engaging in production, but the Guild did grant waivers on a case-by-case basis.

In TV's early days, producer-packagers included Hal Roach Studios, Jack Chertok Productions and Bing Crosby Enterprises, and later Desilu, Four Star Productions and Goodson-Todman. One of the most prolific agent-packagers in '50s TV, Don Sharpe, negotiated a deal to establish Four Star Productions with Dick Powell, Charles Boyer and David Niven each having an ownership interest in the company. He also managed a deal with CBS to air *I Love Lucy*. Sharpe became Desilu Productions' exclusive representative and was essential in having Desilu produce, in addition to the *Lucy* series, *Our Miss Brooks* with Eve Arden. He also was instrumental in helping Douglas Fairbanks, Jr., form his own production company.

The two largest agent-packagers in the early television industry were MCA and the William Morris Agency. In 1952, MCA formed its own production company, Revue Productions, to produce and market TV properties featuring their clients after the Screen Actors Guild gave the firm a blanket waiver to do so. One Revue series, *General Electric Theater*, was hosted by Ronald Reagan during the 1950s and early 1960s. Several episodes of that series were pilots starring MCA clients. The William Morris Agency developed a special relationship with Four Star Productions and directed its clients to that company.

Introduction 5

Most of the television pilots and series described herein were either done by a producer-packager such as Hal Roach Studios, Desilu, Four Star or Screen Gems (Columbia Pictures' TV subsidiary) or by an agent-packager like MCA-Revue. One other producer who figured prominently in the initiation of movie-star pilots and series was Aaron Spelling. As a writer-producer, he got his start working for Four Star on *Dick Powell's Zane Grey Theater*, *The Dick Powell Show* and *Burke's Law*. After leaving Four Star, he formed various production companies with partners like Danny Thomas, Leonard Goldberg and Douglas S. Cramer. As noted in several of the profiles, Spelling had a knack for convincing feature film stars including Bette Davis, Barbara Stanwyck and Van Johnson to try a television series.

There are a variety of reasons why the big screen stars profiled in this book, for the most part, failed to have their projects turn into a series. With the exception of Groucho Marx's *You Bet Your Life* and Barbara Stanwyck's *The Big Valley*, if film actors did eventually star in their own series, it usually lasted for only a few seasons. Some luminaries like Gary Cooper and Joan Crawford were extremely ambivalent about doing a TV series in the first place and backed out of various deals for their own show. Others were unable to find an advertiser willing to sponsor their series. In certain cases, the network could not find a suitable time slot for a movie star's show.

Many involved in the entertainment business have suggested that one of the chief reasons motion picture actors and actresses had difficulty landing their own TV shows is that movie stars are "larger than life." While they establish a presence on the silver screen, their star image does not translate well to the small screen where their personas have to be less extraordinary. This theory seems to apply mainly to female movie stars who attempted a television series in the 1950s and '60s. Other than Lucille Ball, Donna Reed and Loretta Young, movie actresses had little luck starring in their own shows during this period. If they did succeed in getting a series on the air, it was more likely to be a situation comedy than a dramatic series.

The "larger than life" screen personas of actresses such as Bette Davis and Mae West negatively impacted their ability to obtain a TV series. Certainly, West's sex symbol image turned away potential advertisers and networks from her proposed television projects. Desi Arnaz pointed out another reason movie actresses failed as lead characters on television shows, particularly dramas: In a 1962 news article, he indicated that most television writers (and he could have added most producers, network executives and advertising heads) were men. He went on to say that most of the writing that had been done since World War II was concerned with the experiences of men, and women played subsidiary or incidental roles.[1]

Of the 52 actors and actresses profiled herein, 28 are women and only one, Barbara Stanwyck, eventually got the lead in her own dramatic series, *The Big Valley,* which lasted more than a few seasons.

Fred Astaire and Ginger Rogers

"Can't act, can't sing, balding, can dance a little" was the verdict after Fred Astaire's first screen test. Astaire made his movie debut in 1933 in a film called *Dancing Lady* which starred Joan Crawford, Clark Gable and Franchot Tone, Crawford's husband at the time. Astaire would go on to make many musicals during the '30s, '40s and '50s, most notably with his dancing partner Ginger Rogers. The incomparable duo first appeared in the 1933 movie *Flying Down to Rio*. In 1935's *Top Hat*, Astaire portrayed Jerry Travers, who goes to London to headline a show and meets Dale Tremont (Rogers). In their final film together, *The Barkleys of Broadway* (1949), Astaire and Rogers played a husband-and-wife comedy team. Fred and Ginger would rehearse their routines for hours so that on film, their dancing appeared graceful and effortless. As has often been said, Rogers made Astaire appear sexy; while Astaire made Rogers appear classy. Astaire's screen image was that of a suave singer-dancer; Rogers' persona evolved into the self-reliant girl next door.

Unlike many of his contemporaries who entered television, at least as guest stars on anthology series, in the early '50s, Astaire came to TV rather late in his career, mainly because he was still appearing in major films during the 1950s. For the most part, he continued to star in musical comedies with leading ladies other than Ginger Rogers. In 1951 he appeared with Jane Powell in *Royal Wedding*, set at the time of the royal marriage of then–Princess Elizabeth to Prince Philip. A few years later, he starred with Cyd Charisse in *The Band Wagon* (1953), in which he played a stage and screen celebrity hoping for a Broadway comeback. In 1957, he made *Funny Face* co-starring with Audrey Hepburn and *Silk Stockings*, a musical version of *Ninotchka*, with Cyd Charisse. Not until that year did he appear on television: In "Imp on a Cobweb Leash," an episode of *General Electric Theater*, he played conservative businessman J. Willingham Bardley. His character wanted to be president of the firm for which he worked until a mysterious imp appears and turns him into a practical joker who learns to love life. Astaire chose *G.E. Theater* for his first television debut since his talent agency MCA produced the series through its subsidiary Revue.

In 1958, there were rumors that Astaire might appear on a weekly variety series, on NBC Saturday nights as a replacement for *Club Oasis*, a 30-minute show that presented itself as a nightclub with a different entertainment personality hosting each week. But nothing came of this purported deal. Astaire did star in a one-hour live television special in the fall of that year: *An Evening with Fred Astaire*, airing October 17, 1958, was a critical success and received respectable ratings. Astaire was 59 at the time. The special won nine Emmy Awards and was the first show to be recorded on color videotape. Astaire did three other such specials over the years: *Another Evening with Fred Astaire* (1959), *Astaire Time* (1960) and *The Fred Astaire Show* (1968).

When Astaire appeared on TV as other than a singer-dancer, viewers seemed to be less interested in his performances. However, given his desire to work weeks on perfecting his dance routines and given the physical demands on a dancer's body as a dancer advances in age, it is not surprising that Astaire did not want to host a weekly variety show but instead opted to display his acting talents in a TV series.

In 1961, after *Astaire Time*, he signed on for his own weekly series as host and sometimes actor on ABC's *Alcoa Premiere*. Alcoa was hopeful that viewers would tune in just to see Fred even if he wasn't singing or dancing. When he was approached about doing the series, Astaire commented that he "didn't want to do it the cliché way, of just standing up there and introducing a show. But the way we do it I'm a storyteller on the scene. ... The thing that gets me most about TV is the time, the pace—and you want it that way. I love movies, they're the greatest of all, but the approach [between films and television] is totally different."[1]

About the series, Astaire told entertainment correspondent Army Archerd, "The shows will not be 'messages,' but we hope they will be of consequence and contribute something. Alcoa is great about the ideas—just as Chrysler was great in giving me a free hand in the three musical shows."[2] Astaire starred in two first-season episodes. In "Moment of Decision" (November 7, 1961), he played a magician who feels unwelcome when he purchases a house next to an estate with a snobbish owner. The neighbor bets Fred's character that he can't escape from an airtight cellar. In the February 1962 installment "Mr. Easy," Fred played a Wall Street tycoon who retires at the height of his success.

During the anthology's second season, Astaire starred in three episodes. He appeared as a war hero turned con man who helps an Air Force buddy's family in "Guest in the House," the Devil, who runs his domain like a Madison Avenue advertising firm, in "Mr. Lucifer," and a down-on-his-luck musician who thinks he may have murdered a fellow musician in "Blues for a Hanging." Alcoa pulled its sponsorship of the series due to its ratings and a new corporate policy no longer sponsoring entertainment shows. In addition to episodes starring the likes of John Wayne, the series may be best remembered for premiering the pilot "Seven Against the Sea," which would become the Ernest Borgnine teleseries *McHale's Navy*.

Publicity photograph of Fred Astaire, dated September 4, 1964, and released by NBC to advertise Astaire's "first TV musical comedy," "Think Pretty," a pilot for a proposed weekly situation comedy. It was broadcast on October 2, 1964.

After the demise of *Alcoa Premiere*, Astaire pursued a situation comedy to be produced by Revue. The half-hour sitcom, suitably titled *The Fred Astaire Show*, would combine humor with occasional music. "This is the only thing I haven't done," remarked the actor, "and that was what attracted me."[3] Patterned somewhat on Astaire's real life at the time, the comedy, tagged for the 1964–65 season on NBC, was to be about a retired actor-dancer who owns a record company. In real life, Astaire did own Ava Records, named after his daughter.

The pilot aired as an installment of *Bob Hope Presents the Chrysler Theatre*. Titled "Think Pretty," the show, helmed by Jack Arnold, was scripted by Garry Marshall and Jerry Belson from a story by Bill Persky and Sam Denoff. All four writers were known for scripting episodes of *The Dick Van Dyke Show*. Garry Marshall later created many hit comedies, including *Happy Days*.

Astaire played Fred Addams, a record company executive and former movie star and dancer, who is attempting to sign the nation's hottest comedian Mickey Marshall (Louie Nye) to his Addams Record label for a comedy album. Addams needs a hit recording to keep his company in the black. Marshall's manager, Tony Franklin (Barrie Chase, Astaire's dance partner on his TV specials), a former professional dancer, wants the comedian to re-sign with his current label, and Marshall relies on her sage advice.

Fred and his assistant Don Corbin (Roger Perry) meet with Tony at a nightclub where Marshall performs. Fred asks her to dance, and, while dancing, she informs him that she is not interested in having her client sign with Addams Records. Fred decides to record a live comedy album about surfing with Mickey at the club to show Tony the kind of work his company can do. To keep her occupied and away from the club while the recording is being made, Fred takes Tony to his studio where he sings a new song, "Think Pretty." Tony becomes irate when she finds that Mickey injured his hip while doing the record and is in the hospital. Fred and Don go to Mickey's hospital room to complete the album. After hearing the recording, Tony relents and permits Addams to sign her client. Fred and Tony dance to the "Think Pretty" record, an original composition written for the pilot.

In addition to the pilot focusing on the Fred Addams character's work life, there are scenes of the character's home life. Addams lives in a mansion with a maid named Hannah (Doris Kemper) and his teenage daughter, Lori (Linda Foster). He has a cat named Martha at home and one named George at work.

Roger Perry, who played Astaire's assistant, remembers that making the show was great. "Fred Astaire has to have been one of the nicest men in the business.... He was genuine ... and a genius to boot.... The other plus was

Louis Nye.... I have never laughed so hard in my life. Every day, he was hilarious. And it wasn't forced, wasn't 'put on.' He was just a very funny man."[4]

Despite the talented writers associated with the pilot, it had its weaknesses. Barrie Chase told Astaire, "It's probably the worst script I've ever read. This is just awful." Astaire replied, "Well, thanks, because I worked with the writers on it." To which Chase responded, "This show has what I call ingredients ... it has a dance number at the end of the show, and other ingredients, but that doesn't make a show."[5]

Although *The Fred Astaire Show* never became a series, comedy writer Ron Friedman, who crafted episodes of *The Andy Griffith Show*, *All in the Family*, *The Odd Couple* and *Happy Days*, later developed a treatment for another situation comedy starring Astaire. Like the one described above, this treatment was also based on an aspects of Astaire's real life: his love for horses and horse racing. (When it was written, whether it was ever presented to Astaire, I do not know.) Astaire was passionate about horse racing and in 1980, seven years before his death, he married jockey Robyn Smith.

In the presentation for (the other) *The Fred Astaire Show*, Astaire would play Thomas Ellison "Tommy" Rittenhouse, a former playboy from a wealthy, conservative family who now spends his time training and breeding race horses. Because of his career choice, his family has cut him off financially. Tommy owns Lucky Star Farm. Living nearby is one of his clients, Alicia Trowbridge Hapgood, a young widow with a daughter named Alexandra or Lexa for short. The daughter, 15, loves horses and Tommy, much to her mother's dismay. Lexa likes riding one of the horses at Tommy's farm, Spit 'n' Polish—a crazy horse with his own individual spirit. Lexa's mother owns Spit 'n' Polish. Lydia Baylor Trowbridge is Alicia's mother and Lexa's grandmother, a warm, outgoing, openly adventurous woman who very much likes Tommy. Often Lydia and Tommy conspire to outwit Alicia, her stuffy friends and her attorney Russell Prescott, who disapproves of Tommy, racing and horses. The African-American Wishwell Watson, a former entertainer, helps Tommy run the farm.

Friedman summed up his presentation thusly:

> This series will also show much of the inside view of the racing world—from horse auctions to jockey selection, horse training and the majestic, risk-taking sport of racing itself. But all stories will devolve about the relationship of Tommy Rittenhouse to the interesting, attractive people—and—horses named Against this background, which also features a singular horse like Spit 'n' Polish and stars so sophisticated a charmer as Fred Astaire functioning in stories which concern a world he knows intimately, we'll all be legends in our own time.[6]

Astaire never attempted another television series of his own. But in the final season of Robert Wagner's *It Takes a Thief*, he portrayed Alistair Mundy, the con-artist father of Wagner's character Alexander Mundy in five episodes. According to Astaire, Wagner phoned and asked him to appear on the show. "I'm always flattered to be asked. This is an out-and-out ball to do. I love to work with Bob. He's a heck of a nice guy, dedicated, and I've known him since he's a kid."[7]

Astaire was nominated for an Academy Award for Best Supporting Actor for his portrayal of a con man in the 1974 film *The Towering Inferno*. His final movie appearance was in *Ghost Story* (1981) with Melvyn Douglas and Douglas Fairbanks, Jr.

After starring with Astaire in their memorable 1930s movies, Rogers branched out to become a dramatic and comic actress in her own right in features such as *Kitty Foyle* (1940) for which she won a Best Actress Oscar. Her other movie appearances included *Roxie Hart* (1942), *I'll Be Seeing You* (1944) and *Dreamboat* (1952). Rogers starred in very few musicals after the ones she had done with him.

As with several other movie stars profiled below, Rogers had very mixed feelings about becoming a TV series regular, particularly during the 1950s when the typical series produced 39 episodes a season. She attempted various formats for her own show, but none ever seemed to work out to her liking.

In late 1951, CBS negotiated a five-year deal with Rogers for a 30-minute series which was expected to premiere on the network some time after April 1, 1952. While a specific format was not set, the network indicated that Rogers would sing, dance and/or act in each episode, but she would not be appearing as the same character each week. The network also said that she might do condensed versions of movies such as *Kitty Foyle* if the TV rights to these films could be obtained. Rogers and the network still had to determine if the series would be filmed or aired live. CBS bought approximately 150 story properties including novels, plays and musical comedies from which to select material for the show. The actress was to receive $3500 for each installment and 50 percent of the net residuals for reruns. Although a deal was negotiated, no contract was ever signed by the star. About a year after announcement of the arrangement, Rogers put an end to the deal because CBS would not, according to the actress, permit her to select the stories in which she would appear. The network said that the real reason the deal collapsed was because Rogers was too busy making movies to have time to star in a TV series.

Another year went by and Rogers looked at doing a CBS series produced by John Guedel, who produced Groucho Marx's *You Bet Your Life*. It was tentatively titled *For the First Time*. The concept was to recruit actors from community theaters across the country as a supporting cast for Rogers. Each week there would be different actors recommended by drama coaches and theater operators. No series resulted.

Speaking to *Variety* in 1955, Rogers remarked that she was "a little nervous about 39 pictures in a row." She also said that she didn't like the idea of simply hosting a series, feeling that "you become a well-dressed broom, and you don't contribute any talent."[8] Rogers was under consideration as one of the hosts of Dick Powell's proposed reboot of *Four Star Playhouse* in 1957 but apparently maintained her position on not wanting such a role.

Being courted for a series by both CBS and NBC, Rogers was in discussions with producer Harry Ackerman in 1956 and 1957 to star in a comedy series produced by his Ticonderoga Productions for CBS. The series was to be called *Love That Channel*. Given Ackerman's background as a network executive, the situation comedy may have dealt with working at a television station or network.

In talking about the Ackerman proposal as well as the possibility of alternating with Dinah Shore on NBC's *Chevy Show* in 1957, Rogers said, "Ten weeks ago I turned down the offer made my agent by Henry Jaffe [producer of *The Chevy Show*], but they persist in keeping those reports alive. It's unfair, unkind, unjust. Jaffe made an offer, we didn't like it; there was no counter-offer." She added, "Every summer breeze has brought Harry Ackerman into my house with a pilot script. Unfortunately they have not been things I want to do.... I would enjoy starring in about six hour-long live shows."[9]

Speaking of "live" shows, NBC apparently picked up on this comment and made a pilot of a half-hour music-variety show starring Rogers in December 1958. Written by Alan Handley and Will Glickman, it was directed and produced by Handley, who previously did the Dinah Shore variety shows. Featured in the pilot were Ricardo Montalban, Burr Tillstrom and his puppets Kukla and Ollie, the Ray Charles Singers, dancer Dante di Paulo and the Nelson Riddle Orchestra. NBC thought about scheduling the series on Tuesday nights at 8:30 or on Fridays at 8:30 but apparently nothing worked out.

In 1960, Rogers seemed on the verge of becoming a television star on her own weekly sitcom *The Ginger Rogers Show*. It would be produced by Twentieth Century-Fox and Rogers' own company, Lincoln Productions, for a premiere in fall 1960. Norman Z. McLeod directed the pilot based on a script written by Valentine Davies, known for writing *Miracle on 34th Street*.

On the series, set in San Francisco, Rogers would play twin sisters Margaret Harcourt, a writer, and Elizabeth Harcourt, a fashion designer (and the more free-spirited of the two). Charlie Ruggles appeared as their uncle, Eli Harcourt. Upon returning from Spain, Margaret learns that her sister has fallen in love with Mario Chellini (Cesare Danova), but he has dumped her.

She decides to teach Mario a lesson by pretending she is Liz and acting like the kind of woman he is really attracted to. She plans to make him regret that he broke up with her sister. Gardner McKay, who was starring in the hit ABC series *Adventures in Paradise*, appeared as himself as Margaret's date at a party to make Mario jealous. Later, Liz sees Margaret dating Mario dressed in clothes like the ones she wears and goes to the party that her sister and Mario are attending. She changes places with Margaret and, when Mario asks Liz to marry her, she says "no."

At the end of the pilot, Ginger Rogers described the format of the proposed series, saying that in most episodes only one of the twins will be featured to give a greater variety to the stories. Liz will be involved in comedy situations, Margaret in more dramatic stories, but occasionally both characters would appear on the same episode as they did in the pilot.

The pilot, which never sold, was eventually broadcast on CBS on July 22, 1963, as part of *Vacation Playhouse*, a summer replacement series featuring unsold pilots.

Rogers's final attempt at her own series was in 1972 when producer-game show host Ralph Edwards wanted to put together a syndicated talk show with Ginger as host, patterned after the successful Dinah Shore talk fest. However, as with her other attempts, nothing came of this endeavor.

Rogers' last TV appearance was in the 1987 *Hotel* episode "Hail and Farewell" where she played a psychic. The actress passed away in 1995 at 83-years of age.

Joan Blondell

Joan Blondell is one of the most underappreciated and versatile actresses from the Golden Years of Hollywood. She began her film career in the 1930s, appearing in such features as *The Public Enemy* (1931), playing Mamie, the girlfriend of James Cagney's friend Matt, and *Gold Diggers of 1933* in which she appeared as a torch singer. In the 1940s, the actress was featured as Aunt Sissy in *A Tree Grows in Brooklyn* (1945) and as Zeena, a mind reader, in 1947's *Nightmare Alley* with Tyrone Power. She played Katharine Hepburn's friend and co-worker in the Tracy-Hepburn romantic comedy *Desk Set* (1957). Toward the end of her career, she played supporting roles in *Grease* (1978) and in the 1979 remake of *The Champ*. As she aged, Blondell gracefully transitioned from a leading actress to a character actress unlike many of the other leading ladies from the 1930s. Her star image also changed from a warm-hearted, wisecracking dame to a warm-hearted, wisecracking mother or mother surrogate.

As described in the actress' biography,

> Hers was the three-dimensional face on a two-dimensional screen. She was full of surprises, one moment as tough as Joan Crawford, the next as fragile as Margaret Sullavan, and the next as saucy as Mae West.... She could even cry on cue, a talent sorely envied by Bette Davis. She excelled in a wide variety of genre pictures, including mysteries, romantic comedy, film noir, musicals, Westerns, screwball comedies, family dramas and satire.[1]

Her first husband, cinematographer George Barnes, was an Academy Award winner for Alfred Hitchcock's *Rebecca*. Blondell's second spouse, actor Dick Powell, went on to head one of the most successful television production companies in the 1950s and '60s, Four Star Productions. Her third husband, Mike Todd, won an Academy Award for *Around the World in 80 Days* (1956). Blondell divorced Powell before he made his millions as the head of Four Star and divorced Todd before he became rich and famous. As a result, in order to earn a living, she had to ply her trade as an actress for most of her life.

The actress did become a supporting player in two relatively short-lived TV series; she attempted many more pilots as either the lead character or a supporting one. Her first success as a regular on a TV series was in ABC's

Here Comes the Brides in 1968. In this comedy-adventure series set in 1870s Seattle, Washington, she played Carlotta "Lottie" Hatfield, bar and hotel owner as well as a cook. It ran for two seasons. Blondell's character helped to settle problems when lumberjacks brought 100 marriageable women to Seattle as possible brides for the men. Nominated for an Emmy as Best Actress in a Drama for the first season of the series, she lost to Barbara Bain from *Mission: Impossible.*

Blondell later became a regular on the NBC drama *Banyon,* set in 1937 Los Angeles. Robert Forster starred as private detective Myles Banyon with Blondell playing Peggy Revere, the owner of a secretarial school. (Hermione Gingold had that role in the pilot.) Revere's school was located in the same building as Banyon's detective agency, and she provided him with a new secretary each week. *Banyon* lasted for only half a season in 1972.

Blondell's first attempt at a series of her own was a pilot originally titled *Calamity Jane* but changed to *The Pussyfootin' Rocks* when aired as an episode of *Schlitz Playhouse of Stars* on November 21, 1952. In this comedy–Western, Blondell, assuming her wisecracking dame persona, appeared as Calamity Jane along with Buddy Ebsen. (Tom Ewell originally was announced for the part but Ebsen took over.) Written by Luther Davis, produced by Edward Lewis Productions and directed by Robert Aldrich, the pilot was shot in Mexico City. The storyline had Calamity Jane meeting a smuggler (Ebsen) who is transporting illegal aliens into the U.S. He explains that the rocks she sees moving are really immigrants covered with canvas. A gang of masked robbers captures Jane, the smuggler and the immigrants. However, she manages to escape as the U.S. Border Patrol comes to the rescue. Actress Kathleen Freeman appeared as the robbers, the Ripplehissian brothers, as well as their mother.

Joan Blondell's publicity photograph for her final television series, NBC's *Banyon,* which ran from September 1972 to January 1973. The actress appeared in eight of the 15 episodes.

In 1954, Blondell made a pilot for Revue called *The Joan Blondell Show*. She played Joan Preston, a one-time Broadway star, married to banker Ted Preston (John Sutton), who, for some unexplained reason, had a British accent. Also in the cast were Ellen Corby as Frankie, their maid; Susan Whitney as Ellen, the Prestons' daughter; and Rodney Bell as Huey Duckworth, Ted's banking colleague. Joan Preston, who tends to overdramatize, thinks that the magic has gone out of her marriage. She plans a romantic evening with her husband to celebrate their fifteenth wedding anniversary. However, Ted works late at the office and misses the dinner at home. He had given his credit card to Huey Duckworth, who was taking wealthy Henrietta Mosley (Madge Kennedy), a potential client, to dinner. The following day, the busboy from the restaurant where Huey and Henrietta had dinner comes by the Prestons to drop off a purse he thinks belongs to Joan. Joan concludes that her husband was not working late but instead took another woman out to dinner. Confusion ensues with Ellen, Joan and then Ted all visiting Henrietta Mosley's house to find out what really happened the night before. Finally, Huey explains to Joan about the prior evening.

The pilot was directed by Rod Amateau and written by Joe Connelly and Bob Mosher (creators of *Leave It to Beaver*). NBC considered adding *The Joan Blondell Show* to its Saturday night line-up in place of a series called *The Duke*, but that never took place. The pilot eventually aired as an installment of *General Electric Theater* on June 5, 1955, under the title "Star in the House."

In 1959, Blondell landed the lead role in a comedy pilot developed by Jess Oppenheimer, one of the creators of *I Love Lucy*. Called *The Jacksons*, the sitcom, earmarked for the 1959–60 season on NBC, concerned a wife (Joan, assuming her warm-hearted mother image) whose husband Pat (J. Pat O'Malley), a factory manager, had just retired and whose daughter Marilyn had recently married. Unusual for a TV show at the time, Joan and her fictional husband shared the same bed. The couple now finds that they have little to do, particularly Joan. She goes to see a doctor because she's depressed. In the waiting room, she meets a pregnant woman who is having problems knitting baby clothes. Joan decides she can help but, inevitably, Pat finds the knitting and assumes that his wife is fantasizing that she is pregnant. The truth comes out when the couple visits the doctor again. As the doctor remarks, Joan's maternal instincts still need to be satisfied which, if the pilot had become a series, no doubt would have gotten her into many funny situations. Written by Oppenheimer and Leo Solomon, the pilot was helmed by John Rich.

About the same time, Blondell was under consideration to co-star in a pilot to be produced by Desilu, *You're Only Young Twice*. The concept was kind of the opposite of *The Jacksons*: In this proposed series, a retired couple has to continually deal with the problems of their children and grandchildren. Actor Melvyn Douglas was a candidate to play the husband opposite Blondell, but the roles ultimately went to George Murphy and Martha Scott.

During the final season of *The Real McCoys* with Walter Brennan and Richard Crenna, she appeared as Aunt Winifred Jordan on three episodes of that series. Winifred was Louise Howard's (Janet DeGore) visiting aunt. Louise was a love interest for Richard Crenna's character Luke McCoy after Kathleen Nolan (who had played Crenna's wife Kate) left the comedy. Reverting to her wisecracking dame persona, Blondell's Aunt Win was an outgoing, sexy former Broadway dancer to whom the men on the series were attracted and who made the women jealous.

When Vivian Vance left *The Lucy Show*, Blondell was cast in back-to-back episodes as a possible replacement for the Vance character. She played Joan Brenner, Lucy's next-door neighbor, an actress. However, apparently Ball did not get along well with Joan. During the taping of the second episode, the two actresses traded insults with Lucy saying, "I thought you were a comedienne. Can't you turn any of those lines to be funny?" Blondell responded, "If they were written in that vein, I could do it, but these are straight lines. There is nothing I can do except feed *you* the lines."[2] The audience was shocked when the scene ended and Lucy told Joan that the scene stunk. Joan replied, "F--- you, Lucille Ball!" and walked out. Needless to say, Blondell did not become a regular on *The Lucy Show*.

Set in Hollywood during the 1920s, *Hooray for Hollywood* was a sitcom pilot for CBS shot in late 1963 and aired on June 22, 1964. It focused on the experiences of Jerome P. Baggley (Herschel Bernardi), head of World Goliath Studios. Blondell played Miss Zilke, his ever-loyal secretary who also narrated the show. In the credits, it said, "Also starring Miss Joan Blondell." The co-stars included Marvin Kaplan as Munroe, Baggley's brother-in-law and lackey, and Joyce Jameson as Vonda Renee, the studio's biggest star. The storyline dealt with Baggley's competitor, Leviathan Pictures, learning that Vonda's contract would expire soon and wanting to entice her away from Goliath Studios for $1 million. When Baggley realizes this, he offers her a $3 million movie about Marie Antoinette. The bankers who support the studio learn of the money involved and threaten to fire Baggley. He informs them that the new contract Vonda signed is with him personally and not with the studio, and so they beg him to stay. Produced by Warren Lewis, the pilot was directed by Barry Shear based on a script by Sheldon Keller. It was a joint production of Desilu and Don Sharpe Productions.

In 1966, Blondell co-starred in a comedy pilot based on a *McCall's* magazine story by Harriet Frank, Jr. The project, called *And Baby Makes Three* (also known as *Baby Crazy*), starred James Stacy as Peter Martin Cooper, a new pediatrician setting up practice at a medical center complex. Dr. Cooper's girlfriend Jennie Winton (Lynn Loring) is a student nurse. Blondell appeared as Joan Terry who, while interviewing for the doctor's nurse's position, tells him that "my mother drank and Father took in laundry." She sells herself as a mother surrogate, saying that she will bring maturity to an office headed by a young doctor. Also practicing in the complex was Dr. Charles Norwood (Gavin MacLeod), a dentist.

A Little League Team visits Dr. Cooper's office. Jimmy, a team member and the doctor's nephew, complains of a problem with his elbow. Terry gives him pointers on pitching the ball to reduce stress on his elbow. She then accompanies the team to the game to help them.

The series title came from the title of the college thesis Dr. Cooper had written. Richard Crenna produced and directed the pilot from a script by Jack Marlowe and Bill O'Halloren. The pilot was produced by Bing Crosby Productions in association with Pendick Enterprises—Richard Crenna's company, named after his wife Penni and himself.

Blondell made another 1966 sitcom pilot, *Ace of the Mounties,* about a straight-laced Royal Canadian Mounted Police Constable, Wade Terhune (Ron Hussman), with a lazy St. Bernard named Ace who never obeyed his master. Ace was the dumbest dog in the Mounties' kennel, but he had a strong jaw and sharp teeth. The dog would only move when told to "sit." Blondell was featured as Ma Devereaux, owner of the local trading post, in this comedy take-off on *Sergeant Preston of the Yukon*. Others in the pilot included John Williams as Inspector Nigel Fairchild, to whom Terhune reported, and Susan Yardley as Gabby Derereaux, Ma's daughter and potential love interest for Terhune. Written by Chris Hayward and Alan Burns, the pilot episode titled "Call of the Mild" was produced by Blondell's late ex-husband Dick Powell's Four Star Productions for ABC.

The storyline involved Terhune dealing with fur traders trying to cheat the Indians and the trader's boss Dirk Sangler (Simon Oakland). The Mountie has the traders pay up and leaves the money with Ma Devereaux for safekeeping, but he soon learns from Gabby that Ma needs help fending off Sangler and his men who want to get their money back. Terhune spots explosives and asks Ace to carry the dynamite to the stove in the saloon where Dirk and his boys hang out. Instead, Ace puts the dynamite in Ma's stove just as Dirk and his gang enter the trading post. After the explosion, Terhune captures the men and thinks that Ace, buried under some wood, is dead. But the dog is just sleeping. Subsequently, Terhune learns that Spangler is one of the most wanted criminals in that part of Canada, thereby making Terhune a hero.

Ron Hussman enjoyed working with Blondell on this project, saying she had respect for the acting profession and that he had a really good time making the pilot.[3] The pilot was shot in a canyon near Los Angeles which the production company sprayed with artificial snow to look like Canada in the winter. Hussman believes that the pilot never became a series because it was aimed for an early time slot on ABC's schedule and the network had no openings for a comedy aimed at youngsters.

Again teaming with actor-producer Richard Crenna, Blondell made another pilot for ABC titled *Mrs. Thursday*, written by Richard M. Powell (no relation to Dick Powell). She appeared as Ellen Thursday, a long-time cleaning lady for Dunrich Corporation in New York whose owner, George Dunrich (Kennan Wynn), died and left her his mansion, money and business. Mrs. Thursday learned of Dunrich's death from his young business associate, Mr. Hunter (Phillip Clark). Dunrich had three ex-wives, Bibi (Monique Van Vooren), Margo (Patricia Cutts) and Sheila (Sandra Warner). In his will, Dunrich gave Mrs. Thursday the discretion to share any of his $100 million with his ex-wives under the stipulation that they not protest his will. Ellen decided to run the Dunrich Corporation herself with Mr. Hunter as her business adviser, and she continued the ex–Mrs. Dunriches' allowances provided they all took jobs. Mary Wickes played Edna, a cleaning woman and Ellen's long-time friend.

This pilot was based on a hit British series of the same name. The proposed series almost made it onto ABC's Saturday night schedule for the 1967–68 season. *Mrs. Thursday* was penciled in at 9:30 p.m. after *The Lawrence Welk Show* and before the Western *Iron Horse*. However, the network decided that the additional advertising revenue they might make by extending their prime time line-up to end at 11:00 p.m. instead of 10:30 p.m. wasn't worth the cost of an additional series, and so *Mrs. Thursday* was bumped from the fall schedule.

In 1967, Blondell went to Hawaii to appear in a drama pilot called *Kona Coast* starring Richard Boone as sea captain Sam Moran. She played former alcoholic Kittibelle Lightfoot, manager of the Refuge, a home for reformed drunks. When her brother, Moran's shipmate, died from injuries received in a fire on Moran's boat, her sibling left his share of a boat he co-owned with Kittibelle to Moran, meaning that Moran became a reluctant partner with her.

In the unsold pilot, Blondell was billed third after Boone and Vera Miles who played Dr. Melissa Hyde, a marine biologist and Moran's former love interest. The plot deals with Moran's estranged daughter dying from a heroin overdose with Moran determined to learn who gave her the lethal drug. The culprit, Kryder (Steve Ihnat), knows that the Boone character will not stop until he finds him, so he sets fire to Moran's boat and then tries to kill him. But Moran finds him and has him arrested. The pilot was written by Gil Ralston, based on a story by John D. MacDonald, and directed by Lamont Johnson. When the pilot didn't sell, additional footage was added to release it as a movie. Blondell reportedly told her daughter that Boone was "crude, impolite and cruel. He was mean and degrading." But she did enjoy working with Vera Miles.[4]

After Marlo Thomas' *That Girl* ended its run on ABC, writer-director Bill Persky created a proposed sitcom for Ted Bessell, who had co-starred as Thomas' boyfriend on her series. Persky, the creator of *That Girl*, developed *Bobby Parker and Company* for Bessell. According to Persky, he had always loved Blondell as an actress and specifically wrote the role of Bobby's mother for her.[5] In the pilot, made in 1971, Bessell played a travel agent with a wife, Dayna (Marj Dusay), father (Tom D'Andrea) and mother (Blondell). When something was on his mind, he imagined that his wife and parents were with him. They all accompanied him to his periodic appointments with his psychiatrist (Tom Poston) where Bobby talked about his fears and the correct thing to do.

Blondell's character was a loving, caring mother whose son Bobby could do no wrong. Her character wore a black dress with white ruffles and an apron. She carried a mixing bowl stirring its contents with a wooden spoon and had lines like, "I've never been happy a day in my life and I've enjoyed every minute of it." Referring to her son, she said, "He's too good—that's his curse." Tom D'Andrea, who played Bobby's father, had starred as Luther Gillis with Blondell's sister Gloria on the long-running 1950s series *The Life of Riley*.

The pilot, made for NBC, never became a series because the network said they could not risk putting on a show about someone in analysis. This was before *The Bob Newhart Show*, about a psychologist and his patients, became a hit. The *Bobby Parker and Company* pilot finally aired in 1974.

Joan Blondell's final acting appearance on television was in the miniseries *The Rebel*, about the American Revolution. It aired in 1979, the same year that she died at age 73 from leukemia.

Stephen Boyd

Born in 1931 in Northern Ireland, William Millar changed his name when he became an actor by taking his mother's maiden name "Boyd" and using "Stephen" (a favorite name in his family) as his first name. His most famous role was that of Messala, Ben-Hur's childhood friend, in the 1959 movie *Ben-Hur*. With leading man good looks, Boyd began his acting career on the stage and in British films. One of his first roles was as a Nazi spy in the movie *The Man Who Never Was* (1956). He garnered critical and public fame appearing in the 1957 French movie *The Night Heaven Fell*, as Brigitte Bardot's love interest. Before *Ben-Hur*, he had roles in *The Bravados* (1958), as a convict awaiting execution, and in *The Best of Everything* (1959), as a paperback book editor.

In the 1960s, Boyd appeared in a number of movies including 1962's *Billy Rose's Jumbo*, where he portrayed the son of a circus mogul, *The Oscar* (1966) playing a manipulative star who tries to win an Academy Award, and *Fantastic Voyage* (1966) as a CIA agent. Originally cast as Anthony in Twentieth Century–Fox's *Cleopatra* with Elizabeth Taylor, Boyd was replaced by Richard Burton after production was shut down due to Taylor's illness. As his biographer states,

> At the beginning of the 1960s, Stephen Boyd was basking in the bright lights of international glory and acclaim following *Ben-Hur*. Ten years later, the light had faded significantly, with less and less plum roles coming his way. He would always work but it was the quality of the work that became questionable. His appétit for quality had not diminished. However, finding decent roles in decent movies was becoming a tough call.[1]

In late 1972 and early 1973, Boyd filmed a TV crime pilot playing the main character Steve Cutler, a former cop, CIA agent and Justice Department official now living in Key West, Florida, and spending most of his time fishing with his friend Candy (Woody Strode). Cutler had made big money solving a kidnapping case and so didn't have to work regular hours. Also in the pilot were Shug Fisher as Sam Olsen, Cutler's cook, and Sheree North as Brandy, the bartender at Sloppy Joe's Bar where Cutler and his friends hung out. *Key West*, written and produced by Denne Bart Petitclerc (aka Anthony S. Martin), was directed by Philip Leacock for Warner Brothers.

The story revolves around an ex-con, Prescott Webb (Ford Rainey), who, as he is dying, wants Cutler killed. Cutler had put Webb in prison for ten years for stealing government funds, but Webb was paroled after serving only two years. Webb's personal secretary Ruth Frasier (Tiffany Bolling) visits Cutler to give him a safety deposit box key. She advises him that it would be a mistake to open the box, which, of course, he does. He finds another key inside the box. Later, Cutler receives a visit from Senator Scott (William Prince) who offers to give him $250,000 for the key. Steve then meets with General Tom Lucker (Simon Oakland), who knows the Senator, and informs Steve that the key is related to something he did years earlier. The general's wife confesses that the key leads to documents that Webb possessed about a case in the Far East that involved the Senator, the general and Steve. Cutler discovers that Ruth is more than Webb's secretary; she is really Webb's daughter, and the key is to Webb's wall safe. Ruth takes the key while Steve is sleeping and goes to her father's estate to open the safe. The safe is booby-trapped, and Ruth dies in the explosion. Steve tells the Senator and the general that

Woody Strode (left) and Stephen Boyd (right) in a scene from the pilot *Key West*. They are surrounded by unnamed actors playing henchmen and by actress Sheree North (with her back to the camera).

Webb had hired a contract killer to murder them if the booby-trapped safe did not kill them. The Senator and general were involved with Webb in his theft of the government funds, and he wanted to exact revenge on them for having him jailed. They both are murdered by the contract killer.

Although filming of *Key West* was completed in January 1973, Warner Brothers, thinking there was too much dialogue in it, had more action scenes added. Despite this change, the pilot did not sell. NBC finally aired it on December 10, 1973.

After the pilot failed to become a series, Boyd continued to act in made-for-TV movies (including 1975's *The Lives of Jenny Dolan* with Shirley Jones) and on TV series such as *Hunter* and the original *Hawaii Five-O*. His final film appearance was in the critically acclaimed 1977 British crime drama *The Squeeze*, where he played a gangster. In 1977, at the relatively young age of 45, Boyd died of a massive heart attack while playing golf at a Northridge, California, country club.

Claudette Colbert

Claudette Colbert began her acting career with an appearance in the 1927 movie *For the Love of Mike* as the love interest of a college athlete. Usually playing humorous, stylish, intelligent women, Colbert would go on to star in many romantic comedies in the 1930s and 1940s including *It Happened One Night* (1934) in the Oscar-winning role of a pampered heiress who falls in love with newspaper reporter Clark Gable; *The Palm Beach Story* (1942) in which she portrayed identical twins both in love with the same man (Joel McCrea) who also has an identical twin; and *The Egg and I* (1947) with Fred MacMurray as her husband who wants to become a chicken farmer. Colbert also appeared in dramatic roles such as the lead in Cecil B. DeMille's *Cleopatra* (1934) and as an upper-middle-class housewife and mother whose husband volunteers for military service in the World War II drama *Since You Went Away* (1944). The latter seemed to influence Colbert's selection of roles for possible television series. She was in her fifties in the 1950s, and both of her major efforts at a TV series involved her playing mothers.

Seeing that other film actors were making profitable deals to star on TV and that a series which lasted a few years could result in residuals for the reruns, Colbert indicated that appearing on TV "sounded very appealing. I had visions of working for three years and then sitting on my patio and collecting the money."[1] Her first attempt at a TV series was Screen Gems' *Leave It to Liz* in 1954. In the pilot episode "While We're Young," Colbert played Liz Hopkins, a widow whose 15-year-old daughter Katie (Eilene Janssen) wants to date the new basketball coach at school, Gig Sperry (Tab Hunter). Liz thinks Katie is too young to go on dates. When the coach stops by to discuss the matter with Liz, he ends up asking *her* to go to a dance with him instead of Katie. Liz decides to attend the dance after Katie tells her that she is old enough to be Gig's mother. However, then Liz has second thoughts and agrees that her daughter should attend the dance with Gig. She permits Katie to go, while she goes with Dr. Tyler McManus (Patric Knowles), whom she has been seeing.

J. Watson Webb, Jr., directed the pilot based on a teleplay by Stanley J. Wolf and Paul Crabtree from a story by Wolf. Rockhill Productions was to produce the series. Colbert attempted to negotiate a three-year contract with NBC for the show, but for a variety of reasons the deal fell through. Her husband wanted an escape clause in the contract should Colbert find the work on the series too tough. Colbert also did not want to appear in commercials for the series' sponsor, Toni hair products. Furthermore, according to Colbert, the network indicated that the potential series needed more comedy. NBC may have been looking at Colbert as the next Lucille Ball, thinking that a series title like *Leave It to Liz* should be about the misadventures of a wacky mother. "I can do a pratfall whenever it's called for," explained the actress. "But my kind of comedy is the brand I did in pictures like *The Egg and I* and *Family Honeymoon*. There has to be a reason for the slapstick; otherwise it just looks silly."[2]

Colbert's series was tentatively scheduled for Saturday nights at 8:30. When NBC would not agree with her demands, the network extended the run of *The Duke*, a series about a professional boxer, in that time slot. Colbert later denied that she turned down *Leave It to Liz* because she wouldn't do commercials. However, the actress did indicate that she was afraid of trying to do 39 episodes which, in the '50s, was the usual number produced in a year. "I just don't think there is enough good material to supply 39 shows a season," the actress stated. "Once you get on the treadmill, you don't have time to work over the scripts and make them better. If you get one good one out of ten, you're lucky."[3]

Colbert then considered hosting a dramatic series for CBS, but that project never came to fruition. She was considered for an all-star anthology series similar to *Four Star Playhouse* with different stars hosting and appearing in episodes. However, instead of four Hollywood stars, CBS program chief William Dozier wanted six stars. In addition to Colbert, Joan Fontaine, Joseph Cotten and Donna Reed were being considered. While each episode would have had its own story and star, the six leads would be seen in the same locale and there would be a threading-together of the stories. Colbert seemed to like the concept of being a rotating host, saying, "[T]he best plan for a dramatic actress is to be on every third week, as they do on *Four Star Playhouse*.... I think it's wrong for a dramatic actress to attempt 39 shows a year because you just cannot do that many good programs."[4] *Six Star Theatre* failed to become a series. (In 1960, Four Star Productions attempted a similar anthology series, *Six Star Playhouse*.)

Colbert later made another sitcom pilot, *The Claudette Colbert Show* (aka *Mrs. Harper Goes to Congress* or *Welcome to Washington*) in which she played newly elected Congresswoman Elizabeth Harper, who moved to Washington, D.C., with her husband, history professor Paul (Leif Erickson), and her children Susie (Shelley Fabares) and Billy (Eric Anderson). Maudie Prickett played her secretary Alfreda, who didn't like it that the new representative was a female. The pilot, produced by Norman Tokar, was written by Inez Asher and Whitfield Cook. Colbert invested $50,000 of her own money in the project that was produced by her company Colbert Enterprises and filmed by Desilu in 1957.

The storyline dealt with the problems the new Congresswoman faces on her first day in office. Playing a stylish, confident female, Colbert's character learns that there is more to being a representative than voting on legislation. On the way to Washington, Paul finds that the apartment the family was to move into has already been rented. Leaving his wife at her new office, he and the kids try to locate another apartment without telling Liz what they are doing. Liz has to contend with a constituent who is pushing for legislation to build better houses for non-migratory birds while preparing to meet with Representative Grinnell, the assistant party whip. When she learns that the apartment her family thought they would rent has been taken, Liz and Alfreda begin phoning to find a place to live. In the end, Grinnell, who owns apartment buildings, locates a place for the family.

Apparently, advertisers rejected the pilot fearing that Congress would be upset over the way it was portrayed. However, the pilot did air as part of a summer series of unsold pilots on September 30, 1958, and again on August 23, 1960.

Colbert's final TV appearance was in the 1987 mini-series *The Two Mrs. Grenvilles*, appearing as the wealthy mother-in-law of Ann-Margret. Claudette Colbert died in 1996.

Gary Cooper

In most of his movies, Frank James "Gary" Cooper was the epitome of the ideal American hero. Initially an extra and stunt man, Cooper quickly became a leading man in Westerns during the silent era. In his first sound picture, *The Virginian* (1929), he played a good-natured cowboy. He also appeared in adventure movies and dramas like *The Lives of a Bengal Lancer* (1935) in which he portrayed a lieutenant in charge of newcomers to the 41st Bengal Lancers stationed in India. In the '40s, his natural and underplayed acting style won him roles as a champion of the common man in *Meet John Doe* (1941) and *The Pride of the Yankees* (1942), where he had the role of legendary baseball player Lou Gehrig. Cooper won two Oscars for Best Actor for in *Sergeant York* (1941), as one of the most decorated soldiers in World War I, and *High Noon* (1952), where the actor played a town marshal forced to face a gang of killers alone. In 1954, Cooper formed his own production company, Baroda Productions, with financier Paul V. Shields and attorney I.H. Prinzmetal to make features including *The Wreck of the Mary Deare* (1959) and The *Hanging Tree* (1959).

As with many movie stars, he explored the possibility of a television series in the early 1950s because of the large financial return from a long-running show. In 1951, *Broadcasting* noted that Cooper

> has been discussing a TV series with the William Morris Agency in New York and Hollywood. He would be producer and in control of the TV film package as well as its star, if plans work out. A series of 40 30-minute films yearly would be produced at an estimated cost of $20,000 each.
> Of particular interest to the star is the fact that the prolonged running time of a TV series in the expanding market will provide him with a large annual income for many years.[1]

No series resulted from such discussions. With TV Westerns all the rage in the late 1950s and with Cooper's screen persona so strongly tied to the Western genre, ABC announced in February 1957 that it was negotiating with the actor through Allied Artists to produce and occasionally star in a one-hour Thursday night Western series. Thirty-nine episodes of *Western Theatre* would be made with Cooper establishing his own company to help produce the series.

When an agreement for a Gary Cooper series could not be worked out with ABC, Cooper's representatives approached CBS with the same concept of a one-hour Western adventure series with Cooper hosting and narrating but, in this case, not starring in any of the episodes. Supposedly, Cooper wanted to be paid $50,000 for each installment. The deal being negotiated would have been for three years beginning in 1958. The projected series would have been produced by Cooper's production company Baroda Productions along with Ashton Productions, a company Cooper formed with the three Mirisch brothers. In April 1957, CBS even selected a time slot for the series: 10:00 p.m. Wednesday nights beginning in January 1958. The series would alternate with the anthology *The United States Steel Hour*.

However, a few months later, in July 1957, Cooper backed away from the idea of having his own series. Undisclosed tax obstacles were cited as one reason. But in a 1957 news article, Cooper said he'd had second thoughts about hosting a TV show:

> In such a master of ceremonies job, you're selling a lot of things besides the product of your show's sponsor. You're selling the show itself. You're selling yourself. And you're selling, in a way, your own movies. My feeling is that it's bad business for me to do it. ... I know more about movies than television. I'd be moving into a competitive business. You can't do television with one hand. If you go into it, you should go in with all four feet. Besides, I'm a lazy son of a gun.[2]

Cooper continued to make features. In his final movie, *The Naked Edge*, a 1961 British-American production, he played the victim of a blackmailer who accused him of murder and theft. Perhaps if Gary Cooper had lived longer, he might have later reconsidered appearing on his own TV show, but he passed away in 1961 from cancer.

Joan Crawford

No movie actress had more ambivalence about appearing on a weekly television series than Joan Crawford. Born Lucille Le Sueur, her first appearance in a motion picture was as a body double for actress Norma Shearer in the silent movie *Lady of the Night* (1925). In Crawford's last silent picture *Our Modern Maidens* (1929), about mismatched sweethearts, she starred with Douglas Fairbanks, Jr., who would become her first husband in June 1929.

Crawford became a major movie star in films including *Possessed* (1931) with Clark Gable where the actress played a factory worker who becomes a wealthy lawyer's mistress, *Rain* (1932) as Sadie Thompson, a prostitute, *The Women* (1939), appearing as a perfume counter clerk who has an affair with the husband of a New York society woman, *A Woman's Face* (1941) as a blackmailer with a facial disfigurement whose life is changed by plastic surgery, and *Mildred Pierce* (1945) in which she gave an Oscar-winning portrayal of a long-suffering mother with an ungrateful daughter. Her movie career started to taper off in the 1950s as was the case with other aging female film stars coincidental with the advent of television. However, she made a comeback in the successful 1962 movie *What Ever Happened to Baby Jane?* as the wheelchair-bound former actress whose sister Jane (Bette Davis) is the sibling from Hell. Like Davis, Crawford played ambitious, independent women in her film roles — equally comfortable playing the victim or the victimizer.

According to *Broadcasting* magazine, in 1952, Crawford submitted a five-year TV proposal to the major networks asking for $200,000 per year for 26 half-hour episodes of an anthology series plus 50 percent ownership of the vehicle.[1] No network accepted Crawford's proposal because of the price.

The following year, *Variety* reported that Crawford turned down an offer to star in a half-hour TV series based on *Mildred Pierce*.[2] Crawford indicated that she would be willing to appear in that role in a one-shot special on radio or TV but not as a recurring character because of the movies she had scheduled. Later that same year, *Variety* indicated that Crawford almost accepted a deal for a dramatic series to be sponsored by Proctor & Gamble on a minimum two-year, no-option basis.[3] But the actress bowed out when she landed three motion picture commitments.

In 1954, Crawford formed her own production company and produced a pilot called *The World and I* in association with her talent agency MCA where she played a journalist roving the world for stories. At the time, she stated that she did not feel that because she would be seen on television on a weekly basis that people would stay away from her movies. "My only competition will be from others on TV, and I don't think I have to concern myself, about competing in both media." As with Claudette Colbert and Gary Cooper, Crawford said that her chief reason for doing a series was to assure her of a permanent income from its reruns. "I began to earn top money only after the big taxes came in, and the government last year took 83 percent of my

Joan Crawford as a journalist in a scene from *The World and I*, her only pilot. She would have played the same character on a weekly basis if it had become a series.

earnings. This year, it will be more, and as a result I'll have barely enough left for living expenses."4 Crawford felt that the ideal arrangement was for her to do a TV series of 39 episodes and one movie a year.

Written by Andrew Solt and directed by Rod Amateau in early 1954, *The World and I* featured Crawford as Mary Andrews, a reporter with a syndicated column doing human interest stories. Her boss Jeff Davis would like to marry her, but she still grieved over the loss of her husband in the Korean War. While driving to Edinburgh, Mary gets a flat tire. A stranger, Tom Wickers (John Sutton), helps her change the tire and she offers him a ride. He reveals that he was just released from prison after serving 17 years for murder. Over the car radio, Mary hears that a man has escaped from a nearby prison and begins to fear that Wickers may be the escapee despite the fact that he tells her that, if she feels uncomfortable with him in the car, she can let him off anywhere. She then picks up an American soldier, Corp. Ray Johnson (Chuck Connors), who is on his way to get married, thinking that he may help her with Wickers. However, the soldier arrives at his destination before she has a chance to ask for help. Wickers makes a pass at her, confirming her fears. Later, Mary's car is stopped for speeding by the police who inform her that the escaped prisoner has been captured. Wickers shows the police official papers relating to his release. Mary has to apologize to him for how she acted.

The producers indicated that *The World and I* did not turn into a series because no network time slot could be found for it. The pilot did not show the lead character in the most favorable light. Normally, any effort with the intent of becoming a weekly series should not present the main character as a victim of his or her own somewhat irrational fears. Furthermore, although it was set in Great Britain, Mary Andrews drove an American car on what looked like an American highway in the West and didn't always drive on the left side of the road.

The *World and I* pilot aired as an installment of Revue's *General Electric Theater* on October 31, 1954, under the title "The Road to Edinburgh." Apparently, Crawford was not informed beforehand that it would air. When she learned about it, she commented, "You'd think they would tell me about it. After all, I own it."5

In 1956, Crawford told Dave Kaufman of *Variety* of two offers—one from Screen Gems and one from NBC—to star on her own series. At the same time, she expressed her mixed thoughts about television. "I don't know whether I'm going to tackle TV or not. I force myself to look at it, and I'm terrified at its mediocrity." Crawford went on to say,

> Irving Briskin [Screen Gems] wants me to do a series, and promised to have writers work on stories for six months of shows, and that he would look for just the right

property for me. I said fine—then I won't have to start with something like five stories. You can work hard enough without the added frustration of "Where is the next script?"

NBC in New York also has offered me a series, in which I would star in 18 pictures, with two other stars each in 18 other pictures in a rotating star type of show. They offered me a three-year deal, and I'm considering it now. I would own the show, and would line up the two other stars. If I take this series, which would be shot in New York, I would like to use members of the Actors Studio like a repertoire [sic] theater.... I wouldn't think of going on TV unless I owned the whole bloody thing.[6]

A few years later, Crawford negotiated a deal with NBC to star on her own anthology series. *The Joan Crawford Show* (aka *Joan Crawford Theatre* and *Joan Crawford Presents*) was earmarked for the 1959–60 season. Crawford would host all 39 episodes and star in 20 of them. She wanted at least 40 scripts to choose from before going into production with the series, saying, "I'm not going to end up with a nervous breakdown working hard and doing lousy scripts."[7] The episodes were to be filmed in Hollywood, but the actress would host and do the commercials in New York so she could be near her husband Al Steele, head of Pepsi-Cola. Crawford was to be a co-producer along with game show producers Mark Goodson and Bill Todman. However, the producers couldn't interest any sponsor in the proposed series.

Crawford was also under consideration as one of the hosts for Four Star Productions' proposed *Six Star Playhouse* in 1960, but this project offered to CBS never went forward.

For the 1961–62 season, William Dozier of Screen Gems attempted to strike a deal with the actress for a series in which she would play an attorney based, in part, on the original radio serial, *Portia Faces Life*, which concerned a widowed attorney (her husband was murdered by criminal elements that he had been trying to expose) who fought corruption in her home town. *The Joan Crawford Show* was to be produced by Joseph Naar and Elliot S. Loustein for CBS, but by September 1961 the deal was dead. *Variety*'s Dave Kaufman commented, "Miss C's opinion of SG [Screen Gems] in this matter isn't printable."[8]

Having dealt with almost every television production company in Hollywood to no avail, Crawford tried once more with Dick Powell's Four Star Productions for a series. In 1962, she was reviewing scripts for Powell's NBC anthology series, seeking two scripts to star in for producer Aaron Spelling. Evidently she didn't find any scripts to her liking because she never appeared on that series.

Crawford made a guest appearance in the 1964 pilot *Royal Bay*, which featured Paul Burke as Barney Stafford, a young lawyer in the seaside town of Royal Bay. Charles Bickford appeared as Burke's father, Hugh. Bickford's character had three other sons including a psychologist played by Richard Carlson. The concept of the proposed series was that each episode would feature the exploits of one of Stafford's four sons. Crawford, who helped produce this pilot, plays Della Chapelle, whose daughter Jenny (Diane Baker) suffers from a rare skin disease that causes extreme sensitivity to daylight which is why Della conducts most of her business at night. Crawford would not have been a regular if the project had become a series. However, she may have made guest star appearances on the proposed show. Released as a theatrical feature and later broadcast on television, *Royal Bay* was titled *Della* (aka *Fatal Confinement*) to focus on Crawford's character which is probably why some think that this project was an unsold pilot for a Joan Crawford television series.

In 1969, Crawford guest starred in the pilot for Rod Serling's *Night Gallery*. It was produced by Universal which now included Revue Studios. She played wealthy Claudia Menlo, blind since birth, who blackmails a surgeon into performing an eye transplant so she can see for at least part of one day. Just as she begins to see, a major power blackout plunges her apartment into total darkness. The segment was one of Steven Spielberg's first directing assignments. After Crawford met him, she called the head of Universal, Lew Wasserman, asking why such a young director had been assigned to her. Wasserman responded, "Joan, if you're unhappy, don't mention it because they won't replace him, they'll replace you."[9] According to Spielberg, after that, he had no problems with Crawford during the filming.

Joan Crawford's final TV appearance as an actress was in a 1972 episode of the Gary Collins series *The Sixth Sense*. Ms. Crawford died in 1977 at age 72.

Bette Davis

When she first started in movies in the early 1930s, Bette Davis was described as a "little brown wren." According to the actress, "ash-blonde hair was considered brown in Hollywood in those days. It was the era of *very* bleached blonde hair—thus the title 'little brown wren.'"[1] Regarded as one of the greatest American motion picture actresses of all time, Davis appeared in almost all movie genres from comedies to crime thrillers to romantic dramas. The only genre she never tackled on the silver screen was Westerns. The actress is probably best remembered for her romantic dramas. Her characterizations often overshadowed the storylines of the films.

Bette Davis' first notable screen appearance, as a vulgar waitress who descends into prostitution, was in 1934's *Of Human Bondage*. The following year, she won a Best Actress Oscar for her performance in *Dangerous* where she played a tempestuous actress. She won the award again as a spoiled Southern belle in 1938's *Jezebel*. In addition to her two Oscars, she was nominated for *Dark Victory* (1939) in which she portrayed a Long Island socialite who learns she is dying, *The Letter* (1940) playing a murderess, *The Little Foxes* (1941) appearing as a scheming Southern aristocrat, *Now, Voyager* (1942) as a repressed Boston heiress who transforms herself into an independent woman, and *Mr. Skeffington* (1944), as a faithless beauty. Davis was also Oscar-nominated for 1950s pictures in which she played aging actresses, *All About Eve* (1950) and *The Star* (1952). In her big comeback film, *What Ever Happened to Baby Jane?* (1962), she received her final nomination as a character who holds her crippled sister (Joan Crawford) captive in an old mansion.

Embodying strong, capable, independent women in her movie roles, Davis' attempts at her own television series reflected this screen persona and that may be why networks and advertisers resisted picking up her pilots. Male actors in her TV pilots had secondary roles to her on-screen characterizations. Bette Davis was perceived as too "high voltage" for the "cool" medium of television.[2]

Like many film stars in the early days of TV, Davis was in great demand from TV producers to star on her own show. In August 1952, Jack Hellman in his *Variety* "Light & Airy" column reported that Davis would play a continuing character, a "New Jersey Portia," on her own series for which she would receive $2500 per half-hour. This project never saw the light of day.

After she appeared on the Hal Roach-produced series *Telephone Time*, *Variety* indicated in April 1957 that Davis would star on a weekly half-hour anthology series, *The Bette Davis Show*, to be produced by Jerry Stagg. She would introduce each episode and act in some of them. This project also never got off the ground.

Her episode of *Telephone Time*, "Stranded," was based on a true story: Davis played Beatrice Enter, a Minnesota schoolteacher stranded in the schoolhouse with her pupils during a blizzard. She is able to lead her students out of the building to meet a rescue party.

Davis' next attempt at a TV series, *Paula*, co-starred her husband, actor Gary Merrill. The pilot, shot in 1958, had Davis playing Paula Brand, a New York theatrical agent married to playwright David Brand (Merrill). Paula attends a play that marks the debut of Clay Alexander (Tom Pittman). The son of an iconic actor, Clay is unsure that he will perform as well as his father Barkley (Ian Keith). Paula discourages his father from talking to his son before the play, but Barkley visits him anyway in his dressing room. When Clay goes on stage, he is petrified and forgets his lines, leading to bad reviews and the play's producer wanting him fired. The next day, Casey Ryan, Paula's theatrical agent partner, tries to talk Clay out of quitting. Paula and Barkley find Clay in a bar and they too encourage him to return to the stage. After Paula gives him a pep talk, he goes back to work. Allen H. Miner directed the pilot which was written by Lou and Peggy Shaw. Merrill's part was very small: His character appears at the beginning, attending the play with his wife, and at the end, helping a character with an idea for a play. Re-titled "The Starmaker," it aired on March 11, 1958, as an episode of *Studio 57*. According to Davis,

> The night before Gary and I started the actual filming on "Paula," our living room at the Chateau Marmont, where we were staying, caught on fire. Had not someone in a nearby room seen the smoke billowing out our window, we would have been asphyxiated by morning. I often wondered why I was saved. My career at this point was practically nil—only TV offers, scripts of which were mostly inferior. My only desire for living were my children.[3]

Davis had 100 percent ownership of the pilot which would have resulted in large returns for her if the project had run for several seasons. Davis felt that playing a theatrical agent opened up a wide range of opportunities for her character, from comedy to drama. Lack of work in movies prompted the actress to consider this TV project. She said, "It's a man's era in movies today. All the scripts I read focus mainly on the man's part. They're stories about wars, and things like that. There hasn't been a woman's picture in an awfully long time. If a gal wants to work today—and I certainly do—TV is it."[4]

Davis starred in another pilot that was broadcast as the October 28, 1959, episode of the hit Western *Wagon Train*. In "The Elizabeth McQueeny Story," Davis played the title role, an assertive, well-dressed woman who joins the wagon train with nine young women: Roxanne (Maggie Pierce), Danielle (Danielle Aubry), Nina, Lynn (Lynette Bernay), Jeannie, Joyce, Mary, Anna and Diana. This was Davis' second appearance on the series. (Her first was in "The Ella Lindstrom Story" where she appeared as a pioneer woman with seven children. In that episode, her character thinks she is pregnant again but instead discovers she has a malignant growth.)

In "Elizabeth McQueeny," the Davis character says she is going west to open a finishing school for girls, but Major Adams (Ward Bond) later finds that she is really an actress who plans to open a "palace of entertainment" with her girls as dancers. Indians deliver to the wagon train a "Count" Roberto Del Falcone (Robert Strauss) whom they say is a thief. The count joins the train as McQueeny's driver. Madame diagnosis an outbreak of spotted fever when a young man, infatuated with Roxanne, falls ill. McQueeny and her other girls help tend the sick until almost everyone recovers except for Roxanne, who dies from the fever. In the end, McQueeny and her girls perform a can-can dance for the men, raising more than eyebrows.

This episode, written and directed by Allen H. Miner (who had directed *Paula*), had been conceived as a stand-alone pilot called *Madame's Palace*, taking place in 1800s Las Vegas. Making it an episode of *Wagon Train* reduced the cost of the project and guaranteed a wide exposure. However, this exposure did not help turn *Madame's Palace* into a series.

In early 1963, Jack Webb, famous as Sgt. Friday on TV's *Dragnet*, became the head of Warner Brothers Television. His goal was to reinvigorate the division which had supplied many popular series (*Cheyenne, Maverick, 77 Sunset Strip*, more) to ABC in the late '50s. By the time Webb was named top man at the TV division, Warners had only a few series on television. One of his first actions was to sign Davis to star in an hour-long dramatic series called *Morgan and McBride*. Davis would play a lawyer with William Shatner as her partner. Writer Fay Kanin created the concept for the potential series with Robert Dozier writing the pilot script. To entice Davis to sign with Warner Brothers, the studio, for which she made so many movies in the '30s and '40s and then attempted to get out of her contract, gave her a stake in owning the proposed series which was unprecedented for the company.

However, no pilot was ever produced. The following year, Warners was still shopping the series around trying to get actress Greer Garson to play the female attorney with Peter Falk as her co-star. *Morgan and McBride* appears to have been very similar in concept to a pilot Kanin wrote in 1972, *Heat of Anger*, about an attorney and her younger male partner. Originally to star Barbara Stanwyck, the pilot was made with Susan Hayward due to Stanwyck's sudden illness at the time.

Davis' next series project was a 1964 sitcom pilot, *The Bette Davis Show* (also known as *The Decorator*), produced by Aaron Spelling for Four Star Productions. Viewers knew it was supposed to be a comedy because of the everpresent laugh track. In the pilot, Davis plays an interior designer named Liz who lives briefly with her clients in order to become accustomed to their tastes as she redecorates their homes. Richard Kinon directed the pilot from a teleplay by Cy Howard and Matt Crowley, based on a story by Howard. Mary Wickes played Viola, Liz's assistant.

A wealthy judge (Ed Begley) from Oklahoma wants to hire Liz for $10,000. Since Liz is heavily in debt, she takes the job under two conditions: She must be given carte blanche when decorating and must live with the client during the redecorating process so that the home will reflect the client's personality. The judge's daughter Missy (Davey Davison) is to be married, and the judge wants Liz to redo the farmhouse he and his wife lived in when they married. He is giving it as a wedding gift to his daughter and her fiancé Jim (James Stacy). The judge hopes that Liz will show his daughter the good life so she will decide not to marry her less-than-prosperous fiancé. However, Liz encourages Missy and Jim to elope to avoid Missy's father planning all details of the wedding. Liz does redecorate the farmhouse like it was when the judge and his wife Mabel lived there. Naturally, the judge likes what she has done.

In the pilot, Davis did her best "Bette Davis" impersonation, smoking a cigarette in almost every scene. If the pilot had gone to series, each week a new guest star would appear as Liz's client.

Reflecting on the pilot, Davey Davison recalled that the first day when the cast sat around a table to read the script, there was an Oscar on the table to remind everyone of Davis' award. Bette said that its backside looked like her husband's. Davison also remembered that Davis

> was very focused. Friendly, but concentrated. In the mornings when I would see her in makeup, I'd say "good morning" and move on to take care of my own business. I never stopped to make small talk.... One morning I picked some wild flowers growing outside the sound stage and as I passed her in makeup I gave them to her. She was pleased. Some time later that morning she came to me, sat down and started talking. She spoke of her home in Connecticut and the flowers there. She spoke about her daughter, B.D., and her grandchildren, of whom she was so proud, and of Gary Merrill being the love of her life. She was warm and funny and kind.[5]

Davison's last shot of the day one day was a close-up. The producers told Davis that she could leave for the day and that someone else would read the off-camera lines to Davison, but Davis insisted that she would read the lines to help the young actress. According to Davison,

> We sat next to each other in the half darkness on some old wooden steps away from the set while the lights were repositioned for my close-up. We talked 45 minutes or so about acting and actors. She told me her first important picture, *Of Human Bondage*, was with Leslie Howard who was a big movie star. She was excited to be working with him. That didn't last, however, because in their scenes together for her close-ups he stood off camera delivering his lines while reading a book. After that she swore she would never treat [an] actor as he had treated her. And that she would always do her off-camera lines. So late, late at night, she stood playing our scene, working as brilliantly off-camera as she had on camera, for my close-up.[6]

ABC, the network for which the pilot was made, decided against making it a weekly show.

In 1971, Davis made two pilots. The first, *Madame Sin*, co-starred Robert Wagner, who executive produced the project. Davis' Madame Sin made money by taking on various assignments from wealthy people trying to manipulate world events. She lived in a castle on an island off Scotland and used the money she earned to run a think tank comprised of scientists engaged in unusual research such as memory manipulation and sonic wave devices to control people. Appearing in heavy blue eye shadow with her hair in Gorgonic braids and dressed all in black with white pearls, a Eurasian-looking Davis camped it up as this woman of mystery. The Japanese-American Citizens League objected to this portrayal of Asians, saying that it presented a stereotypical picture of them as wily and evil.

Madame Sin captures ex–CIA agent Anthony Lawrence (Robert Wagner), who is grieving the loss of his fiancée Barbara, thought to be killed by Chinese agents. Madame Sin has a special job for Lawrence: hijack a Polaris submarine for one of her clients by kidnapping the sub commander so the commander's mind can be manipulated by Madame Sin's scientists in order for him to turn over the submarine to her. The kidnapping and brain manipulation proceed as planned. Meanwhile, Lawrence finds that Barbara (Catherine Schell) is really alive and living at Madame Sin's estate. After returning the commander to his sub, Lawrence plays dead to get away from Madame Sin's henchman. However, he loses his hearing thanks to the sonic devices the henchman uses on him. Stealing a boat, Lawrence warns the authorities about the impending hijacking of the sub. They believe him and relieve the commander of his duties. Madame Sin's plan fails, and she and her staff vacate the castle. Only Barbara is left behind. She returns to Lawrence—and poisons him as instructed by Madame Sin. Madame's next plan is to steal the crown jewels of Britain.

David Greene directed *Madame Sin* from a script he wrote with Barry Oringer, based on a character created by Lou Morheim and Barry Shear. Oringer wrote the early drafts of *Madame Sin* but, as he indicated, "thereafter had nothing to do with it. David Greene, a good director, unfortunately also fancied himself a writer and pretty much turned the script into a piece of crap."[7] This pilot was filmed in Scotland and London, England. When the project was not picked up as a series, ABC aired it as a Movie of the Week in 1972. Abroad, the film was released to theaters.

Davis' second pilot of 1971, *The Judge and Jake Wyler*, focused on retired judge Davis, who now runs a detective agency, and her ex-con partner Jake Wyler (Doug McClure). It was written by Richard Levinson, William Link and David Shaw, and David Lowell Rich directed. Levinson and Link were the forces behind the popular *Columbo* detective series. Davis' Judge Meredith was almost the polar opposite of the one she portrayed on *The Bette Davis Show*: Wearing horn-rimmed glasses with her auburn hair pulled back into a single pigtail, her character mainly sat behind a desk making phone calls while McClure's Jake Wyler did all the footwork. Since Judge Meredith suffered from severe allergies and was also a hypochondriac, she had to stay indoors with the windows closed. The judge could not stand cigarette smoke, and when Wyler came to visit her, he had to be vacuumed and wear a white smock. She also relied on secretary Chloe Jones (Barbara Rhoades) and household assistant Quint (James McEachin).

The story followed the case of Robert Dodd (Kent Smith), who had hired the judge to find out if his wife Caroline (Lisabeth Hush) was having an affair. When Dodd returns from a business trip, Wyler informs him that not only is his wife seeing another man but also that she has left Dodd. Dodd collapses and is admitted to a hospital for nervous exhaustion. He is later found dead in his hospital room. The police think he committed suicide, but Dodd's daughter Alicia (Joan Van Ark) hires Judge Meredith to prove that her father was murdered. If murder is shown, then Dodd's wife will receive triple damages from his insurance policy. However, if he committed suicide, no money will be paid out.

The list of suspects is everyone who visited Dodd in the hospital, including his business partner James Rockmore (John Randolph), who informs Wyler that Dodd's business trip involved a secret mission for the State Department with Dodd receiving a letter from a writer living in Albania asking for asylum in the U.S.; Dodd's second wife Caroline; her paramour Frank Morrison (Gary Conway); and Anton Granicek (Eric Braeden), an Albanian government representative. Through a process of elimination, Dodd's killer turns out to be ... none of the above. All of the suspects found Dodd dead upon visiting him. Frank Morrison thought that Caroline had murdered her husband and so made it look like he committed suicide. However, the real murderer was Dodd's daughter Alicia, who wanted Meredith and Wyler to prove that Dodd did not commit suicide and that Caroline had murdered him so that Alicia would end up with the insurance policy payout.

The Judge and Jake Wyler was one of Joan Van Ark's first TV films. As she recalls, one of her initial scenes to be shot involved her character meeting with a lawyer to discuss her father's will. The scene did not include Davis' character. Van Ark said that she felt immense pressure doing the scene without giving anything away (i.e., that her character was the real murderer).

> As we rehearsed, already dressed in an expensive black designer suit, sitting across from the lawyer at his desk, I could see Ms. Davis hovering ... watching us as we rehearsed the scene.
> The lines ... the scene ... everything felt stiff, and I knew that uncomfortable vibe might indicate my guilt to the audience ... and tip the story.
> As I started to leave to let them light the set in preparation to shoot, Ms. Davis edged over to the director and whispered something in his ear.
> The next thing I knew, the wardrobe department was on the set with two to three beautiful *black* wide-brimmed, elegant hats with lovely black veils ... my "widow's reeds."
> We three ... Ms. Davis, the director and I ... decided on the perfect hat, which in every shot effortlessly guaranteed the audience's sympathy. It took all the pressure off by allowing me to play the scene, simply saying the lines, no other "layers" needed. The hat and the veil did all the work.
> I will never forget what she did for me. What she taught me about "camera" ... what a gift she gave me. And when it was all done ... the scene was perfect. And so was Ms. Davis.[8]

NBC considered adding *The Judge and Jake Wyler* to its rotating detective series *Wednesday Night Mystery Movie*—a companion to its *Sunday Night Mystery Movie*. However, the network passed on turning it into a series. When the pilot didn't sell, Universal added more scenes so it could air as a two-hour TV movie. In 1973, the script was resurrected for the movie *Partners in Crime* with Lee Grant and Lou Antonio. This attempt also failed to become a series.

In early December 1972, Davis signed with MGM to star in another comedy pilot, *Hello Mother, Goodbye* for NBC. The Jack Sher-Bud Freeman script had Davis playing the possessive mother of two adult sons and a daughter. When she drove through the gate on the MGM lot, there was a banner: "Welcome Bette and Jimmy" (Jimmy Stewart was filming one of his *Hawkins* TV movies on the lot). Davis remarked, "I was finally co-starring with Stewart

... even if only on a banner—plus we had a date for lunch. I told Jimmy I had waited 40 years for a date with him. One must never give up one's dreams! They do come true!"[9]

In *Hello Mother, Goodbye,* Davis starred as Teresa Mullen, a sprightly senior wearing sunglasses and a scarf in the opening scene where she recklessly drives an old "woody" station wagon. Teresa, a widow, was proud of her son Bobby (Jack DeMave), a New York City sportscaster, and her daughter Carolyn Kibbee, married to a doctor with young son Peter (Vincent Van Patten) and young daughter Sue (Erica Petal). She was less thrilled with her other son Kenneth (Kenneth Mars), with an ex-wife Judy, who had quit a well-paying engineering job to run a novelty business. For Mrs. Mullen's birthday, her offspring buy her a one-year trip around the world; Mullen's neighbor Leona Rheinquist (Lurene Tuttle) will accompany her. Meanwhile, Kenneth is upset that the lease on the warehouse where he stores his novelty items is going to cost more than he anticipated. His mother wants him to move into her house while she is away. He agrees and uses the basement as his warehouse. As might be expected in a situation comedy, Teresa returns unexpectedly from her trip, and mother and son have to co-habitat together for at least a year.

"It was heaven to do," Davis remarked upon completing the pilot. "The MGM-TV people are gentlemen. The director was Peter Hunt, who is marvelous. The cast was great. The sets were magnificent. It was the most fun I've had acting in many years. The day after we finished, I got up and felt regret that I didn't have to go to work. That hasn't happened to me in years."[10]

NBC failed to place this series on its fall 1973 schedule, but MGM hoped that the network would pick the series up as a midseason replacement. It didn't happen.

Davis' next attempt at a TV series was an NBC mini-series, *Family Reunion,* that aired on October 11 and 12, 1981. Written by Allan Sloane, based on the *Good Housekeeping* article "How America Lives" by Joe Sparton and directed by Fielder Cook, this TV pilot concerned Elizabeth Winfield (Davis), a schoolteacher who retires after 50 years of service. She lives in the family home in Winfield, a small New England town founded by her ancestors. As a retirement gift, she is presented with a bus ticket for unlimited travel. After she receives a letter from her sister's family stating that she is going to be the godmother when her grandniece gives birth, she decides to use the ticket to visit her various relatives across the country, taking with her a former students, Richard Cooper (played by Davis' real-life grandson J. Ashley Hyman, 11 years-old at the time).

Meanwhile, Elizabeth's nephew Chester Winfield (David Huddleston), a U.S. Senator, along with her grandnephew, are planning to build a shopping mall on undeveloped land near Elizabeth's home that has been in the Winfield family for years. Chester doesn't want his aunt to find out about the project, knowing that she would be against it. When she returns from her trip, Elizabeth finds men surveying the undeveloped property for the shopping center. She asks one of her former students, James Cookman (John Shea), now an attorney, to try to stop the project and also plans to invite all of her relatives to a reunion in Winfield. Together with Cookman, Elizabeth attempts to win over to her side the relatives, who have shares in the undeveloped land, to prevent the mall from being built. Addressing the crowd, she says that this will be their last reunion and tells them that it is up to them to honor the family name. Cookman explains that they will be losing their family heritage to the development. Her relatives end up voting the majority of shares against the project.

Left to right are James Brolin as Peter McDermott, Bette Davis as Laura Trent and Connie Sellecca as Christine Francis in the pilot for ABC's *Hotel*. When Davis recovered sufficiently from strokes she suffered after making the pilot, the actress appeared in two more feature films, *The Whales of August* (1987) and *Wicked Stepmother* (1989).

In voiceover narration at the end, Elizabeth Winfield says, "We cannot know what the future holds, but whatever comes, Winfield and Winfielders will face the future together," setting up the possibility of a dramatic series chronicling the lives of Winfield family members as well as residents of Winfield. *Family Reunion* was the last pilot in which Davis played the central character.

In early 1983, Davis was featured in what would be her last attempt at a television series. Produced by Aaron Spelling and E. Duke Vincent, the two-hour ABC pilot *Hotel* was like a land-locked *Love Boat* centering on stories of the guests at a San Francisco hotel, the St. Gregory. The stories were more dramatic than those on *The Love Boat*. The pilot was directed by Jerry London and written by John Furia, Jr., and Barry Oringer. The latter had co-written Davis' *Madame Sin* pilot.

The hotel staff included manager Peter McDermott (James Brolin) and his assistant Christine Francis (Connie Sellecca). As Laura Trent, owner of the hotel, Davis appeared in just a few scenes, unlike her previous series projects in which she was the main character. Her first scene with the Brolin character involved her concerns with his hiring of an ex-convict as head of hotel security and with how hard McDermott works.

Later in the pilot, Laura Trent, who lived in the posh hotel penthouse, becomes involved in a case of McDermott encouraging a prostitute, gang-raped at the St. Gregory, to file criminal charges against the young men, including the son of a frequent guest at the establishment. Trent defends McDermott's actions in front of the rich businessman. At the end of the show, Trent permits a married couple, workers at the St. Gregory, to use her suite while she is on business in Los Angeles.

James Brolin said of Davis, "Her beauty was always the beauty of personality rather than mere physical beauty. Those eyes, the widest and most hypnotic in Hollywood history, have lost none of their flare and fascination."[11]

Hotel was the only pilot that Davis made that was actually picked up by a network. The actress was to be featured in seven of the first 13 episodes. However, tragedy struck Davis when, later in 1983, she was diagnosed with breast cancer and underwent a mastectomy. She then suffered four strokes which caused paralysis and slurred speech. Although she wanted to return to *Hotel*, her lengthy rehabilitation prohibited it. Anne Baxter, as Victoria Cabot, Laura Trent's sister-in-law, was added to the series in place of Davis. Baxter appeared on the series for the first two and a half seasons before dying at age 62 of a brain aneurysm. *Hotel* lasted until 1988. Davis outlasted the series by over a year, passing away in October 1989 at age 81.

Irene Dunne

Versatile actress Irene Dunne's first movie was the little-known *Leathernecking* (1930), a comedy for RKO. Dunne played a society girl pursued by a Marine private. The actress went on to star in *Cimarron* (1931), one of the best Westerns ever made, which won three Oscars. In it, she appeared as a wife and mother of a family that witnesses the transition of Oklahoma from a territory to a state. The actress also starred in other classic films including *Back Street* (1932) about a single woman who has a long-term affair with a married man; *Roberta* (1935), a musical with Fred Astaire and Ginger Rogers, and *The Awful Truth* (1937), a comedy about a soon-to-be-divorced couple who go to great lengths to disrupt each other's new romances. In the next decade, Dunne starred with Cary Grant in *My Favorite Wife* (1940) as a woman who returns to her family after having been shipwrecked on an island for a number of years and in *Penny Serenade* (1941) about the struggles of a married couple to start a family. She also appeared in such iconic films as *Anna and the King of Siam* (1946) as a tutor for the king's children, *Life with Father* (1947) as the wife and mother of an 1880s family in New York City headed by William Powell, and *I Remember Mama* (1948) as the mother of a Swedish immigrant family.

When movie roles of equal caliber failed to materialize after her Oscar-nominated turn in *I Remember Mama*, Dunne tried television. She began her TV career by hosting the CBS anthology series *Playhouse of the Stars*, sponsored by the Schlitz Brewing Co. The series had started as a one-hour presentation in 1951 but was reduced to 30 minutes beginning in April 1952 when Dunne began her hosting duties. Initially, actress Joan Bennett was to preside over the anthology, but this arrangement fell through with Dunne taking over for the series of 26 dramas originally to be titled *Irene Dunne Television Theater*.

Referring to her career as a TV star, Dunne remarked, "I love it! Making films for TV is as exciting as making them for theaters. I have nothing against live television either, though I'd rather see a good, finished product on film."[1]

The actress was paid $8250 per episode for hosting, which totaled $84,000 for what amounted to about three weeks work. She would have also received a share of the residuals when the episodes were rerun. After six months, Dunne ceased association with the series; thereafter, one of the stars of the weekly drama introduced the episode.

In December 1952, Dunne had discussions with Harry Ackerman, head of CBS entertainment, about starring as Christine Fair in a sitcom titled *Vanity and Mrs. Fair*, to be written and produced by Frank Galen. Originally, CBS had tried to interest Claudette Colbert in a radio version of the series which dealt with the owner of a beauty salon called "The Vanity." Nothing came of the idea of Dunne starring in this proposed vehicle.

Christine Fair was a widow with two children, Bobby, nine, and Karen, 15. Clarence, Mrs. Fair's father, helped her run a small cosmetics firm manufacturing Fair's own brand. Sybil Trout was Christine's best friend. In Frank Galen's pilot script, Christine and Sybil pose as chorus girls in an attempt to interest H.K. Wheeler, Jr., the offspring of the owner of H.K. Wheeler and Son, in distributing Christine's cosmetics.[2] After Allen Webster, a newcomer in town, recognizes Christine and her friend, she has to admit her scheme to Wheeler, who says he would never touch her line of cosmetics. But when a potentially incriminating photo of Wheeler and his assistant carousing with the "chorus girls" is shown to him, he changes his mind and makes a deal with her.

In real life, Dunne was a devout Catholic which may be the reason she made a pilot in 1954 titled *Sister Veronica*, about a nun who was the superintendent of St. Mark's Hospital. Dunne's character had to solve not only the hospital's problems but also those of its patients. In the opening, Sister Veronica is trying to fix a hospital dumbwaiter. Claire (Stephanie Griffin) is being admitted suffering from a fractured skull after falling on the front steps of her father-in-law's mansion. Claire had been trying to see her husband Scott Averill (John Hudson), from whom she is separated; her father-in-law didn't want his son to marry her in the first place. To avoid publicity, the father-in-law demands that Claire be treated in his home and not at the hospital. But the doctor and Sister Veronica indicate that Claire cannot be moved. Sister Veronica wants to give the marriage a chance to work. Scott comes to see his wife and declares that they will never be separated again. Claire regains consciousness and reveals that she is pregnant. Seeing how much in love the couple really is, the father-in-law drops his objections to the marriage. The pilot was produced by Michel Kraike for Screen Gems with Ted Post directing from a script by Erna Lazarus based on a Vivian Crosby short story in *Ladies Home Journal*. The unsold pilot aired as an episode of *Ford Theatre* on April 15, 1954.

In 1962, Dunne starred as interior decorator Margaret Henderson, a widow and mother of two college-age offspring, in a pilot titled *Go Fight City Hall*. Attempting to remove a traffic hazard in her community, Margaret runs into bureaucratic red tape. She then enters politics as a reform candidate. Her son Tony (Bart Patton) and her daughter Melissa (Stephanie Hill) help her with the campaign against sitting committee man Woody Purvis (Allyn Joslyn). After a judge, who encouraged her to run, is endorsed by her opponent, he asks her to withdraw from the race, but she refuses. At a town hall debate, she is asked a question planted by her opponent about how her husband really died in World War II. Margaret has to reveal that he wasn't killed in action but had a nervous breakdown after being in several battles, went berserk shooting his gun at his fellow platoon members, and was finally shot by his platoon sergeant. Purvis' smear backfires with Margaret being elected. Directed by Don Mankiewicz and written by Charles Haas, the pilot was produced by Stanley Rubin and broadcast as an episode of *General Electric Theater* on January 28, 1962.

In an interview with newspaper columnist Hal Humphrey, Dunne denied that *Go Fight City Hall* was a pilot for her own TV series. "They wanted it to be but believe me, it is not a pilot for a series. When I was at the Revue Studios filming this show, I felt so sorry for all those people who were there doing series and knowing they were unable to do their best. It just can't be done every week, can it? … I think of the lonely lives they must lead. They are so busy with the series that they have no time to do anything else."[3] Perhaps Dunne denied that *Go Fight City Hall* was a pilot because she knew it didn't sell before it aired on *General Electric Theater*. It ended up being Dunne's final TV acting appearance.

Later in 1962, Dunne was reportedly selected to star in a projected one-hour series called *Three Angel Way*, written by Barbara Chain and to be produced by composer Jule Styne, responsible for musicals such as *Gypsy* and *Funny Girl*. Somewhat similar in theme to Dunne's *Sister Victoria* pilot, *Three Angel Way* was to focus on the activities of three nuns, but no pilot was ever produced.

Dunne received a Kennedy Center Honor in 1985 for her contribution to the arts. She died in 1990 at age 91.

Nelson Eddy and Jeanette MacDonald

Singer-actors Nelson Eddy, a baritone, and Jeanette MacDonald, a soprano, are best known for the movie musicals they made together in the 1930s and 1940s. Their first feature was Victor Herbert's *Naughty Marietta* (1935) with Eddy playing a mercenary leader who saves MacDonald from being kidnapped by pirates. Probably their most memorable picture was *Rose Marie* (1936) in which MacDonald appeared as a Canadian opera singer who learns that her younger brother has killed a Mountie. Sgt. Bruce (Eddy) of the Royal Canadian Mounted Police is sent to capture the brother. MacDonald and Eddy made six more films for MGM including *Maytime* (1937) about the tragic love story of a Parisian opera singer (MacDonald) who falls in love with an American student (Eddy), *Sweethearts* (1938) focusing on married Broadway stars who contemplate careers in films, and *I Married an Angel* (1942), their final movie, with Eddy as a wealthy playboy who dreams he marries the perfect woman—an angel (MacDonald)—but finds that her perfections and truthfulness are inconvenient.

After making his TV debut on *The Alan Young Show* in 1951 where he sang and acted in a comedy sketch, Eddy starred in a 1952 comedy pilot called *Nelson Eddy's Back Yard!* playing a version of himself: a singer living in Alta Vista, California, with his manager Barney (Chick Chandler). Eddy's home bordered the property of Gloria Bryant (Jan Clayton), a widow who worked in a department store and used to be a singer. Her young sons Tommy (Sammy Ogg) and Freddy (Richard Eyer) were typical boys who liked to play cowboys and Indians and often ventured into Eddy's backyard.

The pilot began with Eddy just back from a tour and working out with his manager while listening to his recordings. Tommy and Freddy burst into the living room and tell Nelson that they want him to appear at their junior high school that evening to participate in a concert benefit for a schoolmate named Lawrence who needs money to move to Montana for his health. Nelson reluctantly agrees. He sings "Wish You Were Here" and then asks Gloria to come up on stage to duet with him on "Wonderbar." After the sell-out concert, Eddy returns home. Mr. Lipscomb, representing the city attorney's office, stops by to inform him that he cannot keep livestock on his property. Nelson has no idea what Lipscomb is talking about. When Gloria, Freddy and Tommy stop by, the boys reveal that they purchased a gift for Lawrence with part of the proceeds from the concert: a pony that he can ride in Montana, and they put the animal in Eddy's backyard. The pony gives birth just as Nelson is going to propose marriage to Gloria. The proposal goes unsaid. The never-sold pilot was written by Lou Houston and Alan Dinehart, Jr., and directed by Dinehart.

During the 1950s and 1960s, Eddy toured the country with his nightclub act. While performing at a Palm Beach, Florida, club in 1967, he suffered a cerebral hemorrhage and died at age 65.

Jeanette MacDonald died two years earlier, on January 14, 1965, of a heart attack. Her last TV appearance was in a 1959 episode of Jack Paar's *Tonight Show*. Like Eddy, after her film career, she appeared mainly in concerts and in musical theater.

MacDonald was offered her own TV music series in the early 1950s. With some regret, the singer remarked, "I, who found guest shots nerve-wrecking, wouldn't dream of taking on 15-minute, twice-a-week singing programs I was offered. I couldn't fancy myself appearing in anything so unpretentious. Dinah Shore, who accepted a similar offer when it came along, showed better sense...."[1]

Like Eddy, MacDonald made a comedy pilot that never became a series. Not as autobiographical as Eddy's pilot, MacDonald's attempt at a sitcom did portray her as a singer who liked to help people. The pilot, *Prima Donna*, broadcast as an episode of *Screen Director's Playhouse* in 1956, was written by MacDonald's husband Gene Raymond and Peter Milne and directed by David Butler. MacDonald's character, Martha Blessing, meets a boy named Johnny (Alfred Caiazza) who happens to have a great singing voice. She wants Johnny to audition for a role in a movie. Johnny's parents want him to be a baseball player. Martha invites his parents to dinner to discuss her plans for the boy, unaware that the parents are baseball manager Leo Durocher and his wife Laraine Day. When the Durochers arrive, Martha thinks they are paying her a surprise visit and tries to get them to leave. Eventually she realizes they are Johnny's parents. Johnny and Martha perform a duet for them.

If the pilot had become a series, MacDonald's co-stars would have been Jane Darwell as Lena, her cook, Jacqueline deWit as Emmy, her secretary, Jerome Cowan as Lewis, her agent, and Jack Lomas as Tad, her piano accompanist.

MacDonald's final flirtation with a television series of her own was a docudrama based on famous figures in music history and the people who influenced them. It was developed with writer Donn Mullally. MacDonald wanted to host a series of documentaries profiling such musical luminaries as Jascha Heifetz, Gian Carlo Menotti and Puccini. Each installment of the proposed series would be capped with MacDonald interviewing a celebrity about the person profiled. It never came to fruition.

Douglas Fairbanks, Jr.

The only offspring of silent film actor Douglas Fairbanks and his first wife, Anna Beth Sully, Douglas Fairbanks, Jr., began his career in silent features. He played Joan Crawford's longtime sweetheart in the 1929 picture *Our Modern Maidens*. The two actors married that year and divorced four years later.

Fairbanks, Jr., played in the iconic features *Little Caesar* (1931) as Caesar's (Edward G. Robinson) friend, *The Prisoner of Zenda* (1937) as kidnapper Rupert of Hentau, and *Gunga Din* (1939) as one of the three male leads along with Cary Grant and Victor McLaglen. In 1949, Fairbanks wrote, produced and acted in *The Fighting O'Flynn* as an Irish poet and freedom fighter battling Napoleon's army.

With the help of packager Don Sharpe, Fairbanks formed his own production company, Dougfair, in the early 1950s to produce movies as well as TV shows. One of the first TV pilots he made was initially called *International Theatre* for NBC in 1952. Fairbanks served as host and narrator as well as starring in approximately 27 of the 156 installments of this anthology series with many of the episodes shot in England. The series went through a few title changes—*Douglas Fairbanks, Jr. Theatre* and *Douglas Fairbanks, Jr. Presents* before it was syndicated by NBC under the title *Rheingold Theater*. It ran from 1953 to 1957.

Fairbanks' production company was unique at the time for filming his pilots in Europe, particularly England. He was well known on the continent, having been decorated by several European governments for his World War II military service. Filming abroad reduced costs.

Maybe because his father starred in a number of adventure films such as *The Mark of Zorro* (1920), *Robin Hood* (1922) and *The Thief of Bagdad* (1924), Jr. had a predilection for proposing TV projects with action-adventure themes. His only project that became a series, besides his anthology show, was *Terry and the Pirates*, a syndicated adventure based on the Milton Caniff comic strip, which lasted 18 episodes. Terry Lee (John Baer) and his sidekick Charles C. Charles nicknamed "Hotshot" (William Tracy) worked for Air Cathay operated by Chopstick Joe (Jack Reitzen) in the Orient. As airplane pilots, they became involved in various adventures flying people to different destinations in that region. In several episodes, Lee had encounters with his nemesis, the mysterious and beautiful Dragon Lady (Gloria Saunders).

Fairbanks would have less success with several other adventure-themed pilots. One was based on a radio series on which he starred, *The Silent Men*. A typical episode of the radio show would begin with an announcer saying, "The National Broadcasting Company proudly presents Douglas Fairbanks' production of *The Silent Men*, transcribed stories of the undercover operation of the Special Agents of every branch of our federal government and their relentless fight against crime."

Fairbanks would then open an episode by identifying the setting and the role he would be playing, and saying that only the names and places are fictional. Although Fairbanks acted in all episodes, he generally played a different government agent in each. In one episode he might be Immigration Agent George Stenson, in another Treasury Agent Bill Foster, and in still another, CIA Agent Henry McAdam. He portrayed agents from virtually all branches of the government, such as the Department of Commerce Enforcement Division, the Postal Service, the Federal Narcotics Bureau, Department of Defense, ATF, FBI and the Civil Aeronautics Administration.

In adapting the radio series for TV, the idea of the same actor playing different roles in each episode was abandoned. Although the concept of one actor appearing as various characters in different episodes of an anthology series was common in 1950s TV, this generally occurred when the stories varied widely in their themes—romance, comedy, mystery, etc. To have the same person play different main characters in a series dealing with the same theme—government undercover agencies—would have been very confusing to the viewer, and so the TV pilot for *The Silent Men* became *The Silent Man* with the lead character, portrayed by Robert Ayres, being a CIA agent named Dick Bosworth.

In the unsold 1952 pilot, Bosworth's boss assigns him to investigate the disappearance of American journalist Ben Cummings behind the Iron Curtain. Bosworth flies to the country posing as a stamp collector and meets his contact, Nadia. He is assigned a government monitor named Prevna. Soon he learns that Cummings was arrested for espionage and is in prison. Bosworth is able to get into the prison and attempts to escape with Cummings, but Prevna catches them and takes the pair to his headquarters. Nadia appears, seemingly in cahoots with Prevna, but Prevna lets Cummings and Bosworth escape. Both Prevna and Nadia are part of an underground movement against the government.

The pilot for NBC was helmed by Terence Fisher, who directed from a script by Gil Doud. *The Silent Man* subsequently aired as an episode of Fairbanks' anthology series in 1954.

Another unsuccessful pilot produced by Fairbanks in 1952 was *Foreign Legion*, written by Anthony Bartley and directed by Daniel Birt. The project starred actor Charles McGraw as Sergeant Flint of the Foreign Legion. A Foreign Legion patrol team is attacked in the Sahara by tribesmen led by Amir Dhow (Martin Benson), who kidnaps one of the team. Sgt. Flint is sent to rescue the Legionnaire and finds Yasmine (Mara Lane), the daughter of the chief of another tribe.

While this pilot never became a series, Bartley, who was married to actress Deborah Kerr from 1945 to 1958, produced a series about the French Foreign Legion in 1956 titled *Assignment Foreign Legion*. This anthology series featured Merle Oberon as a news correspondent narrating (and occasionally appearing in) stories about the men of the Foreign Legion. It lasted 26 episodes.

In 1956, Fairbanks' company filmed a pilot based on Bulldog Drummond, played by Robert Beatty. The Drummond character was a World War I veteran who became an adventurer after the war. Directed by David McDonald and scripted by Irving Rubine, the Fairbanks' pilot "The Ludlow Affair" was set in London and filmed there. Harriett Ludlow (Greta Gynt) contacts Drummond about her scientist husband Felix (Michael Anthony) who has been kidnapped. Felix developed a formula for a new antibiotic which the kidnappers want in exchange for his release. The kidnappers warn Mrs. Ludlow not to go to the police, which is why she visits Drummond.

Drummond and Mrs. Ludlow are being monitored by the kidnappers. At night, someone breaks into the Ludlows' safe and steals the formula. The next day, Drummond informs his assistant Kelly (Michael Ripper) that he was the safecracker. Drummond phones Mrs. Ludlow, disguising his voice, and demands money for the return of the formula. Kelly supposedly turns over the formula to Mrs. Ludlow, while Drummond tails the person who has been shadowing her. He then discovers that Mrs. Ludlow hired the kidnappers to get rid of her husband so that she and Roger Benning (William Franklyn), the doctor's assistant, could control the formula. Drummond frees Dr. Ludlow from a house near the Ludlow home, and Mrs. Ludlow and Benning are arrested.

Fairbanks had a tentative deal with ABC Film Syndication to sell *Bulldog Drummond* to local stations but the sale never materialized. The pilot did subsequently air as an installment of *Douglas Fairbanks Presents*. In 1957, Don Sharpe resurrected the idea of doing a *Bulldog Drummond* series and decided to film another pilot, but this effort never got off the ground.

Another project that aired as a segment of *Douglas Fairbanks Presents* in 1956 was based on the tales of the Arabian nights. In an episode called "Scheherazade," produced and directed by Howard Huth and written by Irving Rubine and Selwyn Jepson, Hugh Williams appeared as Shayer, vengeful ruler of Baghdad, who finds that his wife has been unfaithful. After the execution of his wife and her lover, Shayer takes more than 700 of Islam's most beautiful women for his brides. However, since he believes that the only chaste wife is a dead one, he has all of his wives beheaded the morning after the wedding. Then he meets Scheherazade (Maya Koumani), who outwits the ruler and punishes him for his actions. Fairbanks considered expanding this pilot from 30 minutes to an hour, but the pilot never sold.

Also, in 1956, Fairbanks set a co-production deal with Television Programs of America (TPA) for a *Captain Kidd* series to star Anthony Dexter. Dexter, who had starred in the movie *Valentino*, and looked similar to the silent screen heartthrob, had previously played Kidd in the feature *Captain Kidd and the Slave Girl*. Others in the cast included Denton De Gray as Scar, Danny Green as Morgan and Christopher Lee as the governor. Directed by Dennis Vance for Douglas Fairbanks Productions Ltd., this project also didn't turn into a series. The pilot later aired as an episode of the syndicated series *Chevron Hall of Stars* in 1956.

Fairbanks came up with a novel idea for producing potential TV series that foreshadowed the movie of the week concept. His company produced some theatrical films that were to serve as "dry runs" for prospective TV series. He intended to work out any problems on the features and then convert them into series after they appeared in movie theaters in England. Three such properties that were to be made into movies were *A Place of Execution*, *Counselor at Large* and *Privateer*. Only one, *A Place of Execution*, could be confirmed as actually produced, under the title *The Hostage* in 1956. *The Hostage*, with Ron Randell as airplane pilot Bill Trailer, involves the kidnapping of the daughter of the president of San Tanio, a South American country. A revolutionary leader in the country has been arrested for the murder of the head of the police and is due to be executed. President Pablo Gonzuelo (Carl Jaffe) receives a note that his daughter Rosa (Mary Parker), living in London, has been kidnapped. She will be released if the president stops the execution of the revolutionary leader. Bill Trailer is contacted by the kidnappers to act as go-between between them and Scotland Yard and to convince Rosa to make an appeal to her father for the revolutionary's reprieve. When Trailer is placed in the same room as Rosa, the two try to come up with ways to escape. The president signs the execution order, while Trailer finally escapes after Rosa is taken by the kidnappers to be hanged from a street lamp in front of the San Tanio embassy in London. Trailer arrives with Scotland Yard detectives in time to save her.

The movie was made very cheaply using stock footage and newsreel clips for many outdoor scenes. Directed by Harold Huth, it was written by Alfred Shaughnessy, based on a 1953 British television series, *A Place of Execution*. Presumably, if a series had resulted from the movie, it would have followed the adventures of Bill Trailer.

Fairbanks' production companies continued to develop pilots in the late 1950s after his anthology series came to an end. At the time, he said that his multiple production activities didn't give him enough time to act as host and producer of *Douglas Fairbanks Presents*.[1] One such pilot, *Tramp Ship*, was done in 1957. The production company chartered a freighter to use as a "floating stage" for this proposed series. Home base for the series was London but episodes would have been filmed all over the world. The pilot was written by Norman Reilly Raine, who created the *Tugboat Annie* series of movies. Another such project intended for the 1958–59 TV season was *Police Boat*; I could not find details about its storyline.

Also in the late '50s, Dougfair Productions joined with Sol Lesser to produce a pilot called *The Gaucho*, based on the silent film starring Fairbanks, Sr. Shot in Mexico, the pilot focused on the life of an Argentinian cowboy played by Carlos Rivas. At least three scripts were written for the proposed series: "The Troubadour" by Polly James, "The Stampede" by Milton Raison and Arthur Brown, Jr., and "The Matchmaker," also by Raison and Brown.

One of the last pilots in which Fairbanks was involved as a creator, but not as a producer, was called *Three Wishes*. A departure from his adventure-type projects, it was a sitcom—something like a forerunner to *I Dream of Jeannie*, but with the genie male and his mistress female. Starring Uruguayan actor Gustavo Rojo as the genie and Diane Jergens as Annie, his mistress, the storyline had Annie traveling to Boston to marry Henry (George Grizzard). As a wedding gift from her Uncle Jonas (Wallace Ford), owner of a New York City antique shop, Annie selects an antique Arabian lamp. When she rubs the lamp, out jumps a genie willing to help with her problems. She wishes for a new outfit including a mink coat to impress her husband-to-be. After arriving in Boston, Henry questions where she got the new clothes. Annie shows Henry the lamp and conjures up the genie, but the genie is invisible to everyone but Annie. Later Henry finds a man's suit that the genie had left in Annie's hotel room which makes Henry even more suspicious. The wedding is called off, and Annie returns to her uncle's antique shop.

Don Sharpe-Warren Lewis Enterprises produced the unsold pilot for NBC in 1960. Andrew McCullough directed from a script by Robert Riley

Crutcher. *Three Wishes* was based on an episode of *Douglas Fairbanks Presents* titled "The Genie" in which Fairbanks appeared as the spirit. In the episode, a beautiful young girl discovers that her grandfather, who runs a curio shop, has had a lamp delivered from Tangier. Every time he rubs the lamp, a genie appears ready to grant his every wish.

Fairbanks gave up producing in the 1960s and returned to acting with roles in both TV and films. His final motion picture was 1981's *Ghost Story* with Fred Astaire and Melvyn Douglas. Fairbanks passed away in 2000.

Jose Ferrer

Born in Puerto Rico in 1912, Jose Ferrer made his movie debut as Charles VII in *Joan of Arc* (1948). The film starred Ingrid Bergman in the lead role. Ferrer later won an Oscar for his portrayal of poet and swordsman Cyrano de Bergerac in the 1950 film of the same name. The actor went on to memorable portrayals as artist Toulouse-Lautrec in *Moulin Rouge* (1952), composer Sigmund Romberg in *Deep in My Heart* (1954), the defense counsel for the mutineers in *The Caine Mutiny* (1954) and the Turkish Bey in *Lawrence of Arabia* (1962). In addition to the Academy Award, Ferrer won several Tonys for his performances and directing of Broadway plays.

In early TV, Ferrer reportedly wanted to be a producer. An item in the April 11, 1951, *Variety* stated that he had purchased the rights to the *Horatio Alger* series and wanted actor Wally Cox for the lead. Ferrer also bought the rights to Irvin S. Cobb's *Judge Priest* short stories for a possible series. Priest was an eccentric judge in rural Kentucky, portrayed on the movie screen by humorist Will Rogers. In addition, Ferrer was planning a show called *The Creative Personality* featuring psychologist Dr. Fredric Wertham. None of these projects ever resulted in a series.

Another of Ferrer's proposed TV series was *Royal Performance*, a 1952 concept that he would produce, direct and occasionally star on.[1] The show would have featured a single actor on camera alone performing excerpts from classic or contemporary works. For example, one episode would be devoted to actor Peter Lorre dramatizing the murder and escape scenes from *Crime and Punishment*. Another installment would focus on Broderick Crawford appearing as a businessman whose world is collapsing around him from *The Big Deal*. Joan Crawford may have starred on an episode describing the circumstances of her broken marriage from *Love Will Out*. *Royal Performance* would have been produced by Columbia Pictures for NBC.

MGM signed a deal with Ferrer in 1960 to star in a 60-minute series based on the exploits of Agatha Christie's Belgian detective Hercule Poirot. Ferrer would both produce and star in the drama which was slated for the 1961–62 TV season on CBS. Episodes were to be shot on locales throughout Europe.

Originally, MGM contemplated a 30-minute anthology series titled *Agatha Christie* but abandoned this concept when Ferrer appeared on the scene. But by December 1960, Ferrer left the project without apparently filming a pilot. CBS had concerns over the cost of filming episodes in Europe.

The network was still interested in a series based on the Poirot character. In 1961, a 30-minute pilot was made with Martin Gabel in the lead. When it was screened privately, the reaction was negative. It eventually aired as an episode of *General Electric Theater*.

Ferrer's later attempts at his own TV series were projects that combined his talent as a leading man with unconventional characters. He played an angel in the half-hour comedy anthology pilot *Everything Money Can't Buy* (1974), written by Bernie Slade and directed by Carl Reiner. The actor was the only regular on a show that intended to demonstrate what humans would wish for if an angel were to grant them their hopes and dreams.

The pilot, titled "Mr. Right" (aka "Very Special People"), centered on single, self-sacrificing San Francisco deli worker Doris Moroni (Brenda Vaccaro). She's dating Ernie Hancock (Peter Bonerz), who won't commit to marriage.[2] Riding the bus to work one day, she gives up her seat to an elderly man which brings her to the attention of Mr. Angel (Ferrer). He comes into the deli, introduces himself, stops time and explains he would grant her anything money can't buy. Mr. Angel, wearing a bowler hat and a carnation in his lapel, gives Doris his business card, asks her to contact him, and then leaves. Doris sees him again and decides she wants to meet a new guy—a knight in shining armor. The next thing she knows, Doris is saved from a mugging by a handsome professional golfer named Chris Livingstone (Bert Convy). Doris tells Ernie that she has met another guy, and she and Chris continue to see one another. Ernie follows them on their dates, becoming more and more jealous of their relationship. Meanwhile, Doris begins to see that Chris is not as perfect as she thought. He wants to control all aspects of her life once they are married. After Chris proposes marriage, Ernie proposes to Doris as well, but she says she already said "yes" to Chris. At the wedding, Doris has doubts. During the ceremony, Ernie arrives at the church, says he objects to the marriage and declares his love for her. Doris runs to him and they kiss. In the final scene, Doris thanks Mr. Angel and says she got her knight in shining armor after all.

The pilot was picked up by ABC as a series for the 1974–75 TV season and scheduled for Thursdays at 8:00 p.m. However, in June 1974, ABC announced that Ferrer was being replaced. Michael Eisner, the vice-president of ABC for program development and production, said, "We are changing the character and are going in a new direction on the series, and Ferrer is not right for it. He is a fine actor and this is in no way a reflection on him."[3] Subsequently, the courts delayed a change to the Prime Time Access Rule which would have given the networks an extra hour on Sundays to schedule their programming. Each network had to drop an hour of programming from its fall schedule. In ABC's case, one of the series to go was *Everything Money Can't Buy*. However, the network later brought the series back as a mid-season replacement with Carl Reiner as the angel and with a new title, *Good Heavens*. It lasted 13 episodes.

In 1978, Ferrer starred in a three-part pilot for CBS titled *The Return of Captain Nemo*, produced by Irwin Allen seemingly in an attempt to revive a version of his movie and television series *Voyage to the Bottom of the Sea*. Underwater intelligence experts Lt. Jim Porter (Burr DeBenning) and Comdr. Tom Franklin (Tom Hallick) discover Nemo's ship, the *Nautilus*, while participating in war games in the Pacific and awaken Nemo (Ferrer), who has been in suspended animation for over 100 years. Nemo appears none the worse for wear with a head of silver hair and a full beard. He had been searching for the lost continent of Atlantis when the *Nautilus* ran onto a reef because of a tidal wave. Once the *Nautilus* is freed from the reef, Nemo goes off to find Atlantis and also pursue Prof. Waldo Cunningham (Burgess Meredith), the proverbial evil genius with his own state-of-the-art submarine, the *Raven*, who has trained nuclear missiles on Washington, D.C., and is demanding $1,000,000 in gold bullion. Using a laser beam, Nemo destroys Cunningham's nuclear missiles, but then he has to prevent the professor from going after nuclear waste and scattering it throughout the oceans. In the last part of the pilot, Nemo finds Atlantis, but his nemesis Cunningham kidnaps him along with the king of Atlantis. The professor wants to extract every bit of the captain's knowledge by tapping his brain and then destroy every capital city in the world so he can become the leader of the planet. Nemo stops Cunningham's evil plans by destroying the *Raven*.

This pilot was to be the first story arc in a planned *Captain Nemo* series, but since it aired to low ratings, the series never went forward. The pilot was released theatrically as *The Amazing Captain Nemo*.

Reminiscing about working with Ferrer on *Captain Nemo*, actor Tom Hallick recalls that the actor was a delight. Hallick also stated that the turnover among executives at CBS hurt the project. "Half were fired and if a project isn't theirs ... it doesn't get made."[4]

Having portrayed an angel in *Everything Money Can't Buy*, Ferrer played a devil named Victor Noble in *The Covenant*, a NBC movie pilot broadcast in August 1985. His character was the head of the wealthy Noble banking family in San Francisco. It seems that in 1500 B.C., the Aryans made a pact with evil. The Sanskrit word for Aryan is "noble." The Noble family—the most powerful banking family in the country—was the keeper of the Aryan covenant whose power passed through the females of the family. The Nobles used the power of the covenant to control people and events for their own personal gain, while the covenant protected the family. They maintained a sacred fire in the basement of their bank, engaged in sorcery and financed global terrorism. Victor's wife Dana (Jane Badler), who had supernatural powers, had previously been married to his brother. (Victor killed his brother to marry Dana.) Her fraternal twin sister Claire (Michelle Phillips) was married to Eric (Bradford Dillman), Victor's son by a previous marriage. Stefan (Kevin Conroy), Claire and Dana's brother, was fond of Angelica, his niece and Claire's daughter. Zachariah (Barry Morse), a judge, had been assigned by the forces of good to destroy the Nobles.

The storyline of the pilot focuses on whether 18-year-old Angelica will be told about the covenant now (usually the family waits to tell their children until they turn 21). The judge had attempted to murder Angelica so she would not be able to inherit and then pass on the evil of the covenant. Dana wants to initiate Angelica now. Victor resists but then changes his mind after Angelica and her parents leave the compound to go to a nightclub over Victor's objections. Claire wants her daughter and husband to leave the compound permanently. With the assistance of David Wyman (Charles Frank), a relatively new employee of the Noble Bank, Claire procures airline tickets. At the airport, Eric is murdered by Dana in disguise. Dana makes it appear that Stewart Hall, another bank employee who had hired David, aided Claire. She convinces Claire to help her get rid of Hall or else she will ask Angelica for help. In the end, David Wyman agrees to work on behalf of Zachariah against the Noble family. J.D. Feigelson and Dan DiStefano wrote the pilot, which was directed by Walter Grauman.

A year after *The Covenant* failed to become a series, Ferrer landed a featured role on a short-lived TV series, *Bridges to Cross*. He played Morris Kane, the acerbic editor of the major news magazine *World/Week*. The stars of the series were Suzanne Pleshette as Tracy Bridges and her ex Nicolas Surovy as Peter Cross, reporters for the magazine. The CBS series lasted only seven episodes. Ferrer then became a semi-regular on *Newhart* as Arthur VanderKellen, Stephanie's (Julia Duffy) father, from 1985 to 1987 and then had a role as Reuben Moreno on the daytime drama *Another World* from 1989 to 1991.

One year before his 1992 death, Ferrer made his final prime-time television appearance as orator Edward Everett in *The Perfect Tribute*, about how Lincoln came to write the Gettysburg Address.

Geraldine Fitzgerald

Irish-born Geraldine Fitzgerald began her American film career in the late 1930s, starring with Bette Davis in *Dark Victory* (1939). Fitzgerald appeared as Ann King, secretary and best friend of Judith Truhenne (Bette Davis). Fitzgerald received an Academy Award nomination for Best Supporting Actress for her role as Isabella Linton in *Wuthering Heights* (1939). Then, after appearances in several 1940s movies, her film roles diminished. During the next decade, she worked on the Broadway stage; the 1960s saw her return to features as a character actress in *The Pawnbroker* (1964), playing a neighborhood social worker in this movie about a Holocaust survivor, and in *Rachel, Rachel* (1968), as a minister.

Fitzgerald made many guest appearances on episodic television beginning in the 1950s with roles on anthology series such as *Suspense* and *Goodyear Playhouse*. In 1983, she played Rose Kennedy in the *Kennedy* miniseries. Fitzgerald received an Emmy nomination for guest starring on *The Golden Girls* in the 1988 episode "Mother's Day."

The actress' first regular TV role was in a summer prime-time soap opera, CBS's *Our Private World,* a 1965 spin-off from the daytime drama *As the World Turns* (CBS was imitating the success of ABC's *Peyton Place*). She played Helen Eldredge, matriarch of a socially prominent and wealthy family living in Lake Forest, Illinois, with whom Lisa Hughes (Eileen Fulton) from *As the World Turns* becomes involved. *Our Private World* ended its run in September 1965. In 1970, Fitzgerald appeared on the ABC daytime drama *The Best of Everything* as Violet Jordan, a warm and loving mother surrogate to the female secretaries on the series.

In the late '70s, Fitzgerald continued with maternal roles, appearing as Margaret McKenna "Peggy" Quinn, wife of New York City firefighter Tom Quinn (William Swetland), in *The Quinns,* an extended family drama pilot. Peggy's father-in-law Sean Quinn, Sr. (Liam Dunn) had retired from the fire department 27 years earlier. Tom and Peggy were the parents of Bill (Barry Bostwick), 39, single and a fire department lieutenant; Michael (Peter Masterson), 38, who taught French and coached basketball at a high school and was married to Elizabeth with four kids; and 45-year-old Rita (Pat Elliott), who had been living in Nebraska with her family until her husband's death. Rita had two children, 21-year-old Laurie, an aspiring actress, and 14-year-old Robbie.

The pilot, which aired as an ABC movie on July 1, 1977, was written by veteran movie-TV scribe Sidney Carroll, directed by Daniel Petrie, and produced by Daniel Wilson. The main storyline deals with Tom's retirement from the fire department, Rita returning to New York and trying to find a job, Bill's romantic entanglement with the wife of his boss, the fire commissioner, and Mike trying to become a surrogate father to nephew Robbie.[1]

Fitzgerald's character is supportive of the family: She attends a ceremony where her husband receives a commendation from the fire commissioner for his service to the city. She sublets an apartment for Rita and her kids to live in until Rita can find a place of her own, and she helps plan her husband's retirement dinner. Her character tries to stop Tom from obsessing about his age. He admits that his entire life has been the fire department and his family. He has no hobbies and is depressed about his future.

Fitzgerald's next TV series project was in 1978 when she taped a 60-minute special for PBS as a pilot for a weekly series featuring her cabaret act. If the special had become a series, she would have played hostess in presenting different cabaret acts each week.

Making her debut at age 71 as a potential regular on a situation comedy called *Mabel and Max*, Fitzgerald appeared as Mabel Oberdeen, a 70-year-old, thrice-married veteran actress who befriended 24-year-old Maxine "Max" Turner (Mary B. Ward). Max had just arrived in New York City to further her acting career. She met Mabel when she was in Mabel's acting class and helped out in the apartment they shared, paying half of the rent. Harry Kanter (Shelly Berman) had been Mabel's agent for the past 40 years, and Paul Oberdeen (Tony Goldwyn) was Mabel's 32-year-old son. Comedian Elayne Boosler and Barra Grant scripted the pilot, which was directed by John Pasquin and produced by Barbra Streisand's Barwood Productions.

The storyline had Paul wanting his mother Mabel to move from New York City to New Jersey to live with her sister. Mabel doesn't want to retire despite the fact that she hasn't acted in a year due to a heart attack. Mabel asks Harry to find her work. Reluctantly, she auditions for a laxative commercial, the only job Harry finds for her. She blows the audition because she really doesn't want to appear in a commercial for a product like "Fiber Life." Mabel then admits to Max that she is afraid of starting over but eventually she does the commercial.

The unsold pilot aired on CBS on July 31, 1987. Director Pasquin says that Fitzgerald was wonderful to work with, "totally directable and charming with a wonderful sense of humor."[2] He remembers one shot in particular, a framed close-up of a black-and-white photo of her, possibly from *Wuthering Heights*, which was on a dresser in her apartment set, and the shot was framed so, as she looked at it, her face was reflected on top of the photo.

The sound stage on which *Mabel and Max* was filmed was the one the actress worked on when making *Dark Victory*. The makeup artist for the pilot, Michael Westmore, was the grandnephew of Perc Westmore, the *Dark Victory* makeup man, and Tony Goldwyn, who played her son, was the grandson of *Wuthering Heights* producer Sam Goldwyn.

Commenting on *Mabel and Max*, Fitzgerald indicated that her character "feels like I do about work." She went on to say, "[H]ere I am, suddenly working on something Barbra Streisand is involved in. I've always been a great fan of hers. Who'd have thought it would happen!"[3]

Fitzgerald's final appearance was in the 1991 TV movie *Bump in the Night* starring Meredith Baxter and Christopher Reeve. After a lengthy battle with Alzheimer's disease, she died at age 91 in 2005.

Joan Fontaine

Joan Fontaine, born Joan de Beauvoir de Havilland, made her first film appearance in the 1935 Joan Crawford feature *No More Ladies* where she was billed as Joan Burfield. Six years later she received her first Academy Award nomination for Alfred Hitchcock's *Rebecca* in which she played the second wife of Maxim de Winter (Laurence Olivier), whom she comes to believe is still in love with his late first wife Rebecca. Fontaine, known for her elegance and refinement, won the Oscar as Best Actress for her starring role in Hitchcock's *Suspicion,* becoming the only actor ever to win an Academy Award for a performance in a Hitchcock movie. In *Suspicion,* Fontaine played a woman who comes to believe that her irresponsible husband (Cary Grant) is planning to kill her. The actress was also nominated for an Oscar for the 1943 film *The Constant Nymph,* about a young girl (Fontaine) who falls in love with a much older, self-absorbed composer (Charles Boyer). Fontaine's sister Olivia de Havilland won Oscars for *To Each His Own* (1946) and *The Heiress* (1949).

Fontaine's first venture into becoming a TV series regular was in 1954 as one of the hosts of a proposed travelogue series, *Holiday,* that was to be produced in Paris by her spouse Collier Young. In addition to Fontaine, Ida Lupino and Edmond O'Brien were to serve as narrators of the 30-minute series. Somewhat ironically, Lupino was the former wife of Collier Young. The pair had divorced in 1951, and a year later Young married Fontaine.

As with other actresses profiled in this book, Fontaine was offered her share of anthology series to host in the mid–50s. She was one of the six stars slated to preside over such a series along with Claudette Colbert. About starring on her own series, Fontaine said, "If I can't find one good script, how can I expect to find 39? It's all a question of material. TV is the best publicity you can get. But you have to think of the quality first."[1]

In 1956, Fontaine reportedly was to be one of the hosts of an anthology series with something of a twist. Three actresses would star on the series with Fontaine hosting dramatic presentations one week, another actress hosting musicals the next week, and a third female star introducing comedies the following week. No title was given for the series, which never came to fruition.

Five years later, Fontaine starred in a pilot for an anthology series which planned to feature stories of romance. *The Ways of Love* was a 1961 presentation on *Alcoa Presents—One Step Beyond* with Fontaine and Warren Beatty and produced by Collier Young. If the pilot had been picked up as a series, Fontaine would have been its host and narrator.

The project featured Fontaine as Helen Grayson, an alcoholic. One snowy day, she invites her husband of 17 years, Harry (Warren Beatty), to their cabin in the mountains and tells him that she doesn't need him or alcohol any more. He leaves and is knocked unconscious in a car accident during a snowstorm. A man then appears at Helen's door looking like a young version of Harry and asks to use her phone. The young man relates a story about his wife giving birth and the baby dying, which had happened to Helen after her marriage to Harry. At the time, Helen thought that her husband didn't want the baby, but the young man says he did. The man leaves. Harry regains consciousness and attempts to free himself from the vehicle. Helen phones her doctor about what she just experienced and asks him to come immediately. On his way, the doctor helps Harry extricate himself from the car. He and the doctor arrive at the cabin, and Helen and Harry reconcile.

John Newland, the host of *One Step Beyond*, directed the pilot from a script titled "The Visitor" by Larry Marcus. If the pilot had become a series, in addition to host duties, Fontaine would act on each episode either as the star or in a supporting role. The series would have had a stock company of actors who would rotate in relative importance in each episode's roles on a weekly basis.

In February 1983, NBC premiered a prime-time soap opera, *Bare Essence* about power and corruption in the perfume business starring Genie Francis from *General Hospital*. Joan Fontaine was to have had a recurring role on this drama as a columnist for a women's magazine. Fontaine did appear on two episodes of *Bare Essence* but in no more, probably because the series lasted for only 11 installments before it was canceled.

In 1986, Fontaine performed on the TV pilot *Dark Mansions*. Aaron Spelling produced the pilot in yet another attempt to turn a movie star from the Golden Age of Hollywood into a TV regular. The project, directed by Jerry London, was written by Robert McCullough based on a first draft script by long-time TV writers Anthony and Nancy Lawrence. Spelling originally wanted Loretta Young to play Margaret Drake, the elegant matriarch of a wealthy ship-building family living in a mansion on Drake Point, Seattle. According to McCullough, he and producer E. Duke Vincent met with Young at her home. She asked him to kneel and pray to God about the venture and wanted references to Christianity added to the script. The producers decided that she wasn't right for the part, and Fontaine stepped in. McCullough called her "lovely and very classy."[2]

The pilot opens with Margaret Drake wanting to write her memoirs and hiring Shellane Victor (Linda Purl) to live in her home to help her. Margaret's husband Alexander (Dan O'Herlihy) is struck by lightning while testing a new boat in a storm; this makes Margaret chairwoman of the board of Drake Shipyards, much to the dismay of her adopted son Phillip (Paul Shenar) who wants to take control of the company and take it public. Phillip is married to Jessica (Lois Chiles) who is cheating on him. They have two teenage kids, Noelle (Melissa Sue Anderson), who is blind, and Cody (Yves Martin) who is adopted. Margaret has a biological son named Jason (Michael York), a widower whose wife Yvette died under mysterious circumstances. Was she murdered, did she commit suicide, or did she accidentally fall off a cliff on the estate? Jason also has two teenagers, Nick (Grant Aleksander), who has anger issues stemming from his mother's death, and Banda (Nicollette Sheridan).

With such an extended family, there were potential conflicts between the Fontaine character and her sons, between the sons themselves, between the sons and their kids, as well as between the siblings and cousins. Thrown into the mix of family conflicts were some gothic elements. For example, despite the fact that Noelle was suffering from hysterical blindness after witnessing Yvette's death, she seems to have second sight and "saw" the death of her grandfather in the storm. Margaret Drake and her late husband had built a duplicate mansion on the estate and abandoned their first house after Margaret had some type of accident. Also, there were unexplained noises in Margaret's current home. Most mysterious of all: Shellane was a dead ringer for Jason's late wife Yvette.

At a party given by Margaret to celebrate the seventy-fifth anniversary of Drake Shipyards, Shellane, unbeknownst to her but with the encouragement of Jessica, wears a gown that Yvette had worn on celebratory occasions. After the initial shock of seeing Shellane in the dress, Margaret and Jason think they hear Yvette's voice coming from a bedroom in the mansion. That is where the unsold pilot ended, but when it aired as a movie of the week, to give the pilot more of a conclusion, a scroll was added stating that Shellane finished Margaret's memoirs, married Jason, and then died in the same place where Yvette's body had been found.

The network and Aaron Spelling were in negotiations to decide if the series should be picked up for 13 or for 22 episodes. The negotiations collapsed after a test audience began laughing at the pilot, thinking it was high camp.

After *Dark Mansions* failed to turn into a series, Fontaine became one of the first movie stars to have her own show on cable TV. In 1987, an announcement was made that she would appear in a weekly show on Tempo Television, one of the first basic cable outlets. She was to have hosted a 30-

minute series interviewing guests including Tony Randall, Harry Belafonte, Richard Gere and Joel Grey beginning in January 1988. I do not know if the series actually premiered; the cable outlet was sold to NBC in 1988 and became CNBC.

Joan Fontaine's last TV acting appearance was in the 1994 Christmas movie *Good King Wenceslas* playing Queen Ludmilla. Fontaine died in 2013.

Janet Gaynor

Janet Gaynor was unique in that she was the only actress to win a single Oscar for appearing in more than one movie. She won the award in 1929 for her performances in the silent films *7th Heaven* (1927), about a romance between a Paris sewer worker and an abused prostitute; *Sunrise: A Song of Two Humans* (1927) in which Gaynor played the wife of a farmer in love with another woman; and *Street Angel* (1928), as a destitute young woman who joins a traveling carnival. Since 1929 was the first year for the Academy Awards, her Oscar for Best Actress represented work for movies made in 1927 and 1928. Her most notable sound film was 1937's *A Star Is Born*, about a rising Hollywood star in love with an actor whose career is on a downward spiral. Gaynor was known for playing sweet, wholesome, young women in her films.

Gaynor retired from acting in 1939, but in the early '50s she returned with appearances in anthology series like *Medallion Theatre* and *Lux Video Theatre*. Having grown older, the actress had to recreate her screen persona by playing mothers and widows instead of young women. In 1957, for example, she had the role of the mother in the musical comedy film *Bernardine* with Pat Boone and Terry Moore.

In February 1961, *Broadcasting* announced that Janet Gaynor and George Murphy would star in a pilot for Desilu called *Sweet Sixteen*. The two actors would play the parents of three kids—a 16-year-old daughter, a younger daughter and a baby son. Suzie Kaye, Barbara Beaird and Donald Washbrook (brother of *My Friend Flicka* star Johnny Washbrook) were cast as the children in this half-hour comedy pilot written by Ed James, creator of *Father Knows Best*, and directed by John Rich. The pilot was filmed at Desilu for Home-James Productions as a possible series for NBC.

After this pilot failed to become a series, Gaynor considered another TV vehicle, this time playing a widow in her golden years. Created by Ted Key, the creator of *The Saturday Evening Post*'s "Hazel" cartoon, *Emma's First National Bank* (aka *Jennie's Bank*) was to star Gaynor as Emma Heppel, a 55-year-old widow living in a brownstone her husband had left her. To help make ends meet, she rented apartments to several eccentric characters including Ivan Kousikofsky, who ran a ballet school, Kimball Barley, a mural artist, Kimball's wife Edith, a sculptress, and Seymour Baron, a 28-year-old musician who gave organ lessons and composed music for unique instruments such as beer bottles and trash cans.[1]

One day, Emma, who lived her life according to her horoscope, met Buttons Popping, a young woman who waited on her in a restaurant. Buttons, a sexy 21-year-old blonde, eventually moved in with Emma to help her manage her affairs. Buttons strove to be a belly dancer.

Emma soon learns that her distant cousin Alexander Groff has died and left her his fortune along with the bank he owned. Evan Moore, the bank's conservative, widowed president, slightly older than Emma, had an 18-year-old son, Benson, who wanted to be a rock musician with a band called the Abominable Snowmen. However, Emma, a soft-touch at heart, wanted a small office in the bank for her and Buttons to make a few loans to people who had been turned down by other financial institutions. Moore assigned Otis Wilson, his 28-year-old protégé and son of a dear friend, to oversee Emma's new loan department. Otis was to keep Emma happy and not allow her to give money away. Emma decided that she would co-sign every loan she made and personally see that whatever ventures she would finance wouldn't fail. The projects financed by Emma always seemed to succeed because she had an almost unfailing insight and confidence in people.

This comedy projected for the 1966–67 TV season was to be produced for Screen Gems by Gaynor's husband, Paul Gregory. Gregory, who married Gaynor in 1964, had produced the movies *The Night of the Hunter* (1955) and *The Naked and the Dead* (1958). I could not determine whether a pilot based on Ted Key's idea was ever made. Contacted by this author on why *Emma's First National Bank* never went forward, Gregory succinctly replied, "My wife nor I found the project worthy of pursuit."[2]

Ted Key had really wanted actress Helen Hayes for the proposed series. In response to his letter asking her to consider the pilot script, Hayes responded, "I do appreciate your writing the TV character for me—and I've been trying for days to screw up my courage to, at least, read the script—but I can't! I'm lazy at this stage—and I hate California. So many of my friends who have undertaken serials have been so unhappy and exhausted—and felt so trapped."[3]

Gaynor's final TV appearance was in a 1981 episode of *The Love Boat*. She passed away in September 1984 as the result of complications from injuries sustained in a 1982 automobile accident with singer-actress Mary Martin.

Stewart Granger

Best known for playing the lead in movies such as *King Solomon's Mines* (1950), *Scaramouche* (1952) and *Beau Brummell* (1954), handsome, dashing Stewart Granger (real name: James Stewart) began his film career in the 1930s with roles such as the son of a lord in the British comedy *So This Is London* (1939). In the '40s, he made features including *Waterloo Road* (1945), appearing as a philandering draft dodger, and *Madonna of the Seven Moons* (1945) where he played a jewel thief. Granger's screen image was that of a swashbuckler-adventurer.

Variety reported in 1959 that Granger had signed a deal with Four Star Productions for his own TV adventure series, *Safari,* to be filmed in Africa. The show was to be produced in association with his production company, Tracy Productions, named after his daughter with his then-wife, actress Jean Simmons. However, later that year, the actor apparently changed his mind about filming a series in Africa since he didn't want to be away from his own animals on a ranch he owned in Arizona.

In 1960, Granger and Four Star announced a new projected half-hour series, *The House of Four Keys*. Granger would portray, what else, an adventurer. I could track down few details about pilot but apparently his character was one of the four Key brothers who ran an art gallery.

In 1970, Granger became a regular on an established TV series when he signed to star as retired Colonel Alan McKenzie on NBC's *The Virginian* in its ninth season. The McKenzie character, a former army major who had commanded troops in Africa, India and other parts of the British Empire, became the new owner of the Shiloh ranch. The Western's title changed to *The Men from Shiloh* with James Drury, Doug McClure and new regular Lee Majors starring on a rotating basis in each episode. Granger's character appeared in 11 of the series' 24 installments. According to his biographer,

> Granger told the *Radio Times* that he coped with this all-action part by showing that he could ride as well as his American co-stars and by doing his own stunts. That way he earned their respect, he stated.... However, it seems he did not earn their love, because he admitted that tempers frayed during the series. "If you've made 70 films

over 39 years, it's not easy to work with a man who's only done one thing in his life—play a television cowboy." This may well have been a not-too-subtle dig at James Drury who had starred in the original *The Virginian* series....¹

After the demise of *The Men from Shiloh*, Granger next tackled the role of famous detective Sherlock Holmes in a 1972 ABC movie pilot, *The Hound of the Baskervilles* with Bernard Fox as Dr. Watson, Anthony Zerbe as Dr. Mortimer, Ian Ireland as Henry Baskerville, William Shatner as George Sta-

Bernard Fox as Dr. Watson (left) and Stewart Granger as Sherlock Holmes in the ABC-TV movie pilot *The Hound of the Baskervilles*, which aired February 12, 1972. Fox is probably better known for his role on *Bewitched* as Dr. Bombay.

pleton and Anne Merrow as Beryl Stapleton. Barry Crane directed the pilot, adapted from the Arthur Conan Doyle novel by Robert E. Thompson. Approaching 60, Granger evidently decided to give up swashbuckling roles to portray more cerebral characters.

The plot follows fairly closely that of the novel with Dr. Mortimer contacting Holmes about the unnatural deaths of members of the Baskerville family dating back to the English Civil War when Hugo Baskerville was killed by a mad dog after offering his soul to the Devil for help in abducting a woman. The most recent victim, Sir Charles Baskerville, died after being attacked by an enormous hound. Sir Henry Baskerville, Charles' nephew, is the heir to the estate since Charles' youngest brother Rodger died in South America, apparently leaving no heirs. Sir Henry has been receiving warning notes from an anonymous source not to move to the Baskerville estate. Holmes and Watson accompany Sir Henry to the estate where they meet neighbors George Stapleton and his sister Beryl. Sir Henry begins to court Beryl. Holmes finds that Beryl is really Stapleton's wife, not his sister, and that Stapleton is Sir Henry's cousin Rodger, the unknown son of Rodger Baskerville, Sir Charles' deceased youngest brother. Rodger wanted to eliminate Sir Henry in order to inherit the estate. George Stapleton (*nee* Rodger Baskerville) is attacked by the hound he had trained to kill Sir Henry and falls into quicksand.

The Hound of the Baskervilles was one of three pilots made for a Universal series to be called *Great Detectives,* somewhat patterned after Universal's *Mystery Movie* series which aired on NBC for several years initially featuring *Columbo, McMillan and Wife* and *McCloud.* The detectives in the proposed new series were to be Holmes, Hildegarde Winters, played by Eve Arden, and Nick Carter, played by Robert Conrad.

Granger's final TV role was a 1991 episode of the James Earl Jones–Richard Crenna series *Pros and Cons* (originally titled *Gabriel's Fire*). In the episode, Granger played a former matinee idol who hires the two detectives to find his lost love (June Allyson). Granger died two years later at age 80.

Kathryn Grayson

Rarely, but it did happen occasionally, film stars would attempt something on television that was light years away from their typical movie image. Such was the case with Kathryn Grayson's first TV series pilot.

Beautiful and ladylike, actress-singer Grayson was most known for her appearances in movie musicals from the 1940s and '50's. Her most famous roles were as the singing daughter of an Army commander in the 1943 film *Thousands Cheer*, one of the stars of 1945's *Anchors Aweigh* with Frank Sinatra and Gene Kelly, and as Magnolia Hawks in the 1951 remake of *Show Boat*. She partnered with Italian tenor Mario Lanza in *That Midnight Kiss* (1949) and in *The Toast of New Orleans* (1950). Supposedly while shooting a scene for the latter film, Lanza attempted to French kiss Grayson; the actress claimed that the situation was made worse by Lanza eating garlic before shooting. She had her costume designer sew pieces of brass into her gloves. When Lanza tried to kiss her again, she hit him with the glove.[1]

In the 1960s, Grayson appeared on stage in musicals like *Camelot* and in the operas *La Boheme, Madame Butterfly* and *La Traviata*. Saying "I'm just tired of musicals without stories—of scripts I'm offered where it says I sing for no reason at all," Grayson's first attempt at a television series was *Lone Woman*, a pilot that aired as part of CBS's *Playhouse 90* in December 1957.[2] This proposed Western drama starred Grayson in an unusual non-singing title role as a Cheyenne princess who marries fur trader William Bent (Scott Brady). Raymond Burr was William's brother Charles. William and Charles Bent were real-life traders who had established a privately owned fort in the early nineteenth century. Ralph Levy produced and directed the pilot from a script by Al C. Ward.

The plot concerned Jesse White (Vincent Price) competing with the Bent brothers' fur trading business in Arizona by threatening violence to those trappers who sold to the Bents. William decides to marry Lone Woman, making him a blood brother and partner in a beaver fur trading agreement with the Indian tribes. His brother Charles resents the idea of William marrying a Native American. However, William really falls in love with Lone Woman, and so wedding plans are made. After White tells the chief of the tribe the original reason Bent wanted to marry Lone Woman, the chief terminates the trading agreement with Bent.

While William is away scouting for furs, White's buddy Jim Kester (Jack Lord) decides to have some "fun" with Lone Woman. However, she shows him so much kindness that he just sits and talks with her all night. Meanwhile, White has killed an enemy of Kester's, but Kester is accused of the crime. Kester's only alibi is that he spent the night with Lone Woman, but he won't dishonor her by saying so. She comes to his defense in court and is backed up by Charles Bent, who watched Lone Woman and Kester talk all night and realized that she is a fine woman. In the end, after White wounds Charles, William kills him.

The original concept for the proposed series focused on Bent's fort (the only privately owned fort in America), which the Bent brothers leased to the army, trappers and others. Episodes would have been based on historical fact with the Bent brothers appearing in only those stories dealing with their exploits. CBS was looking for an adult Western like their hit *Gunsmoke*.

The network abandoned this approach and decided to use the premise for another series it had been developing with Grayson which was titled *Lone Woman* and work the Grayson character into the tales of William Bent and his brother. Rather than shoot a 30-minute pilot, CBS decided to present a 90-minute feature as part of its *Playhouse 90*.

Lone Woman, which would have been a rare Western with a female lead, never became a series. In 1967, Grayson tried again for TV series stardom. This proposed series, tentatively titled *The Kathryn Grayson Show*, would have featured the actress' 18-year-old daughter Patti Johnston in a series about a mother and daughter starring on a major television show. Frank Tashlin, who was dating Grayson at the time, planned to write and direct the pilot, which would have been a feature-length film. During his career, Tashlin directed several Warner Brothers cartoons as well as the live action comedies *The Girl Can't Help It* (1956) and *The Geisha Boy* (1958). The project with Grayson never materialized.

Grayson's final attempt at her own show was labeled a "mystery-comedy" with the 53-year-old actress playing a psychic detective. Robert Guenette and Paul Asselin produced the 1975 pilot. While no series ever eventuated, Guenette and Asselin used clips from the Grayson pilot in the 1976 movie *The Amazing World of Psychic Phenomena*, based in part on the files of Dutch psychic Peter Hurkos. Grayson had been a follower of Hurkos ever since he supposedly helped her locate $40,000 worth of jewels stolen from her hotel room in Chicago. Hurkos' wife Stephany became Grayson's personal manager. In *The Amazing World of Psychic Phenomena*, the actress appears in a segment from the pilot as an unnamed psychic investigator helping the police solve a girl's murder.

Grayson's final TV role was as Ideal Molloy, a resident of Cabot Cove, in three episodes of Angela Lansbury's long-running series *Murder, She Wrote*. The character first appeared in a 1987 installment and then again in two 1989 episodes. Grayson passed away in 2010.

Susan Hayward

Edythe Marrener, screen name Susan Hayward, starred in 65 movies over four decades. At the height of her career, she was the number one female box office star in the world and the top money-earner for MGM and Twentieth Century–Fox. She received her first of five Best Actress Academy Award nominations for the movie *Smash-Up* (1947), about female alcoholism. She was also nominated for *My Foolish Heart* (1949), *With a Song in My Heart* (1952) and *I'll Cry Tomorrow* (1955). She finally won the award for *I Want to Live!* (1958) portraying Barbara Graham, the first woman executed for murder in the U.S. Hayward's most memorable film performances were those in which she played damaged women trying to cope with their circumstances.

Attempting her own TV series, Hayward had roles in two movie pilots in 1972. In both, she played strong, professional females who had been widowed. Written by Fay Kanin and directed by former actor Don Taylor, *Heat of Anger* featured Hayward as a wealthy attorney. (She replaced an ailing Barbara Stanwyck in the lead role; three days into filming Stanwyck had to have emergency kidney surgery.) If it had become a series, the title would have been *Fitzgerald and Pride*.

Jessie Fitzgerald and Augustis Pride (James Stacy) defend Frank Galvin (Lee J. Cobb), who has been arrested for murdering construction worker Ray Carson. Carson had been having an affair with Galvin's daughter Chris (Jennifer Penny). Pride, with an independent spirit, previously worked in the public defender's office. He has his office in the same building as Fitzgerald—a building she inherited from her father. Galvin is accused of pushing Carson off a high-rise building under construction. Pride concludes that Carson, who always lived his life on the edge, wanted a confrontation with Galvin. The two attorneys attempt to show that Carson, a risk-taker, punched Galvin, who went down, and then Carson fell back over the edge of the building. In the end, the jury acquits Galvin.

Hayward liked the fast pace of making TV shows compared to traditional movies. "It's good to get on with the show, without all that sitting around we used to do in making movies," the actress remarked. "It's more fun, from my point of view."[1]

CBS rejected the *Fitzgerald and Pride* pilot, but ABC considered turning it into a series. However, that network ultimately decided not to go ahead with it.

In the same year, Hayward made another movie of the week as a possible pilot for a TV series, *Say Goodbye, Maggie Cole*. The actress starred as a physician whose husband Ben (Richard Anderson) dies suddenly from a heart attack. Having worked in medical research for the past 15 years, Maggie decides to leave Los Angeles for a short-term job as a practicing physician at an inner-city Chicago clinic run by Dr. Lou Grazzo (Darren McGavin). She cares for various patients including a man having seizures as the result of a possible brain tumor. After he undergoes surgery, the tumor is found to be benign. At the clinic, Maggie encounters Lisa, a young girl who works in a coffee shop. Unknown to Maggie, Dr. Grazzo has been treating Lisa for leukemia. Maggie takes a room in Lisa's grandmother's house. When Lisa passes out and is rushed to the hospital, Maggie learns about Lisa's leukemia. The young woman asks Maggie to take care of her. Maggie asks her old boss

Darren McGavin and Susan Hayward as doctors in the pilot film *Say Goodbye, Maggie Cole*. Speaking to the press about the project, Hayward somewhat indicated that the story mirrored who own life in that she had become a widow a few years earlier and went through the same grieving process as Maggie Cole.

Hank (Dane Clark) from Los Angeles about experimental drugs to treat Lisa's disease. Grazzo doesn't want Maggie to begin administering such drugs to Lisa but reluctantly agrees when her current treatments don't work. The experimental drug seems to help Lisa, but then she becomes comatose. Grazzo challenges Maggie to continue to care for Lisa and deal with her possible death, saying that Maggie hasn't yet come to terms with the death of her husband. Maggie stays with Lisa, who eventually regains consciousness for a short time before passing away. In the end, Maggie decides to remain at the Chicago clinic.

Hayward had to dub a scene in which Maggie cries. When she came to the studio for this, her sobbing was deemed too much for television, and so she redid the scene crying four different ways before the director selected the one that was the least wrenching. Hayward remarked, "If they had wanted any other kind of crying, they would have had to call in another actor."[2]

Written by Sandor Stern and directed by Jud Taylor, *Maggie Cole* was produced by Spelling-Goldberg Productions. It was Hayward's final picture. During the filming, she suspected she might have cancer. She was diagnosed with brain cancer in 1973 and died in 1975. She was one of several actors and crew members from the film *The Conqueror* (1956) who passed away from cancer. Others were John Wayne, director Dick Powell, Agnes Moorehead and Pedro Armendariz. *The Conqueror* had been filmed in St. George, Utah, where a cloud of radiation from a nuclear bomb test in Nevada had fallen a year before the movie was made.

Betty Hutton

Blonde, outgoing, ebullient Betty Hutton seemed to perform her heart out in movies and on the stage. She began in films in the late 1930s, graduating to starring roles in comedies and musicals such as *The Miracle of Morgan's Creek* (1944), *Incendiary Blonde* (1945) and *The Stork Club* (1945). Hutton's image was that of a star with boundless energy almost aching for the audience to love and accept her.

From her success in movies of the early '50s, *Annie Get Your Gun* (1950) and *The Greatest Show on Earth* (1952), TV networks wanted her to star in her own series. ABC made overtures to Hutton, but NBC announced in March 1953 that they were close to a long-term deal with the performer to appear on 26 programs a year featuring her singing and dancing talents. Later that year, NBC nixed the deal because of Hutton's demand to be paid up front for future commitments for installments of a variety series. After the proposed NBC series failed to materialize, CBS courted her for a half-hour show. Again her salary demands put an end to negotiations.

Hutton finally made her TV debut in a 90-minute NBC special that aired September 12, 1954. The head of NBC, Sylvester "Pat" Weaver, who initiated the morning program *Today* and the late night series *Tonight*, decided to introduce special programming during prime time. He came up with the idea of presenting "spectaculars": high-budget, original presentations intended to bring a mass audience to the network to view a unique event. He began these spectaculars under the title *Max Liebman Presents*. Liebman had produced NBC's highly successful *Your Show of Shows* that starred Sid Cesar and Imogene Coca.

Hutton headlined the first spectacular, "Satins and Spurs," an original musical comedy with songs by Ray Evans and Jay Livingston and a book by William Friedberg and Liebman. Set in New York City, it was NBC's first color presentation.

Somewhat similar to the movie *Annie Get Your Gun*, "Satins and Spurs" concerned Cindy Smathers, a rodeo star. *Life* magazine wants to do a photo layout and assigns photographer Tony Bart (Kevin McCarthy). As might be expected, he eventually falls in love with Cindy. He invites her out to a supper club for which she buys a special evening gown. At the club, Cindy sings a brassy number and becomes embarrassed when the patrons don't applaud. But Tony thinks she is wonderful. Cindy wants to leave the city, but Tony tells her that she is the one for him. She thinks he is just saying that to get a good photo of her for the magazine. Later, he shows her an advance copy of the spread including a picture of them kissing with a caption that they are going to marry. Tony wants her to leave the rodeo and become a Broadway star, which Cindy does to great acclaim.

The spectacular met with lukewarm reviews. *Variety* said that it bordered between "fair and disappointing" and the initial Trendex rating of ten cities showed that Ed Sullivan's *Toast of the Town* on CBS beat "Satins and Spurs" in the ratings.[1] Final Nielsen ratings placed the special fifth for the week.

The experience of working on this live show caused Hutton to consider retiring from show business. "I've been working since I was three years old," she said, "and I've learned that the goal I originally sought when I began my career is not what I thought it was. The real sense of values, I find, is in being with my family. I've missed being with my kids, Lindsay and Candy, and I don't want them to grow up as I did—alone." The 33-year-old star went on to say about "Satins and Spurs," "It's fine—if you like to work that hard. I've never worked like that in a tight, compact period. TV is a very exciting medium, but it's not for me. It's great for someone with more energy—it's a medium for the younger people."[2]

In August 1955, she negotiated a deal with NBC to be one of the rotating hosts of Tuesday night's *The Chevy Show*. Its hosts, in addition to Hutton, were Dinah Shore and Bob Hope. Her first appearance as host was on a November installment. As a reviewer described, "Intro'd as 'Miss Dynamite,' she lived up to the sobriquet with all the drive of a dervish and rarely gave herself time to catch her breath.... No performer ever tried to do so much in one show..."[3]

In 1956, Hutton was offered the lead in a comedy called *Sis* in which she would have played an older sister who becomes responsible for raising her two younger siblings. She turned the offer down. Actress Nanette Fabray was then considered for the role, which eventually went to ventriloquist Shari Lewis in a pilot produced by Jess Oppenheimer, written by him and Leo Solomon and directed by William Asher. Sis was in charge of her sister Julie (Sheila James) and brother Don (Morris Lippert). Made for NBC, the pilot didn't sell.

Some time in the '50s, Hutton was being considered to star in a comedy developed by Bert Granet to be called *Cassidy Collins and Complexes*, *The Three Collins* or *The Collins Family*.[4] The three Collins were a theatrical act featuring Mary Collins and her partners Mark and Tim. "Collins" was their stage name; they were not related. The act involved slapstick comedy. Mary was experiencing a delayed adolescence which meant that thoughts of men were entering her life. But no matter whom she showed interest in, Tim and Mark behaved like her big brothers and scared them away. Apparently, the Granet treatment was not developed into a script.

Hutton made a pilot in 1957 for Jess Oppenheimer's Burlingame Productions. Initially titled *Hey Mom* and then *That's My Mom*, it starred Hutton as a widow with four kids living in a rented house, part of Magnolia Mansions, managed by Mr. Tuttle (Herbert Anderson) on behalf of his Aunt Emmy Mae Mosley (Nina Varela). The building complex prohibited children and pets from occupying any of the houses but, in a moment of weakness, Tuttle had permitted Betty Beeman (Hutton) and her children Judy (Nancy Randall), Jerry (Steve Stevens), Donny (John Moss) and Bobby (Donnie Baker) to move in.

When Aunt Emmy pays a surprise visit, Betty has to hurriedly clean up the living room to eliminate any signs of children and pets, which includes her character eating dog biscuits pretending they are health food. Aunt Emmy soon finds the kids and the dog and orders the family to move out.

Betty comes up with a scheme worthy of *I Love Lucy*: She'll impersonate a woman named Betty Lou Mason-Dixon from the South, thinking that she can endear herself to the Southern-bred aunt. Using hot water bottles for padding on her behind and assuming a Southern accent, she tells Aunt Emmy that all the children have Southern names, and convinces her to give Betty a lease allowing children and pets. In the process, Betty sits on the aunt's needlepoint, piercing the hot water bottles with the expected results. Aunt Emmy soon finds out about Betty's impersonation and takes the lease from her. The children's dog then retrieves the lease from the aunt so Betty and her kids can stay in their house.

Scripted by Roland Kibbee, the pilot had a lot of physical comedy performed by Hutton and had the actress singing a couple of songs including "You're Nothing but a Hound Dog" and "Carolina in the Morning." Intended for CBS's 1957–58 season, the show was directed by Robert Sidney. At the time, Hutton called Oppenheimer "brilliant. He will handle my TV career from now on. I don't mean just the series. If I do a spec, Jess will produce it, and Kibbee will write it."[5]

According to Steve Stevens, who played Hutton's oldest son in the pilot, Betty made him feel at ease during his audition. "She stood up, walked to me hand stretched out for a welcoming shake. I will never forget her words, 'Steve, just enjoy the moment, are you ready?'"[6] He felt his audition went

Publicity photograph for the unsold CBS pilot *That's My Mom*. Left to right in the inset are Steve Stevens, Nancy Randall, Betty Hutton and Donnie Baker. Producer Jess Oppenheimer seemed to want to make Hutton play a character like Lucille Ricardo in *I Love Lucy*. Courtesy Steve Stevens.

well. Hutton thanked him, hugged him, and said she hoped that they would meet again, which they did when he got the part.

Before the filming of the pilot, Hutton told Steve, "You are here because I fought for you. Remember that, I'm your 'mom,' you need anything, you come to me."[7] During the filming, Hutton would suggest that certain lines be rewritten for her co-stars as well as recommend close-ups for her co-stars' reactions which were not mentioned in the script.

However, after the pilot was shot in March 1957, Hutton decided that she didn't want to be in a domestic comedy telling Dave Kaufman of *Variety*, "I don't like the idea of a domestic series. It's boring; it's not exciting show biz."[8] Hutton soon changed her mind about starring on this type of series because in 1959 she debuted in *The Betty Hutton Show*, where she played Goldie, a showgirl turned manicurist, who inherited a fortune from one of her customers along with guardianship of his three children, a 12-year-old boy and two teenagers, a girl and a boy. Goldie Appleby engaged in antics like disguising herself as a beatnik to attend a party given by her ward Pat and getting back at two con artists posing as foster parents (Goldie had raised money for their supposed orphanage). Filmed by Desilu, *The Betty Hutton Show* was produced by Hutton's own company. The CBS show lasted one season. Hutton insisted on complete creative control of the series; three different producers and two directors had quit by mid-season.

In 1963, CBS was reportedly interested in starring Hutton in a comedy for the 1964–65 season. Created by Cy Howard, the sitcom *Mother Was a Swinger* focused on Hutton as a surfing, motorbike-riding mother of a 17-year-old boy who dates her son's roommate and has a "philosophical" parrot. Referring to the proposed series, Howard remarked, "I know people say that Betty and I are both difficult to work with but show me a happy TV soundstage and I'll show you a cancellation!"[9] Hutton's then-husband Pete Candoli was to write the score for the proposed series and guest star as a musician on the first show. But the network felt that the concept for the series didn't come together and it never appeared on the CBS schedule. The final mention of a Hutton series was in 1964 with a note that Cecil Barker and Ed Simmons were seeking to produce a series starring the actress for the 1965–66 season. Barker had been the producer of *The Red Skelton Show,* Simmons the head writer for that series. There was no mention about the storyline for the Hutton vehicle, and nothing subsequently transpired.

Later in the 1960s, Hutton essentially retired from show business and worked in a Catholic soup kitchen at a parish that helped her with her addictions to alcohol and prescription drugs. Steve Stevens had a brief reunion with Hutton in 1985 when a friend of his invited him and Betty to a backyard barbecue at his Tarzana ranch. By this time, Stevens had become an agent and tried to convince Betty to give him a chance to revive her career. She responded that she was very content with her life and didn't want to ruin it by being the "old" Betty.[10]

Hutton made her last TV acting appearance in a 1977 episode of the Robert Blake detective series *Baretta*. She passed away at age 86 in 2007.

Van Johnson

No leading male motion picture star tried harder than Van Johnson did to get his own TV series after his MGM contract expired in the mid-50s. Johnson was one of the studio's most popular stars beginning with his portrayal of Dr. Randall Adams in *Dr. Gillespie's New Assistant* (1942) and *Dr. Gillespie's Criminal Case* (1943). He then went on to leading parts in such movies as *A Guy Named Joe* (1943), appearing as a novice fighter pilot with a guardian angel (Spencer Tracy). Johnson also starred with Tracy in 1944's *Thirty Seconds Over Tokyo,* about the first retaliatory attack against Japan after Pearl Harbor. Equally adept at comedy and musicals, Johnson appeared with Judy Garland in 1949's *In the Good Old Summertime.* He played one of the mutineers in the 1954 feature *The Caine Mutiny* and starred along with Gene Kelly and Cyd Charisse in the 1954 adaptation of Lerner and Loewe's Broadway hit *Brigadoon*. In most of his films, Johnson had a "good guy" image. In his TV series projects, he usually played congenial father figures with easygoing personas.

Probably Johnson's biggest mistake with respect to television was turning down the lead in Desilu's *The Untouchables,* which went on to become a hit ABC series for a number of seasons. Apparently, the financial deal to play Eliot Ness on the show was not to his liking. Robert Stack got the role in this drama set in Prohibition era Chicago. Reportedly, in 1960, still looking for his own TV series, Johnson sent Desi Arnaz a telegram stating, "I am no longer untouchable."[1]

Johnson's first TV series offer came from the Chrysler Corporation to host *Shower of Stars* beginning on September 30, 1954. CBS's live musical series aired once a month on Thursdays at 8:30. After Johnson turned down the offer, William Lundigan became its host. Johnson made his television debut playing himself on a 1955 *I Love Lucy* episode set in Hollywood with the Lucy Ricardo character becoming his dance partner in his nightclub act.

As early as 1956, Johnson was considering starring in his own series. As with many movie stars at the time going into TV, he wanted an anthology-type show where he would rotate with other stars with each producing their own episodes and starring in three or four installments a year with guest stars featured in remaining episodes. While this concept went nowhere, CBS wanted Johnson to be the permanent host of its prestige anthology series *Playhouse 90*, but no deal was ever reached.

The following year, Johnson attempted to finalize a contract for his own production company, Evan Productions, to shoot 39 episodes of *Van Johnson's Amazing Stories* based on the science fiction magazine of the same name. Johnson would host all of the segments and appear in 20 of them. Presumably the never-realized series would have been for ABC. Dick Powell of Four Star Productions contemplated an adventure series starring Johnson in 1958, but these discussions were not fruitful.

In 1960, Johnson filmed a pilot for ABC in Paris. Actor-dancer Gene Kelly produced it for his Voli Productions. In the pilot, directed by Al Curran from a script by Cynthia Lindsay, Johnson played James Devlin, the owner of a Paris service bureau who attempts to help fellow Americans as they travel abroad although he tends to cause almost as many problems as he tries to solve. Michel (Marcel Dalio) appeared as Devlin's assistant. Billed as a comedy-adventure, the pilot first aired under the title "At Your Service" as an installment of *General Electric Theater* on May 22, 1960.

Hoping for an endorsement for his business, Jimmy Devlin receives a telegram from movie star Gloria Miles (Jan Sterling) asking him to arrange an arrival. Devlin and his assistant meet the plane only to find Penelope Miles (Judi Meredith), the precocious teen daughter of Gloria. Devlin has to act as her guardian until her mother arrives in Paris. Bored with her life as a sheltered teenager, Penny, disguised in a blond wig and change of outfit, slips away from Devlin. She masquerades as "Yvonne" who captures Devlin's romantic interest. He is led on a merry adventure by Yvonne until her mother arrives. Gloria dismisses Devlin without any endorsement for his services, but then Penny as Yvonne devises a plan to win Gloria's stamp of approval for Devlin's business.

In 1965, Johnson starred in a situation comedy pilot based on the 1963 movie *Take Her, She's Mine*. The movie featured James Stewart as the overly protective father of Sandra Dee, a teenager going off to college. In turn, the movie had been adapted from a Broadway play written by Phoebe and Henry Ephron supposedly based on their real-life story raising their daughter Nora Ephron (who went on to be a celebrated writer in her own right).

The Ephrons wrote the script for the pilot which was produced and directed by Richard Murphy. Mollie Michaelson (Charmian Carr), the daughter of Frank (Van Johnson) and Anne (Georgann Johnson), is leaving her hometown Cleveland to attend Hawthorne College for Women in Boston, and her father is still trying to adjust to his daughter being on her own. Mollie becomes what she considers a "sophisticate" while away at school. Meanwhile, her would-be boyfriend Emmett Whitmyer (John Fink), still in Cleveland, pines for her to return. After six weeks at Hawthorne, Mollie flies home for a long weekend. Her dad doesn't recognize her when she gets off the plane wearing all black with pearls and sunglasses and a new hair style. As Frank remarks, "You send off what you think is going to be the first woman president of the United States—and what do you get back? Zilch!"

Emmett asks Mollie to attend a party for his aunt and uncle at a hotel. When Mollie goes to the hotel room with him, she finds that the party was just a ruse to get her alone in the room. Emmett's dad (Frank Maxwell) knocks on the door and takes his son and Mollie to Mollie's home with Mr. Whitmyer instructing his son to explain the incident. Frank learns that nothing really happened. Next a college friend phones Mollie wanting her to come to New York City and then they will drive back to college. But Mollie decides instead to stay home, which amazes her dad.

The pilot, produced by Twentieth Century–Fox, was intended for ABC's 1965–66 TV season on. For John Fink, who played Emmett Whitmyer, it was his first Hollywood acting job and got him his Screen Actors Guild card. Fink believes that the pilot failed to turn into a series because it didn't capture the sharp comedic contrast between the typical all–American upper-middle-class family life and the sophisticated airs of an East Coast elite college student, as the Ephrons' play had done.[2]

Taking a break from TV sitcom pilots, Johnson starred in a 1968 two-hour telemovie, *The Protectors*, a pilot for a series. The series would have starred two other actors on a rotating basis patterned after the somewhat successful NBC-Universal show *The Name of the Game*—a 90-minute drama centered on a publishing empire starring Gene Barry, Robert Stack and Tony Franciosa. Johnson portrayed a police captain who would alternate in episodes featuring a physician played by Brian Kelly and a district attorney. Universal offered Johnson a *Protectors* role after he guest starred on a *Name of the Game* segment. He accepted the role based on the fact that he would be in only one out of every three episodes. The 90-minute drama was earmarked for CBS.

The *Protectors* pilot was released in Europe as a feature under the title *Company of Killers* (aka *The Hit Team*). Johnson appeared as tough-talking Police Captain Sam Cahill, head of the Office of Bureaus and Squads, tracking down hit man Dave Alexander Poohler (John Saxon). Cahill had a wife named Patricia and an 18-year-old daughter, Linda.

The plot involved a business owner, Georges DeSalles (Ray Milland), who hires Poohler to murder Owen Brady (Ray Middleton), the majority stock holder in his corporation. Brady is preventing the company from taking over another firm in which DeSalles has invested heavily. DeSalles needs his board's approval for the takeover so he can remain financially solvent. Cahill's team identifies Brady as the possible target of the hit man and arrests Poohler's associates after a female friend of Poohler's confesses to the police. Cahill takes down Poohler as he attempts to kill Brady. Written and produced by E. Jack Neuman, the unsold pilot was shot in Denver.

Johnson got back to making sitcom pilots with *Man in the Middle*. The 1970 CBS pilot focused on Norman (Johnson), a conservative family man coping with a liberal daughter, Debbie (Heather Menzies), who joins peace demonstrations; an ultra-conservative mother, Belle (Ruth McDevitt), who is into karate and gunmanship; and business partner Harvey (Allan Melvin), who is on a youth trip. Norman's wife Harriet (Nancy Malone) likes to read articles on psychology. The couple also has a son (Michael Brandon). The pilot dealt with Debbie's hippie boyfriend (Elliott Street) of whom dad and grandmother disapprove. They both conspire to break up the relationship.

Ray Allen and Harvey Bullock wrote and produced the project, which was directed by Herbert Kenwith. According to Bullock and Allen, CBS rejected the pilot because the network found it too controversial even though they later launched *All in the Family*. CBS aired the pilot in 1972 as part of a trio of rejected pilots on their *Friday Night Movie*. Bullock and Allen later used the concept for the proposed comedy as a basis for their animated series *Wait 'Til Your Father Gets Home*.

Johnson had a supporting role in a 1972 *ABC Movie of the Week*, *Call Her Mom*, written by Gail Parent and Kenny Solms and directed by Jerry Paris. Johnson played Chester Hardgrove, the president of Beardsley College where "time stood still." Unlike other college campuses during the 1970s with students engaged in the hot political issues of the day, Beardsley students couldn't care less about politics and the Vietnam War. Beardsley students liked to party, particularly the boys at the APE fraternity. The college's motto was "Education Isn't That Bad."

Johnson's President Hardgrove is more interested in show business than in running a college. He likes to appear on talk shows publicizing his latest book and on TV game shows. When the APE fraternity's house mother quits due to the members' behavior, the dean threatens to close the fraternity house unless they find a new house mother very quickly. The members hire a young waitress, attractive Angie Bianco (Connie Stevens). Hardgrove objects to a young woman as a house mother and wants to fire her, but the boys hold demonstrations to keep her. In response to the demonstrations, Hardgrove publicly announces that Angie can remain as house mother, while he secretly plots to get rid of her. After one of the frat members confesses his love for Angie and says he will quit college so they can begin dating, Angie thinks she has become a distraction and decides on her own to leave. Since the college has started to receive donations from parents thanks to Angie's popularity, Hardgrove now wants to keep her. He and the frat set boys trace her to the Chinese restaurant where she is now waitressing and beg her to return.

Gloria DeHaven played Johnson's wife in the movie. Ann Miller and then Cyd Charisse were reportedly first hired for this role. Johnson told columnist Army Archerd that he wouldn't do a series of his own, apparently preferring supporting roles because of the shorter hours. "I waited too long [for my own series]. I couldn't take the long hours unless I had a 9 to 6 deal like Glenn Ford."[3]

Reference books (including *The Encyclopedia of Television Pilots* and *Unsold Television Pilots*) list *Call Her Mom* as a TV pilot, but its co-writer Gail Parent said that she never considered it to be a pilot for a comedy series.[4] Perhaps some producer or network executive thought the movie, if it had big ratings, would have been a good candidate to turn into a series.

In 1983, Johnson went to Britain to star in a six-part mini-series, *The Forgotten Story*, based on the novel by Winston Graham who had authored the *Poldark* stories. Set in the 1890s, the mystery drama concerned an 11-year-old who, following his father's death, has been sent from America to live with his Uncle Joe. The boy is caught up in the lives of the characters who frequent his uncle's restaurant, one of whom is played by Johnson.

Also in 1983, Johnson made his last unsold television pilot for NBC, starring as a wealthy eccentric who, along with his nephew, tried to help people with romance. Titled *The President of Love*, the pilot was written by Chris Thompson and directed by Will MacKenzie.

Johnson played wealthy P. Lazlo Plum, who finds love for the lovelorn and nudges along their romance.[5] He lives with his sister Herbina Plum (Francis Bay) and his offbeat nephew Vanilla "Beany" Plum (Robert Pierce). Herbina manages the family business, Plum Spices, a spice, herb and flavorings company, and doles out money to Lazlo to finance his matchmaking exploits. Lazlo's nephew is the Marketing Director of Love; his secretary is Cassiopia Highthrottle (D.D. Howard), whom Beany finds attractive.

In the pilot, Lazlo befriends Bob Rogers, a down-and-out architect whose latest job is playing Santa Claus in August. Lazlo takes Bob home with him for dinner and introduces the man to Christina, the daughter of Ambassador Nardine whose country produces saffron. Bob and Christina are instantly attracted to one another. Herbina threatens to cut off Lazlo's allowance if he persists in matching Bob with Christina. Beany convinces Lazlo to stand up to Herbina and continue his matchmaking efforts. The ambassador finds Beany and his daughter in what he thinks is a compromising position and wants to kill Beany. Bob makes the ambassador think that he has beheaded Beany, which endears Bob to the ambassador. In the end, Lazlo makes Beany the Vice-President of Love.

"I found him to be a delightful man, brimming with over-the-top energy," said Robert Pierce, who played Beany. Pierce went on to say that Johnson "told me that after my final call-back (in which Van was so kind to read with me before the network brass), on the way to the airport he called the network and informed them that 'Robert Pierce is your guy.'" Pierce also discussed with Johnson the movies that he made in the '40s and '50s. "He said he was doing four or five a year at the time—and that he has never seen *most* of them!"[6]

The original cast of the ABC series *Glitter*. Left to right are David Birney, Morgan Brittany, Barbara McNair, Van Johnson (seated), Kristen Meadows, Christopher Mayer (rear), Arte Johnson and Barbara Sharma. After the pilot was filmed, Johnson was dropped from the cast.

NBC never aired *The President of Love* because, as was related to Pierce, the network had just been sued by singer Wayne Newton based on supposed derogatory comments Johnny Carson made about Newton on *The Tonight Show*. There is a sequence in the *Love* pilot in which Pierce did a purposefully bad impression of Newton, and apparently NBC wanted to avoid any further problems from the singer.

The following year, Johnson finally made a pilot that was turned into a series. *Glitter*, originally about a magazine similar to *People*, concerned the staff of a periodical focused on glamorous personalities and places. Johnson played its editor, with David Birney and Morgan Brittany as Sam Dillon and Kate Sampson, two of its best reporters. In the pilot, reporters cover stories relating to a dying madam and the reunion of a famous dance team in a Palm Springs movie. It was produced by Aaron Spelling and Douglas Cramer. ABC picked up the series for its fall 1984 season. But by the time the program was developed by the network and tested, the decision was made to make it a more serious drama about a newsmagazine like *Time*. Having finally been cast in a pilot that was picked up as a series, Johnson again had the misfortune of not achieving TV series stardom. He was dropped because of the producers' desire to focus on the Charles Hardwick character portrayed by Arthur Hill, a more serious and intellectual character. The change in direction didn't help the series. ABC canceled it after half a season.

Johnson's final appearance on the silver screen was a supporting role as a military officer in the 1992 Fred Williamson feature *Three Days to a Kill*. The actor spent his final years at an assisted living facility in Nyack, New York, where he enjoyed painting. Van Johnson died in 2008.

Buster Keaton

One of *the* major silent film comic actors, Buster Keaton's greatest success as a movie star ended when sound features became prevalent.

Joseph Frank Keaton was born into a family of vaudevillians in 1895. Supposedly, he was given the nickname "Buster" by magician Harry Houdini, who saw the six-month-old falling down a flight of stairs uninjured and without crying. Houdini told Keaton's parents, "That's sure some buster your baby took!" and the nickname stuck.

Among star-director Keaton's legendary silent comedies were *One Week* (1920) about seven days in the life of newlyweds as they attempt to assemble a prefabricated house given to them as a wedding present; *Sherlock Jr.* (1924) in which Keaton played a movie theater projectionist who yearns to become a brilliant detective like Sherlock Holmes; and *The General* (1927) wherein Buster appears as a railroad engineer in Civil War–era Georgia in love with his train "the General" and his girlfriend. The film contains one of the most expensive single scenes of any silent film with Keaton staging an actual wreck of a train (crashing into a river from a burning bridge). In his motion pictures, Keaton had a deadpan, stone face—always stoic while chaos reigned around him.

Keaton's movie career declined with the advent of talkies. He was let go by MGM in 1933 but was later rehired by that studio as a gag writer and also played small roles in movies like *In the Good Old Summertime* (1949) with Judy Garland and Van Johnson, *Sunset Blvd.* (1950) with Gloria Swanson and *Limelight* (1953) with Charlie Chaplin.

In 1949 and 1950, Keaton had his own comedy sketch series broadcast live on local stations in the Los Angeles area. He would perform skits emphasizing his physical skills as a comedian such as hiring a trainer to get in shape for an insurance policy examination involving him handling weights, shooting basketballs into the hoop lying on his back with the hoop behind his head, and engaging in a boxing match with plenty of physical humor. According to a review in *Variety*,

> An old-timer came into his own last night over a new medium. And it looks like television has a new "must-see" program, very likely to become a permanent fixture.

> Buster is the old-timer and the new *Buster Keaton Show* is the vehicle. Keaton has lost none of his touch with the passing years. Little Sad-Face is still one of the really great pantomimists of the era and the television camera proves a perfect medium to catch those mannerisms and expressions, if last night's work was a criterion.[1]

In 1952, Keaton starred in a filmed situation comedy produced by Crown Pictures International titled *Life with Buster Keaton*. On that series, he played a sporting goods store clerk wearing his trademark vest, bow tie and hat. Episodes again emphasized his talents at physical comedy. For instance, in one episode, he and workmate Slugger Jones, a punch-drunk former boxer, get into a tag team wrestling match with two British wrestlers, with Keaton and Jones winning after the two Brits knock themselves out. On another episode, Keaton appears in a community theater production with the daughter of the sporting goods store owner to help raise money to pay a loan and prevent the store from closing. Two bank robbers interrupt the play. Keaton captures them and receives a $5000 reward to save the business.

Keaton came up with an idea for a TV series called *School of Acting* that would have involved improvisational comedy. The star of the show would have been a director-leading man with his own stage crew who would choose members of the studio audience to perform in a one-act melodrama because, as Keaton stated, the dialogue "is automatically funny."[2] The chosen audience members would be sent backstage to rehearse and put on costumes. They then come back on stage to perform the play with scripts in hand. At the end of the episode, the star would announce the play for next week and tell the audience that he hopes they have learned something about the art of acting. Alas, the concept never made it to the pilot stage.

In 1955, Buster traveled to England to co-star in a comedy pilot for Official Films and Sapphire Films for ITV. Thirty-nine episodes were planned starring British comedian Richard Hearne (as a character he had created, "Mr. Pastry") and Keaton as drama teacher Colin Dingle. Several years earlier, Hearne had developed the character of an old man who engaged in physical comedy and dance routines. Mr. Pastry had a walrus moustache and dressed in black with a bowler hat.

The storyline involved Mr. Pastry arriving in London to become an actor. He wants to take acting lessons from Dingle, a down-on-his-luck drama teacher without enough money to pay his rent. Dingle promises to take control of Pastry's career after becoming aware of Pastry's sizable pension. Dingle has Pastry help him leave his boarding house without paying the rent with Mr. Pastry then turning around and renting the same room for both of them, which means that Dingle has to hide every time the landlady comes by. When Dingle realizes that opera auditions are being held, he is determined to get

Pastry a part. Pretending to be the Italian casting director and dismissing everybody but Mr. Pastry and himself, Dingle is successful in obtaining roles as spear carriers in the opera for the two of them. They end up ruining the performance and are thrown out the stage door. *The Adventures of Mr. Pastry* aired on British television in 1958, but no series resulted from the pilot.

At the beginning of the 1960s, Keaton was supposed to become a regular in a series called *Officer Murphy* starring Don Haggerty, mostly known for appearing in Westerns. Thirteen episodes were to be made by Lazy Susan Productions of Los Angeles for syndication. Precisely what the series was to be about, I could not determine, but it appears that no pilot was ever made. As reported by *Broadcasting* magazine, in lieu of a pilot, the producers wanted to take a different approach to giving potential sponsors a look at the proposed series. "Instead of the usual one-episode film, the producers will video-tape five key scenes with supporting continuity-narration by series star Don Haggerty. The five scenes, taken from completed scripts, will give prospects an overall view of the series."[3]

Keaton's final attempt at a TV series, *Medicine Man*, focused on Doc (Ernie Kovacs) touring the Old West selling his tonic, Mother McGreedy's Wizard Juice, with his faithful Indian sidekick Junior (Keaton), who rarely spoke, and with his nephew Chris (Kevin Brodie). In the pilot "A Pony for Chris," written by Jay Sommers and Joe Bigelow and directed by Charles Barton, the nephew wants a pony for his birthday. Meanwhile, a gang of three men is forcing townspeople to give them real money for the difference between the worthless Confederate money they use to purchase something and the actual price of the item. The three scoundrels give Doc $50 in Confederate money for $40 worth of his tonic. Chris thinks that Doc now has the funds to buy him a pony, unaware the money is worthless. Doc comes up with a scheme to convince the three men that the federal government is reimbursing people for any Confederate money they have. The gang then decides to retrieve the money they forced the townspeople to take, thinking that they will have a better deal with the government buy-back program. When the gang learns the truth, they threaten Chris. Then Doc waves his handkerchief and his horse sits on the three men, a trick that Junior taught the animal. Thankful for what Doc did to get their real money back, the townspeople buy Chris a pony. At the end of the pilot, Keaton utters his one line of dialogue ("Sue me!").

In the Screen Gems-produced pilot, the Keaton character did the heavy lifting for Doc and performed a lot of pratfalls. Other story outlines were developed in case the pilot was picked up as a series.[4] In one called "The Six-Second Kid," Doc rescues prospector Kid Dillon, stranded in the desert.

Dillon used to be a boxer, so Doc arranges a match between Dillon and a boxer. Thinking Dillon will win, Doc covers all the bets before finding out that Dillon is too tender-hearted to hit anyone. Doc tries to have the fight called off. To impress Dillon's opponent with his power, Doc has Junior saw through the trunk of a big tree as far as he can, short of having it topple over. Doc and Junior then paste bark over the cut. When the Kid slugs the tree, it falls over. Then his opponent does the same thing with the tree next to it even though it was not tampered with. However, the Kid prevails in the match after he gets super-strength from drinking something called "Ol' Popskull" thinking it is water.

In another proposed story, "Only When I Laugh," Doc helps Dr. Picker, a dentist, and his family after their covered wagon breaks down. Picker is on the verge of starvation, and Chris wants his uncle to save him. To raise money for the dentist and his family, Doc and Junior use the dentist's equipment which includes laughing gas to open their own dental practice. Doc begins pulling infected teeth and charges admission for townspeople to observe the painless dentistry. Junior does a one-man-band bit to entice people to come to the "show." Eventually, Doc runs out of patients. Junior brings Doc a rabbit sandwich for lunch. When Doc bites into the sandwich, he cracks a tooth on buckshot in the rabbit meat. He goes into business again selling admission to his dental practice. Junior hands out free rabbit sandwiches. The audience members then jump up and yell as they bite into the sandwiches.

Kovacs was killed in an automobile accident right after the completion of the *Medicine Man* pilot. Reportedly, ABC was looking at the show as a possible candidate for a series during the 1962–63 TV season. The writers considered finding an actor to replace Kovacs in the project, but apparently the network decided not to pursue it any further.

A movie based on Keaton's life, *The Buster Keaton Story* with Donald O'Conner in the lead role, was released in 1957. A few years later, the Motion Picture Academy presented Keaton with a special Academy Award honoring his lifelong contributions to film comedy.

Buster Keaton's final TV appearance was an uncredited bit on a Lucille Ball special, *Lucy in London*, which aired on October 24, 1966, more than eight months after his death on February 1, 1966, from lung cancer.

Alan Ladd

Alan Ladd appeared in the movie *Citizen Kane* (1941) in an uncredited bit part as a reporter. However, the actor's breakout role was in Paramount's *This Gun for Hire* (1942) as Raven, a hit man who reveals his sensitive side to Veronica Lake's character. He followed that appearance with the film noir hits *The Glass Key* (1942) and *The Blue Dahlia* (1946). Ladd's other major films included *Two Years Before the Mast* (1946) and *The Great Gatsby* (1949). In the 1950s, he starred in one of the greatest Westerns ever, *Shane* (1953), in which he appeared as a former gunslinger. His final screen role was as Nevada Smith in *The Carpetbaggers* (1964). Ladd usually portrayed characters with a cool, reserved persona.

Ladd formed Jaguar Productions in 1953 mainly to produce his own movies. Its first film, *Drum Beat* (1954), starred the actor as Johnny Mackay, who is asked by the Army to attempt negotiations with an Indian tribe about to wage war. Commenting on his company in 1957, Ladd said that he'd formed it "to make pictures in England. Now we spend between $800,000 and $1,000,000 for each picture, and the five we already have produced have grossed around three to three and a half million apiece."[1]

Ladd told columnist Vernon Scott that he hoped that Jaguar would be a legacy for his children and that he wanted to be make two features every year and four TV series. "When I quit acting, I would like to have a healthy company going for the youngsters. I'm not building an empire for that would be pointless. Sue [his wife] and I have enjoyed the greatest of everything." About TV, he said, "I was raised in pictures. If you make the step into television you must do it fully, and very few stars ever come back to pictures. You can't have a career in both."[2]

One of Ladd's first TV appearances in a dramatic role was in an anthology series pilot where he played a police officer. If the pilot had become a series, the actor would have appeared in some but not all of the episodes. The pilot, "Farewell to Kennedy," aired on *General Electric Theater* on November 13, 1955.

Captain of detectives Kennedy (Robert Armstrong), a 30-year veteran of the police force, made one mistake when he accepted a bribe and paid for

Alan Ladd and Kathleen Crowley in the *General Electric Theater* presentation "Farewell to Kennedy," a potential pilot for an Ladd-hosted anthology series. Like many other film stars, Ladd had very mixed feelings about wanting to star in his own TV series.

it with his life. Joe (Ladd), the fiancé of Kennedy's daughter Mary (Kathleen Crowley), sets out to prove that Kennedy actually returned the bribe money. After Joe tracks down the gangster who bribed Kennedy, Kennedy's reputation is restored. Frank Faylen, who later starred as the father on *Dobie Gillis*, played Farber, Joe's partner. Frank Tuttle helmed the pilot based on a teleplay by Harold Swanton from a story by William Fay.

"GE Eyes Alan Ladd Show as TV Entry" read the title of a March *Variety* 1956 item saying that a Western series starring Ladd was under consideration by General Electric for the 1956–57 season. The unnamed half-hour would reportedly have been part of ABC's Tuesday night schedule. Instead of the Ladd series, the network ended up slotting the Western *Broken Arrow* on Tuesdays following the hit *The Life and Times of Wyatt Earp*.

Other than a variety series, Ladd's production company tried almost every television genre to place a series on the medium. None of the pilots his company produced ever became a series.

At the end of 1956, Ladd announced that his company would do pilots for two series. One, based on an idea by Richard Hubler, revolved around the exploits of the Strategic Air Command, the other would be the resurrection of his syndicated radio series *Box 13*. Ladd had starred as newspaperman turned mystery writer Dan Holliday on radio's *Box 13*. To come up with new ideas for his fiction, Holliday placed a newspaper add stating, "Adventure wanted, will go anywhere, do anything—write Box 13." One can only imagine the types of responses Holliday received from various crime victims wanting revenge as well as from other assorted characters.

In 1954, Ladd appeared on an episode of *General Electric Theater* titled "Committed" (aka "Daytime Nightmare") playing Holliday. In the episode, attorney Paul Wells (Whit Bissell) responds to Holliday's ad saying he will pay him $10,000 for a deal that will involve millions. Before he relays additional details, Wells slips Holliday a Mickey, causing him to pass out. Holliday wakes up in a mental institution where the psychiatrist, Dr. Cordell, calls him "Mr. Stokes." Cordell informs "Mr. Stokes" that Wells brought him to the hospital based on the instructions from Stokes' wife Clarice. No one believes Holliday is who he says he is. Mrs. Stokes and Wells had killed her real husband for his money and then made a bargain with Cordell to have Holliday as "Mr. Stokes" killed in the hospital trying to escape. Holliday fights with one of the attendants who is accidentally shot and killed by Dr. Cordell. Holliday escapes, but the doctor reports him to the police as armed and dangerous and as having murdered the attendant. Holliday is able to phone a police lieutenant he knows to come and identify him. The local police are about to shoot Holliday when the lieutenant shows up in the nick of time. Holliday subdues Dr. Cordell and tells the police to pick up Wells and Mrs. Stokes.

For his new television version of *Box 13*, Ladd had hoped that Barry Sullivan would star as Holliday. There were also rumors that Ron Randell was being considered for the part but ultimately actor Bill Leslie won the role.

The pilot was filmed at Paramount. Ladd's Jaguar Productions produced it in conjunction with Aaron Spelling's Caron Productions. Spelling, who at the time also worked for Dick Powell's Four Star Productions, wrote the script. In the late 1950s, Spelling had formed his own production company, Caron Productions, blending his wife Carolyn Jones' first name with his. Jones guest starred in the pilot as a wealthy widow who contacts Holliday when she faces blackmail.

In association with Bilben Productions, a company owned by actor William Bendix, Ladd's company made a pilot for a situation comedy starring Bendix in 1959. Bendix had just completed his role as Chester Riley in the comedy *The Life of Riley* and was looking for another starring vehicle. In *Ivy League*, Bendix played 49-year-old Bull Mitchell, who had retired from the Marine Corps as a master sergeant after 30 years of service. Under the G.I. Bill, Mitchell decides to enroll in an Ivy League college as a freshman. He has trouble adjusting to college life and is considered a "square" by everyone except his landlady Mamie Parker (Florence MacMichael) and her young son Timmy (Tim Hovey). When a cannon used at the school's pep rallies disappears, Bull becomes a hero by finding it. Appearing as college students in the pilot were soon-to-become-famous actors Mary Tyler Moore, Doug McClure and Arte Johnson. The series' concept was created by Jameson Brewer and Dan Nathan, The pilot, written by Everett Freeman, was directed by Richard Whorf.

Commenting on the proposed series, Bendix said that he and Ladd discussed whether he should play the new role very broad as he had portrayed Chester Riley or very honest. "In this new series it poses an actual problem in comedic form. We had a lot of slapstick and unbelievable situations in *Riley*, but people seemed to like it. In the new series, we have more of an honest approach. Whether it will pay off or not is in the laps of the gods."[3] It didn't pay off. While *Ivy League* never became a series, the pilot did air as an installment of *Schlitz Playhouse* under the title "Tell It to the Marines" on February 18, 1959.

Still flirting with the idea of starring on his own series instead of just producing potential TV shows, Ladd was offered his own show in mid–1959. Presumably the series would have been of the anthology type since Lever Brothers wanted a deal for the actor to star in ten of the episodes and host the remaining 29. Ladd countered with the proposal to star on six episodes with no hosting duties. Oglivy, Mather & Benson, the agency negotiating the deal, turned down the counter-offer.

In the early 1960s, Jaguar Productions had plans for several other television projects. *Enigma* was to be a 30-minute mystery-anthology series. The pilot was written by Mike Schreiber and directed by Richard Donner. *Worlds Beyond*, a series about space, was written by Helen and Stanley Scott. *Humor Around the World* was a proposed 60-minute comedy series; while *Fable Time* was a projected 30-minute children's show written by Gwendolyn Burstein. One other proposed series, the half-hour action-adventure drama *Hong Kong Express*, was to have been produced by Robert Fellows, who joined Jaguar in July 1960.

Another project that never went to series, *Third Platoon,* was set during World War II, produced by Jaguar-Caron Productions in association with Paramount. Aaron Spelling wrote and produced this unsold pilot which was directed by Howard W. Koch. Members of the third platoon included Lt. George Bradshaw (Lyle Bettger), an up-through-the ranks soldier, Corp. Mike Hemming (John Goddard), Sgt. Dale Stone (Page Slattery) who, prior to the military, had managed an orphanage, Private Frank Puletti (Johnny Seven), formerly a magician, Private John Victor (Chris Seitz) and Pfc Jess Robin (Richard Newton), whose mother was an alcoholic.

The storyline of the pilot focused on the platoon's mission to destroy a German tank. Private Victor, in charge of the bazooka to take out the tank, is wounded. Bradshaw carries him closer to the tank so he is in just the right spot to fire the weapon. Victor destroys the tank but, in the process, Bradshaw collapses apparently from a gunshot. However, the Army's doctor says he died of a heart attack. Sgt. Stone is put in charge of the platoon.

At the end of the pilot, Alan Ladd, in a voiceover, tells the audience about future stories they will see. The episodes would focus not simply on the war but also on the members of the platoon. Ladd says, "Stories about the third platoon will stick with you for a long, long time." He ends by remarking, "There's a member of the third platoon in every home in America."

While none of these projects would have starred Ladd, a proposed 60-minute Western series tentatively called *Saddle Tramp* may have featured Ladd and three other stars on an alternating basis. After reports surfaced of Ladd starring in this Western, the actor denied he would be featured on any episodes of the possible series. "Television production, remarked Ladd, figures in Jaguar's 1960 plans, but outside of supervising general production, I would play no part in this phase of our operation."[4] As the actor had indicated before, he went on to say that his acting would be confined to motion pictures.

By 1962, Ladd had again changed his mind about starring in a series. He became attached to a project titled *The Man from the Pentagon* written by Charles Skinner and produced by Michel Kraike. Ladd would appear as a trouble-shooter playing a prototype of high government officials in all branches of the service. No pilot was to be made. Two or three episodes were to be completed and shown to networks, thinking one of them would turn the project into a series.

For the 1963–64 TV season, Ladd's production company in association with Ziv and United Artists, produced a pilot for a situation comedy created by the legendary Mel Brooks. Originally called *Dreams of Glory*, the proposed series was renamed *Inside Danny Baker*. The pilot starred child actor Roger Mobley as Danny, who liked to daydream. He wants a motorboat, but his dad, a dentist, instructs him to earn the money for the boat himself. Danny comes up with the idea of turning the family ping pong table into a work of art after seeing that modern art is selling for big bucks. The pilot was directed by Arthur Hiller for ABC. This was the final TV pilot produced by Ladd's company.

The actor-producer passed away in 1964 at age 50 from an acute overdose of alcohol and sedatives.

Hedy Lamarr

> Of all the glamour queens, surely none was more glamorous than Hedy Lamarr. She seemed the definition of the word. Of all the stars of the '40s and early '50s, she was probably the most classically beautiful, with those huge, marbly eyes, the porcelain skin, the dreamy little smile, and the exotic voice that was an artful combination of Old Vienna and the MGM speech school.

So remarked a social historian about the actress from Vienna whose name was originally Hedy Kiesler.[1]

Lamarr became famous in Europe and America mostly for her nude scenes in the Czech-Austrian picture *Ecstasy* (1933) about a young woman who marries a wealthy older man. In her first American feature *Algiers* (1938), Charles Boyer played his love interest. She starred in many movies in the 1940s such as *Come Live with Me* (1941) with James Stewart where she appeared as a Viennese refugee who marries a struggling writer to gain U.S. citizenship, *H.M. Pulham, Esq.* (1941), as a vivacious co-worker with whom Pulham (Robert Young) falls in love, and *Samson and Delilah* (1949), her most successful feature, with Victor Mature as Samson. Her screen appearances declined in the '50s, which led her to consider television.

Of all the movie stars profiled in this book, Lamarr is the only one to have co-invented a secured torpedo-guidance system which she contributed to the U.S. government in the 1940s. Although never used by the government at the time, the invention became the basis of modern anti-jamming applications.

In the October 27, 1952, issue of *Broadcasting* magazine, a brief article reported:

> Going into mid–November production is Victor Pahlen on *Great Loves*, 39 half-hour TV films in color. Starring Hedy Lamarr in historical love stories, interiors will be shot in London and exteriors in the actual European settings. Allowing a 10-day schedule for each film, Edgar Ulmer will direct from scripts by Salka Viertel, Aeneas MacKenzie, Hans Kafka, Noel Coward and others. Miss Lamarr will be costumed by such European courtiers as Fath and Dior. She will receive residual rights plus salary.[2]

Perhaps Lamarr's success in portraying Delilah in *Samson and Delilah* influenced her decision to make a TV series on the great love affairs of history although, granted, the love between Samson and Delilah was rather one-sided.

The first episode of the proposed series, about Queen Esther and the king of Persia, was to be shot in London in 1952. When the series did not work out, scripts for the other episodes were adapted into a feature film titled *The Loves of Three Queens* about Helen of Troy, Genevieve of Brabant and Empress Josephine. The movie was directed by Marc Allegret and Edgar Ulmer, who walked off the set midway through filming in a dispute with Ms. Lamarr. In the first installment, Lamarr appears as Helen of Greece, married to Menelaus (Robert Beatty), king of Sparta. Paris of Troy (Massimo Serato) comes to Sparta and abducts Helen, who falls in love with him. War between Sparta and Troy ensues for ten years. Menelaus fights Troy for Helen with neither the clear victor. However, during the war, Paris dies of his wounds. Eventually, the Greeks sail off leaving behind a large wooden horse as a gift for Troy. As the legend goes, Greek soldiers hidden inside conquer the city. Menelaus returns to Troy but is unable to kill Helen. She returns with him to Greece.

Wearing a blonde wig, Lamarr next portrays pregnant Genevieve of Brabant whose husband Count Sigfride (Cesare Danova) is away fighting a war. Golo (Terence Morgan), a friend of her husband's, makes passionate advances which she resists. He murders Drago (John Fraser), a man trying to save her from Golo's clutches, and claims that Genevieve was having an affair with Drago. Golo has her arrested and held for trial. Upon returning from war, Sigfride refuses to see Genevieve. She goes before the court charged with adultery but refuses to speak. Since her husband doesn't believe she is innocent, she is taken away to be executed. But one of the soldiers asks the executioner to spare her life, and she escapes into the forest where she gives birth and raises her son. Five years later, Sigfride believes that Golo tried to kill him while both were hunting. He engages Golo in a fight to the death and kills Golo, who finally confesses that he loved Genevieve. Sigfride than finds Genevieve and his son in the forest, and they reunite.

In the final story, Lamarr stars as Josephine, in love with Napoleon. Napoleon neglects her, being more interested in affairs of state. After she becomes empress of France and he emperor of France, Napoleon insists that Josephine have children to create a dynasty. When she is without issue, he wants a divorce in order to marry a daughter of a crown head of Europe and have heirs. Napoleon leaves Josephine, who hopes that he is able to father a son.

The movie, produced by Lamarr and Victor Pahlen and originally three hours in length, was severely edited to reduce its running time and was released in 1954. John Fraser, who played Drago in the Genevieve of Brabant segment, gives some insight into why director Edgar Ulmer, Austrian by birth, walked off the project in the middle of filming. During his death scene with Lamarr festooned in a magnificent gown embroidered with pearls and semi-precious gems, the actress pulled Fraser's head away from the camera so the audience would never be able to tell whose head she was cradling. Take after take, Lamarr continued to do this despite Ulmer's protestations. The director threatened to use a double for Lamarr in the scene if she didn't follow his instructions. Fraser recounts that a defiant Lamarr "dropped my head like a cabbage, and firmly putting one hand on the collar of her dress, with one savage wrench she ripped the priceless garment from the neck to the navel. With this gesture, Hedy halted filming for a week. For continuity reasons, the identical material had to be found and the intricate embroidery recreated to make a replica before we could continue."[3]

After *The Loves of Three Queens*, Lamarr made only two more film appearances: as Joan of Arc in the 1957 movie *The Story of Mankind* and as an aging movie star competing with her daughter (Jane Powell) for the same man in 1958's *The Female Animal*.

In the '50s, Lamarr was reportedly in contention as one of the hosts of a proposed TV anthology series conceived by actress-director Ida Lupino as a female counterpart to *Four Star Playhouse* which primarily had male hosts. In addition to Lamarr and Lupino, Paulette Goddard would have been a third host with a male guest star showing up for the fourth week. Each of the females would own a share of the production company with the series to be produced and directed by Jules Bricken. Given the reluctance, at the time, on the part of networks and advertisers to give the go-ahead to dramas starring actresses, it's probably not surprising that this project never got off the ground.

Lamarr was also considered for the female lead in *Buckley,* a situation comedy pilot starring Reginald Gardiner. Produced by Goodson and Todman, the would-be series focused on Gardiner as a genius butler. Written by Edmund Hartmann and directed by Don Quinn, the series was to have Buckley work in the homes of various guest stars. However, instead of Lamarr, the 1955 pilot guest starred Dorothy Lamour.

Lamarr thought of doing a television series in 1957: "TV scared the hell out of me at first… [But] once you get the swing of it, it's fun. I like TV lately. I got to know it. I've had happy experiences guesting on TV, and I'm not scared now."[4] Both nothing came of Lamarr's television series aspirations.

In the late '50s and through the 1960s, Lamarr, attempting to become a TV personality, appeared on several game, variety and talk shows including

I've Got a Secret, *The Tonight Show*, *The Steve Allen Show* and *The Mike Douglas Show*. She even hosted one episode of the ABC rock 'n' roll series *Shindig* in 1965.

One of her final attempts at a TV series stardom was as a regular panelist on a pilot for a game show called *Take My Advice,* made by John Guedel who had produced Groucho Marx's *You Bet Your Life*. The panelists (Lamarr, actor-director Bob Sweeney, comedian-writer Carl Reiner, and psychologist Dr. Loriene Johnson) advised contestants on how to handle various personal problems. Lamarr, Reiner and Sweeney would give humorous and other kinds of answers to a contestant's problems, and the answer that came closest to the psychologist's opinion would win. Lamarr was to be paid $1500 per week for each show plus ten percent of the profits. The 1961 pilot, hosted by George Fenneman, the *You Bet Your Life* announcer, never resulted in a series. Lamarr could never lose her extraordinary movie star persona, making it difficult for middle-class viewers to identify with her.

One of Lamarr's final TV guest shots was on a June 1970 episode of *The Merv Griffin Show*. She passed away in January 2000 at age 85.

Janet Leigh

As the story goes, Janet Leigh (real name Jeanette Morrison) was discovered by actress Norma Shearer who was staying at a ski lodge where Leigh's parents worked. Shearer noticed a photo of the young girl, asked for a copy and showed it to MGM, who signed the 19-year old. Leigh's first movie, *The Romance of Rosy Ridge* (1947), concerned an Ozark family whose head fought on the Confederate side in the Civil War, and their involvement with a schoolteacher (Van Johnson) with whom Leigh's character falls in love. Leigh starred in several classic movies in the '40s, '50s and '60s including the 1949 remake of *Little Women*, *Holiday Affair* (1949) with Robert Mitchum, *The Naked Spur* (1953) with James Stewart, *Houdini* (1953) with her husband Tony Curtis and *Touch of Evil* (1958) with Charlton Heston and Orson Welles. Most notably, she played Marion Crane in the most famous shower scene ever put on film in Alfred Hitchcock's *Psycho* (1960). With the exception of *Psycho*, Leigh's screen image was that of a nice, polite woman.

As her film career slowed, Leigh turned her attention to TV where she often appeared as a wife and/or mother. She played the title character in a 1965 comedy pilot, *Meet Maggie Mulligan* (aka *This—Is Maggie Mulligan*). Maggie was a widowed political cartoonist with a Pulitzer Prize nomination living in New York City raising her teenage son. Friends set Maggie up with dates which she rebuffed, but her son encourages her to pursue a relationship with an FBI agent to whom she is attracted. The pilot was written, directed and produced by Don McGuire. The series, intended for CBS, was to be sponsored by General Foods, but apparently because of an executive change at the network, the show was not placed on the schedule. Leigh never did quite understand what happened to it. "[T]he sponsor liked it and so did I. In fact, I thought it was pretty good."[1]

Also in 1965, Leigh was rumored to star in another pilot for CBS called *Both Judge and Jurie*, to be made by game show producers Mark Goodson and Bill Todman. After this was reported, Leigh stated that, while she had read the script, she had not entered into any negotiations to star in it. She stressed that the script was among many she was considering and that she didn't want to be labeled as already committed to anything.

Two years later, Leigh starred in the sitcom pilot *The Janet Leigh Show* (aka *According to Janet*), written by Leonard Gershe and produced by Jack Chertok. Leigh played Jan Lenox, mother, wife and host of a TV advice show who tried to help viewers with their problems.[2] Jan's husband Tom was in commercial real estate. The couple had two children, ten-year-old Lionel and 13-year-old Polly. Tom's boss was Mr. Hewett, in his sixties; his wife drove Jan up the wall with her comments. Like many TV families, the Lenoxes also had a wisecracking maid, Jessie.

In the pilot, Tom wants Jan to have a dinner party for his boss and their friends including Fred, a key operative in the possible sale of a property that Hewett wants to acquire. However, Fred is separated from his wife Louise, Since the Lenoxes are friends of the couple, Tom and Jan decide to invite Fred first, thinking that Louise will then decline their invitation. But Louise accepts. When Fred, Louise and the Hewetts arrive at the party, Fred is in no mood to discuss the sale of the property. Jan relates a story about two brothers reconciling after being mad at each other. The story prompts Fred and Louise to reconcile, and Fred agrees to discuss the property with Hewett after dinner. Later, Jan admits to her husband that she made up the story about the brothers based on a letter she had received for her TV show.

In still another comedy pilot, *My Wives Jane*, Leigh played Jane Franklin, a married woman trying to balance her domestic life and professional life as a soap opera actress.[3] In the pilot's teaser, Nat Franklin (Barry Nelson, who had dated Leigh in the late 1940s), a doctor in his mid-thirties, and Jane, an actress in her late twenties, kiss and discuss their relationship as husband and wife. The pilot then cuts to Jane (as Laura Holloway) running into the arms of another man: Dirk Bennett (McLean Stevenson), a 38-year-old actor playing Dr. Bruce Holloway on a soap opera titled *The Shining Heart*. Another cut reveals to the audience that Jane is on TV and that she and Nat are watching the program in bed. Nat wants Jane to quit the series since he believes that she is too obsessed with the story and worries that the program is too real for her.

The next day while Jane and Nat are having breakfast, their seven-year-old daughter Molly (Mia Bendixsen) brings the mail to them, referring to Jane as her character Laura Holloway. Nat chastises Molly for this and continues to pester Jane to quit the show. When Dirk arrives to pick up Jane, Molly refers to him as "Mom's other husband" which annoys Nat. While Nat tends to one of his patients who watches the soap opera on the hospital TV, he discovers that Jane (as Laura) is going to have a baby on the show. After fans pester Jane for autographs over dinner at a restaurant, Nat again tells his wife that the show is a disgrace to acting and to medicine. Jane agrees to quit after her character on the soap has the baby, arguing that Laura and Bruce have been waiting so long for a baby. Nat is worried that Molly won't understand the difference between the TV baby and reality and is annoyed that on the program the pregnancy will take only eight weeks. Nat decides to talk to the show's producer, Vic Semple (John Dehner), during his appointment with him the next day. That night Molly tells her parents that she hopes the baby will be a boy.

During his doctor's appointment with Vic, Nat asks him to take Jane off the program. Vic informs him that they were planning to kill her off anyway because they want a younger actress for the lead. After a phone call from Dirk about the next day's script, Jane realizes that they had planned to kill her on the show already, and she is upset at being let go. An 18-year-old actress, Angela Steele (as Alice Wentworth), will be taking over as Bruce's new love interest. Jane is upset and refers to Alice as if she were real. Nat comforts her, saying that he'd never treat her like the show is treating her. Later that week, after Vic calls Nat and Jane to advise them that Angela has lost her voice, Nat confirms that Angela has laryngitis. Vic adds a last-minute scene where Bruce says goodbye to Laura in the hospital, but Jane improvises on live television and calls out to Bruce to say goodbye. Vic is astounded, but Nat seems happy that Jane has done this. Over dinner that night, Vic says they have never had such an audience response, and he wants to keep Jane on the show to have the baby. Nat only lets Jane return if Vic agrees to allow seven months for her to have the baby for medical accuracy. Vic proposes a toast to future twins.

In the tag, Nat and Jane tuck Molly into bed and make sure that she knows the difference between real babies and TV babies. Molly understands but ends the program with a classic soap line that has been referred to throughout the show: "Give it to me straight, Dad."

The pilot aired on CBS on August 1, 1971. It was produced by Edward H. Feldman and written by Larry Gelbart, who later developed the iconic comedy *M*A*S*H*. Speaking of the pilot, Leigh said, "It was going to be on until the daytime soap people told the network: 'You can't make fun of such a lucrative audience.'"[4]

Among the many series produced by the legendary Norman Lear was CBS's *All's Fair* starring Richard Crenna as a conservative columnist who falls in love with a young freelance photographer (Bernadette Peters). The 1976 comedy lasted for only one season. Leigh was to appear semi-regularly on this series as the literary agent and former girlfriend of the Crenna character. Lear had convinced Leigh to take the part. But, on the first day of rehearsal, Leigh felt that the role wasn't what she had expected and didn't see how the character could work. "I didn't want to get into it deeper. So I went to Norman

Janet Leigh and Harry Guardino as husband and wife in the mystery drama pilot *On Our Way*. This was Leigh's final attempt at her own TV series.

and told him how I felt about it." She left the rehearsal, never to return. "It's better to leave in one day than to stay in when it would be much more difficult. The part was not right for me," Leigh recounted. "Sometimes you discuss something you are going to do and it seems exciting, but when you are ready to do it, it's not there."[5] Salome Jens took over the role intended for Leigh.

In 1981, *The Fall Guy*, an adventure series starring Lee Majors as Hollywood stuntman Colt Seavers, debuted on ABC. In his spare time, Colt tracks down bail jumpers. During the initial season, Samantha "Big Jack" Jack (Jo Ann Pflug) assigned cases to Seavers and his associates. Originally, Leigh had the role of the bondswoman but was replaced by Pflug.

Leigh's next TV attempt was CBS's *On Our Way*, a comedy-drama pilot in which she starred as Kate Walsh with Harry Guardino as her husband Sam. Retirees, they decide to travel across America in a motor home. Kate used to run a catering business; Sam was a retired Chicago crime reporter, which meant that their adventures involved some type of mystery. Although not seen in the pilot, the couple had two adult children, Peter and Sarah.

In the pilot, the Walshes travel to Logan, Tennessee, near Memphis. The town is hosting an Elvis Presley tribute. The couple learns that Elvis' stuffed hound dog has been stolen from the local taxidermist. Also, a pair of blue suede shoes has been taken from the local restaurant where they were on display, and the restaurant's owner has been killed. The police find the stuffed dog in the possession of young visitor Steve (Ben Marly) and arrest him for the theft and the murder. Thinking him innocent, the Walshes investigate. Subsequently, the restaurant owner's wife confesses what is really happening: The mayor, with whom she is having an affair, wants everyone to think that the murder was related to the theft of the Elvis artifacts. However, the mayor actually staged the thefts and killed the restaurateur so he could marry his wife and take over the business. Written by Jeffrey Lane, the 1985 pilot was directed by Michael Pressman and produced by Warner Brothers.

In her later years, Leigh continued to appear in films and on television. She also published two novels. Diagnosed with vasculitis, an inflammation of the blood vessels, Leigh died in October 2004.

Peter Lorre

Regarding Peter Lorre, German writer Hans Sahl remarked, "He was a nice guy with no particular characteristics, except for protruding eyes. [They] gave him the look of a demonic, pop-eyed frog and ... predestined him for criminal and gangster roles."[1] Despite yearning to be a versatile actor, Lorre did become typecast as murderers and psychopaths. In his first film *M* (1931), made in Germany, Lorre played the role of a child murderer. His first American movie *Mad Love* (1935) featured Lorre as Dr. Gogol, a crazed surgeon who attaches a knife-murderer's hands to a concert pianist's mutilated stumps.

Lorre did at times break this madman stereotype such as in the Mr. Moto series of detective movies in the late 1930s. Classic movie fans may best remember Lorre being paired with rotund character actor Sydney Greenstreet in *The Maltese Falcon* (1941), *The Mask of Dimitrios* (1944) and others.

Since Lorre was so well-known for playing sinister characters, one of his first ventures into a television series for himself involved meeting with Charles Addams, who had created the Addams Family cartoons, to discuss the possibility of a television horror-comedy show for CBS. Nothing came of these 1953 discussions.

In April 1955, McCadden Productions, owned by entertainer George Burns, filmed a pilot titled *The Getter and the Holder* (aka *Giver and Taker*) starring Lorre and Francis L. Sullivan, based on a play by Sam Neuman. Sullivan bore a striking resemblance to Sydney Greenstreet, who had passed away in 1954. Falcon Productions, whose shareholders included Lorre, Sullivan, Neuman, Irving Yergen and M.P. Moss, co-produced the pilot with Burns' company. Set in Algeria, this whodunit with comedy overtones was written by David Friedkin and Morton Fine, who later produced the TV series *I Spy*.

In the story, Mr. Constantine (Sullivan) and Mr. Cleo Kobe (Lorre) own an antique shop where a man named Robert Stone introduces himself as the curator of the Indo-China museum in Hanoi.[2] Stone is looking for a man named Nelson who stole a Kwan Yin jade statuette from his museum. Constantine agrees to locate Nelson for $5000. Stone gives Constantine $2000 with a promise of the remainder after Nelson and the statuette are found.

To attract Nelson's attention, Cleo spreads the word that he has a jade Kwan Yin. He finds Nelson and says that the story about him having a Kwan Yin statuette was fiction, but that he does have a buyer for the statuette Nelson possesses. Nelson wants Cleo to bring the buyer to him in two hours. Constantine tells Stone that Nelson has been located and asks for the balance of the money. He knows that Stone is an imposter because he used the incorrect gender pronoun in referring to the moon on a Japanese print. He lets Stone follow him and Cleo to Nelson's hideout where Stone strides in with a gun and announces that his real name is Muller. He says the real Stone died in Hanoi but not before telling him about Nelson and the Kwan Yin. Constantine announces that Nelson's Kwan Yin is a fake. Cleo and Constantine then go after a furious Muller, wrestle his gun away from him, and corner both Nelson and him. Back at their shop, Constantine advises the police inspector that he knew that only one true Kwan Yin existed in jade, and it is in Bombay.

After *The Getter and the Holder* failed to be picked up as a series, Lorre attempted another TV venture focused on the antique business. Always short of money and living beyond his means, Lorre starred in a 1958 pilot titled *Collector's Item* as antiques appraiser Mr. Munsey. Vincent Price played Henry Prentiss, owner of the House of Prentiss antique gallery. Jan (Whitney Blake) was their secretary. The idea for *Collector's Item* apparently arose after Price had demonstrated his vast knowledge of art on the quiz show *The $64,000 Challenge.*

In the pilot, written by Herb Meadow and directed by Buzz Kulik, Ivor Hagar (Thomas Gomez) approaches Prentiss about a long-lost *object d'art* called the Left Fist of David. He wants to partner with Prentiss to obtain the artwork from the estate of the recently deceased Mr. Van der Locken. Prentiss and Munsey go to Florida to catalogue and appraise the collection. Prentiss again meets Hagar, a neighbor of the

Vincent Price (left) and Peter Lorre in the presentation films for the potential series *Collector's Item*. After *Collector's Item* failed to become a series, Price and Lorre starred together in the horror films *Tales of Terror* (1962), *The Raven* (1963) and *The Comedy of Terrors* (1964).

late Van der Locken. Neither Prentiss nor Munsey nor anyone else is quite sure just what the Left Fist of David is. Dr. Peasley (Eduard Franz), the curator at the estate, doesn't think that Prentiss and Munsey are needed. Prentiss and Munsey decide to construct a sculpture of a hand and call it the Left Fist of David in order to learn Peasley and Hagar's real motives. Hagar, carrying a pistol, comes to steal the faux artwork but realizes it is a fake. Munsey, Prentiss and Hagar fight over the gun. In the course of the fight, the gun goes off and the bullet hits a chandelier, revealing that it is made of gold and is the real Left Fist of David. Prentiss retrieves the gun from Hagar and shoots him.

The scene with Munsey and Hagar fighting over the gun looked to producer Herb Meadow like two balloons clinging to each other. "They were laughing until suddenly they stopped, both of them, because they had both lost their wind and were so distressed we had to stop. Lorre was very quiet. He just sat, looking off into space, recovering his breath. Gomez was terribly red in the face. I was afraid he was going to have an attack of some kind."[3]

A second pilot of *Collector's Item* was made in November 1957 guest starring Eva Gabor and Andrew Duggan but still featuring Price and Lorre as Prentiss and Munsey. In this pilot, "Appraise the Lady," Gabor appeared as Countess Gia Ferrano while Duggan played Matt Freeland, an oil man in love with the countess. Freeland asks Prentiss to appraise a Florentine chalice that the countess is bringing from Paris. Freeland also wants Prentiss to investigate the countess to see if she is whom she says she is. Prentiss and Munsey look through the countess' belongings upon her arrival. Although they believe the chalice to be genuine, they are not so sure about Ferrano. Prentiss and Munsey realize that the chalice was being used to smuggle jewels into the country and find that the countess and Freeland are working together. The two antiques dealers devise a plan to trap Ferrano and Freeland and find where the countess hid the jewels that were in the chalice. The second pilot was written by James Gunn and directed by Christian Nyby.

The unsold pilots, produced by CBS and TCF Television Productions (Twentieth Century Fox's TV subsidiary), were intended for a series during the 1959–60 season. The syndication arm of CBS felt that maybe, if the series could not find a slot on the network's schedule, it would sell the show directly to local stations. CBS Film Sales thought that there was a growing interest in art throughout the country and that Price's appearance on the lecture circuit after being on *The $64,000 Challenge* showed this. However, nothing came of this endeavor.

Lorre's next TV series attempt was titled *Peter Lorre's Playhouse* with the actor hosting and occasionally starring in some episodes. Initially this mystery anthology series was to be 30 minutes in length but then was changed to one hour. Moffett Enterprises produced the pilot with a script written by John Trayne. Reflecting his sinister persona at the beginning of the initial episode, Lorre was seated with his back to the camera behind a desk wearing a bowler hat and facing a large spider web. He slowly turned toward the camera as he introduced the episode.

Production of an additional 38 episodes was to begin in August 1961 for the 1961–62 season. The show was to be syndicated to local stations. However, talks with Paramount to finance the series fell apart and no additional episodes were made.

Lorre's final TV appearance was in an October 1963 episode of *Kraft Suspense Theatre* called "The End of the World, Baby." He died from a cerebral hemorrhage in March 1964 at the age of 59.

Myrna Loy

During her long career, Myrna Loy made 124 movies. Her first was *Pretty Ladies* (1925) in which the actress, just 20, played a chorus girl. In her early career, Loy was often cast as exotic Orientals. She is best remembered for co-starring with William Powell in the *Thin Man* movies from 1934 to 1947. Loy made a total of 13 films with Powell, including six *Thin Man* pictures. The actress had a very naturalistic acting style, underplaying scenes, reactive more than active. She became known as "the Perfect Wife" not only for her portrayal of Nora Charles in *The Thin Man* and its sequels but also for playing the wife of Cary Grant in *Mr. Blandings Builds His Dream House* (1948) and Fredric March's spouse in the Academy Award–winning *The Best Years of Our Lives* (1946).

Loy is one of the few movie actresses profiled in this book whose initial venture into television was not as the host of an anthology series. In 1953, MCA, the talent agency for Loy and Powell, indicated that both were ready to appear as Nick and Nora Charles in a *Thin Man* TV series. There was even a report that the great-grandson of Asta, the wire-haired dog that co-starred in the original movies, would be in the series.[1] However, Powell, at age 60, confessed that he really didn't want to do a TV series. *The Thin Man* did become a TV show in 1957 with Peter Lawford and Phyllis Kirk playing the husband-and-wife detectives but without the charm of the Loy-Powell pairing.

Loy's other attempts at her own series paired her with a leading actor, but perhaps because the males were not in the league of a Powell or a Cary Grant, none of the pilots became a series. In the mid–50s, Carol Irwin, who had produced the classic CBS dramedy *Mama*, had an agreement with Loy for a weekly filmed comedy titled *It Gives Me Great Pleasure,* based on the book by Emily Kimbrough. Loy played widow Kate Kennedy, a traveling lecturer who yearned to retire and spend more time with sons Tommy and Johnny. Zachary Scott played David Wadsworth, the owner-manager of Wadsworth Lecture Bureau who wanted to marry Kate, but the feeling was not mutual. He would do almost anything to keep his most popular lecturer on the circuit.

The pilot was scripted by Harold J. Kennedy, directed by Ralph Nelson and produced by Revue. Also in the cast were Robert Preston as Jim Tweedy, Lois Bolton as Jim's mother Mrs. Tweedy and Howard Kennedy as Wadsworth's assistant Trumbull. The pilot aired as an April 3, 1955, installment of *General Electric Theater*.

The show opens with Kate again considering retiring from the lecture circuit with Wadsworth talking her out of it. He sends her to lecture in Texas, where she is met by a welcoming committee chaired by Mrs. Tweedy. When her son Jim takes Kate out for dinner, she meets a young boy who gives her the mumps. Sidelined, Kate is unable to have Christmas with her sons. When she is almost recovered, Jim Tweedy tells Kate that he loves her and wants her to quit lecturing and move to Texas. Learning of this, Wadsworth flies to Texas to talk Kate out of the idea. He decides to honor her with his All-American Mom Award instead of giving it to Mrs. Tweedy as he had promised Jim that he would do. Johnny and Tommy present the award to their mother, who changes her mind about moving to Texas and leaving Wadsworth Lecture Bureau.

When this pilot was not picked up, Carol Irwin tried developing a family comedy for the actress originally titled *Minerva* and then *The Myrna Loy Show* on which Lee Bowman would play her husband. The series was to be produced by Screen Gems in 1958. George Oppenheimer wrote the pilot script titled "The Boltons Go to Brackton" and Don Weis directed. Commenting on this potential series, Loy told *Variety*, "It won't just be a comedy, but a mixture of comedy and dramatics. It would be done on film in New York, since my husband lives there."[2]

The Bolton family consists of Minerva Bolton, her husband Luke, a lawyer in his forties, and their three sons, Bruce, the oldest one, Martin, 11 years old, smart and something of a schemer, and five-year-old Ben, who likes animals.[3]

Luke has an offer to leave the legal profession and become headmaster of Brackton School for Boys, which means that the family will have to move. Luke is an alumnus of the school which Bruce currently attends. Mrs. Brackton, the widow of the school's founder, owns the headmaster's house and a sizable portion of the school; she isn't sold on Luke as its headmaster. But after discussing the career change with his family, the Boltons decide to move.

While the family is moving into their new home, Luke receives a call from Adelaide Robey, his new secretary, informing him that Mrs. Brackton wants to meet with him immediately. Luke goes to his office to see Brackton, who had become impatient and left before he arrives. Bruce fights with a schoolmate who doesn't like the fact that Bruce's father is now the headmaster. Minerva breaks up the fight, embarrassing Bruce. Mrs. Brackton then stops by the headmaster's house hoping that Luke is there. She is concerned that Luke has canceled a faculty reception, preferring instead to meet with faculty members in small groups. Minerva bristles at Mrs. Brackton's insistence that nothing at the school be changed. When her husband returns home after Brackton has left, Minerva thinks that she may have ruined his career at the school. The boy who fought with Bruce overheard Minerva standing up to Mrs. Brackton. News spreads and almost the entire school comes to the headmaster's home to welcome the Boltons.

Loy's second attempt at a series was also rejected by the networks. Five years later, in 1963, Loy tried once more to launch a career as a sitcom wife. The project *The Magnificent Montagues* was created by Nat Hiken, best known for developing *You'll Never Get Rich* with Phil Silvers and *Car 54, Where Are You? The Magnificent Montagues* centered on a vain Shakespearean actor, Edwin Montague (Dennis King). To maintain the lifestyle to which he was accustomed, he took a job, at the urging of his wife, as host of a TV kiddie show since he had been unemployed for a lengthy period. Loy again played the "perfect wife," Lily Boheme, also an actress. Pert Kelton was featured as Agnes, the Montagues' maid. As "Uncle Sunshine" on the kiddie show, the acerbic Montague insulted both the sponsors and the audience but nevertheless became very popular.

The Magnificent Montagues started out on radio with Monty Woolley in the lead role. In 1958, Hiken attempted to make a TV version with Sir Cedric Hardwicke and Vivienne Segal in the main roles but was unsuccessful. To show the importance of Loy's casting as Mrs. Montague, Hiken changed the title from the singular, *The Magnificent Montague,* to the plural *The Magnificent Montagues.*

Hiken apparently thought that he may have made a major error in casting Loy in the pilot.

> Throughout rehearsals, Loy glided from one line to the next without the slightest change in expression. Her blank-faced performance worried Nat, but rather than question the respected Hollywood star's approach, he moved onto the soundstage for the first day of filming, hoping that something would change once the camera started to roll. Nothing did. Once again, Loy seemed to sleepwalk through her scenes. Hiken's distress grew—until he watched the rushes. Although apparently apathetic on the set, she glowed on screen, a true master of the understated movie actor's craft.[4]

Hiken shopped the pilot to Desilu, then to NBC, and finally to CBS, but no one would commit to turning the pilot into a series. *The Magnificent Montagues* finally aired on August 16, 1964, as a "special" episode on NBC.

Loy's final acting appearance was in "Sidney and the Actress," a 1982 episode of the Tony Randall comedy *Love, Sidney*. She appeared as Vera Lonnigan, a movie idol of the Randall character. Loy passed away in 1993 at the age of 88. She had received an Honorary Oscar for career achievement two years earlier.

Chico, Groucho and Harpo Marx

Beginning in vaudeville before graduating to Broadway and then to movies, the Marx Brothers made a series of wildly antic and hilarious movies from 1929 through the '40s. Julius Marx was given the nickname "Groucho" because he wore a grouch bag for valuables around his neck. Groucho, with his bushy eyebrows and moustache, always smoked a cigar. Leonard Marx loved the ladies (the chicks) and so was dubbed "Chicko," later "Chico." Chico adopted a persona of a rural Italian immigrant wearing shabby clothes and an Alpine hat. Adolph Marx played the harp, hence his appellation "Harpo." He never spoke on stage, in the movies or on television. Wearing a curly blonde wig, he communicated by honking a horn or whistling. There were two other, lesser known brothers: Milton, a sickly child who wore galoshes or gumshoes at the first hint of rain and was nicknamed "Gummo," and brother Herbert, who received the name "Zeppo" (its derivation is not known). Zeppo, who appeared in the early Marx Brothers films, was the group's straight man. Groucho was famous for his wisecracks and non-stop talking, Chico for his piano-playing, and Harpo for being a mime. Groucho, Chico, and Harpo basically maintained their screen personas throughout their movie and TV careers.

In the brothers' first film *The Cocoanuts* (1929), they ran a hotel. Their other notable movies included *Animal Crackers* (1930), focusing on a search for a missing painting during a party in honor of African explorer Capt. Spaulding (Groucho), *Horse Feathers* (1932). centered on a college football game competition with the new president (Groucho) of Huxley College hiring two bumblers (Chico and Harpo) to help win the big game, and *Duck Soup* (1933) with Groucho, playing the president of the bankrupt country Fredonia, declaring war on neighboring Sylvania over the love of wealthy Mrs. Teasdale (Margaret Dumont, Groucho's foil in several pictures).

In 1950, both Groucho and Chico Marx attempted television series. Groucho's show, *You Bet Your Life*, a quiz show which had begun on radio in 1947, made a very successful transition to TV, running for 11 seasons on NBC.

It was a "semi-scripted" show with the contestants interviewed beforehand so that Groucho could come up with what seemed to be spontaneous ad libs when he spoke with the contestants on air. For his game show, Groucho modified his movie persona to become a TV personality with whom viewers could feel more comfortable. He was less frenetic than in the movies and less prone to start trouble. On TV he acted as "the bemused moderator."[1]

Brother Chico's TV projects were less successful. In 1949, he made a comedy pilot called *Papa Romani* where he played the title character, the head of an Italian-American family including his wife Josephine (Argentina Brunetti), young son Mickee (Jeff Silver) and teen daughter Lucy (Alice Ann Kelley). Chico continued with his Italian accent and wore his trademark hat throughout the show set in New York City. In the pilot, aired on January 9, 1950, the Romanis get their first telephone. Mama Romani doesn't want it because she thinks only bad news is communicated through the device. When she tries to make her first call, she injures her finger in the dial and, at the insistence of neighbor Mrs. Greenstreet (Margaret Hamilton), she goes to the hospital. Mrs. Greenstreet wants to wait by the phone for her brother-in-law to call about his wife, who is about to give birth. Mr. Pinto (William Frawley, later Fred on *I Love Lucy*) stops by, saying he is the vice-president of a linen company whose phone is out of order and who wants to use the Romanis' new phone to conduct business. Mr. Pinto turns out to be a bookie whose clients begin calling and placing bets on horse races. When Pinto receives a call warning him to leave the apartment, Romani begins taking his phone calls as the police arrive and arrest him. Mickee calls the mayor's office to have his dad released, and all ends well. The pilot was written by George Panetta and directed by Frank K. Telford for Jerry Fairbanks, Inc., and Official Films.

When the pilot failed to sell, Chico became involved with another television show for ABC, initially titled *Sugar Bowl* and then called *The College Bowl*. It premiered in October 1950 and ran until March 1951. (It's not to be confused with the quiz show *The College Bowl*, hosted by Allen Ludden and then Robert Earle, pitting two college teams against each other in a test of their knowledge.) In Chico's musical comedy *College Bowl* series, he played the benevolent owner of a college campus soda shop frequented by students who sang and danced. A young Andy Williams, making his first appearance on a TV series, played a student.

In 1959, writer Philip Rapp devised a pilot for Groucho, Harpo, and Chico, *The Deputy Seraph*, "Seraph" being a combination of the words "sheriff" and "seraphim" (an order of angels). Groucho played the motorcycle-riding Deputy Seraph who, with the assistance of "Able-bodied Cherub"

(Harpo) and "Angel Second Class" (Chico), tried to help mortals. The three angels would take over the spirits of people who then would assume Marxian characteristics such as raising their eyebrows and smoking cigars (Groucho), playing the piano (Chico) or chasing women and playing the harp (Harpo). Groucho was still involved with *You Bet Your Life*, so if *The Deputy Seraph* had gone to series, he would have appeared in only one out of every three episodes.

Taking into account the ages of the brothers Marx at the time (Chico, 72; Harpo, 71; and Groucho, 69), Rapp's concept for the potential series involved other actors each week taking on the personas of the brothers so that they would not be burdened with carrying an entire episode.

About 16 minutes of outtakes from the pilot exist, all featuring Groucho, Chico and Harpo. The opening shows Harpo playing his harp on a cloud with Chico at the piano performing "When the Saints Come Marching In." Groucho arrives on a motorcycle—sometimes on the seat; other times just holding onto the handlebars with his body in the air. Groucho is assigned to help a man and woman as described below and enlists Chico and Harpo's assistance.

The scenes with the brothers were to be filmed in Hollywood with the balance of each episode being made in England by J. Arthur Rank productions. During the filming of the Marxes' scenes, Chico had great difficulty remembering his lines. As Rapp indicated, "He wasn't acute, but if a guy blows a line, you do it again." Rapp's son said, "Chico really wasn't alert," and recalled Chico repeatedly blowing a line "and making Groucho madder than hell."[2]

In the pilot script, the brothers are assigned a case on the French Riviera: An American, Paul MacDowell, must marry Linda Pavane by 8:30 that evening.[3] MacDowell hates women, and Linda is engaged to be married to casino operator Andre Lazar. Linda's guardian, her Uncle Cesar, a concert pianist, will not permit her to marry anyone. Cesar controls Linda's estate, and therefore she can't marry without his consent. Paul is a composer who wants Cesar to perform his compositions, but Cesar refuses to see him.

Paul eventually goes to the casino where Cesar is gambling and starts to play next to him. Thanks to the angels, Paul begins winning while Cesar continues losing. After Cesar asks for more credit from Andre Lazar, Andre reveals to Cesar that he knows that Cesar is embezzling Linda's fortune for gambling. Given this, Cesar consents to Linda's marriage to Andre. But she is not happy that Andre wants to marry so quickly. The couple meets Paul in the casino. Paul and Linda used to be in love but broke up when Cesar refused to allow them to marry. At a rehearsal for his concert, Chico's persona takes over Cesar's playing. Harpo's persona becomes the harpist, and Groucho's the conductor. The ensuing confusion causes Cesar to confess to everyone that he stole from his niece and is allowing her to marry a fortune hunter. As the wedding ceremony is about to commence, Andre pressures Linda to marry him or else he will turn her uncle over to the police as an embezzler. Paul intercedes, hitting Andre on the chin, and Linda rushes to Paul's arms. They marry; Cesar later plays Paul's concerto at his concert.

Harpo (left) and Chico Marx in costume for "The Incredible Jewel Robbery," a possible pilot that aired as an installment of *General Electric Theater*. Groucho had only a brief scene with Harpo and Chico at the end of the episode. This was the final appearance of the three Marx brothers together.

In November 1960, Phillip Rapp and the Marx Brothers brought a $565,750 lawsuit for breach of contract against six defendants including Sol Lesser Productions, J. Arthur Rank, Sidney Box and James Swan who were to back Rapp financially in producing the comedy series. The suit charged that the brothers had an oral contract for 39 *Deputy Seraph* episodes but when the time came for the defendants to post an advance of $42,500 for the scripts, the contract was repudiated. In addition to Harpo, Chico and Groucho, Gummo Marx was also included as a plaintiff since he served as the business manager for his brothers. Rapp never got a settlement because Chico was uninsurable due to hardening of the arteries. Without insurance coverage for Chico working on the series, the project died. "Nobody told me about Chico," Rapp said in retrospect, "he was always so lively around the [Hillcrest Country] club."[4] Chico passed away in 1961 at age 74 from arteriosclerosis.

On March 8, 1959, Harpo and Chico appeared on an episode of *General Electric Theater* titled "The Incredible Jewel Robbery," written by Dallas Gaultois and James Edmiston and directed by Mitchell Leisen. Initially titled "Best Laid Plans," the episode had almost no dialogue. The duo breaks into various neighborhood stores to find materials to pull off a jewel heist. Harpo steals two cans of paint from a paint shop, cable from a radio and TV store, and a ring of baloney and a bagel from a deli. Chico takes lights and other hardware from an auto parts store and a police uniform from a costume shop. They drive to an isolated spot where, with the stolen materials, they turn their automobile into a police cruiser. Harpo uses the hole in the bagel to dot i's above the words "city" and "police" on the side of the car. Harpo, dressed like Groucho, goes to a jewelry store and holds up the jeweler who sets off the burglar alarm. Chico arrives in his *faux* police vehicle, handcuffs Harpo and drives off with him and the jewels. A pedestrian flags them down to help a pregnant woman get to a hospital. A real police car drives up beside them and the officer notices that Chico's cruiser has white letters on the side spelling out "City Police" against a black background whereas real police vehicles have black letters against a white background. The pair is arrested and in the final scene, the real Groucho appears and speaks the only line of dialogue in the episode: "We won't talk until we see our lawyer."

Although "The Incredible Jewel Robbery" is cited in both Lee Goldberg's book on unsold television pilots and Vincent Terrace's *Encyclopedia of Television Pilots*, it's not clear how a continuing series would have been based on this episode. Would such a series have been an anthology with the brothers appearing as different characters in a unique story each week or would they continue to play the same characters as in the *General Electric Theater* episode? Apart from appearing with his brothers in these TV pilots, Harpo never attempted a series of his own, no doubt because of the difficulty of constructing a continuing show based solely on the type of character he played. Harpo Marx died in September 1964.

Producer Henry Jaffe, responsible for the series *The Dinah Shore Chevy Show* and *Shirley Temple's Storybook,* announced in 1958 that he was preparing a 30-minute TV series based on *The Magical Monarch of Mo,* from books written by L. Frank Baum of *Wizard of Oz* fame. The series would be for the 1959–60 TV season, but Jaffe wanted to produce a one-hour episode of *Shirley Temple's Storybook* as the pilot.

While no episode of the Temple series was made showcasing "Mo," a year later (June 1959), *Variety*'s Jack Hellman reported that Jaffe was working on a special to star Broadway actor Cyril Ritchard as the Monarch of Mo based on a script by Gore Vidal.[5] In the Vidal script, Mo is a fantasy land where everything the citizens need grows on trees.[6] The daughter of the Monarch of Mo, Princess Pattycake, has literally lost her temper and so is very difficult to get along with. The inhabitants of Mo keep their tempers in lockets and consider them very valuable. Tim Tom, a handsome hunter from the Haunted Forest, wants to marry the princess and vows to find her temper. The Monarch and Tim Tom, both disguised, go to meet the Monarch's adversary, King Scowleyowe, and negotiate a performance in exchange for a temper from his collection. The Monarch is able to obtain his daughter's temper from the king, and Tim Tom and Pattycake marry.

Another year passed with no *Monarch of Mo* special. Then in 1960, Jaffe entered into a partnership with Groucho for the production of a Mo TV special that "eventually may be developed into a series."[7] Frank Gabrielson and Bob Dwan wrote the teleplay for the special to be called *Groucho Marx in the Magical Monarch of Mo.*

This version of Mo was quite different from Vidal's. Groucho played George Smith who, in his dreams, became the Monarch of Mo. George was married to Queenie, a bit of a nag, and has three daughters, Patty, Rosemary and Jane. Snope, the Smiths' next-door neighbor, became the devious Royal Gardener.

In George's dream, Patty Smith falls in love with Prince Tim Tom of Glow. The Royal Gardener's daughter Sandra also wants to marry the prince. The Royal Gardener conspires with Tim Tom's mother, the Queen of Glow, to demand from the Monarch a million dollar dowry. Tim Tom and the Monarch scheme to ask good Witch Fortuna for the dowry. She saves the day by showing them that a money tree is growing in their garden. In the end, the Monarch speaks directly to the camera:

Bet you think I'm going to wake up now, don't you? Don't be silly—why should I leave Mo?—and I've got too much growing for me here. I guess you've probably all got a place like this in your dreams. Someplace where things are easier and happier and certainly not half as cockeyed as they are in what we call the "real world." [Groucho picks a cigar from a cigar tree and smokes it.] Anyway, I hope you find your land of Mo someday and when you do [as he used to say on *You Bet Your Life*], tell 'em Groucho sent you...[8]

NBC tried to find a sponsor for this special. In a promotional brochure for the show, the network indicated that a single vendor could sponsor the hour for $200,000. The brochure emphasized the success of the TV airings of *The Wizard of Oz* (as well as fantasy specials like *Peter Pan* and *Cinderella*) along with Groucho's popularity. However, no sponsor could be found. The special never aired.

Right before Chico's death in 1961, *Variety* announced that the Marx Brothers would reunite in the TV series *The Three Marx Brothers* for the 1962–63 season. Screen Gems had signed the brothers to voice lifelike puppets of themselves, recreating some of their famous sketches. The figures were to be made by Tri-Cinemation, Inc., which had been recently purchased by Screen Gems. The new half-hour weekly series would use stop-motion filming techniques to give movement to the puppets. Chico had apparently recorded some voice characterizations for his puppet before he died; Harpo's puppet likeness would simply whistle. The proposed series never got off the ground, but there would be other attempts to recreate the magic of the brothers' routines through animation.

When Groucho's *You Bet Your Life* was ending, he filmed a pilot for another such program in January 1961. Similar to *You Bet Your Life*, *What Do You Want?* combined talk show elements with a short quiz. George Fenneman, Marx's *You Bet Your Life* announcer, continued in that role for the new pilot. The idea behind the series was that people would sit with Groucho and describe their hopes and desires. One of the guests on the pilot wanted to be the first woman president of the United States. Mother and daughter Beth and Betty hoped for husbands who loved cats and music and had at least $5000 in cash. Beth and Betty brought eight of their 15 felines out on stage to meet Groucho. At the end of each conversation, the quiz was about current events with the contestants given the choice of answering the question correctly for $1000 or taking $400 if they decided they couldn't answer the question.

While *What Do You Want?* did not become a series, a similar show called *Tell It to Groucho* did premiere on CBS in January 1962. Fenneman was not part of this show; a young man, Jack Wheeler, and a young woman, Patty

Harmon, were Groucho's assistants. (Both had been *You Bet Your Life* contestants.) Guests would be interviewed by Groucho and then play a game that involved being shown a photo for a split second and trying to guess what it depicted. If they guessed correctly after seeing the photo for one-eighth of a second, they would win $500. If not, the photo would appear for half a second for $250 for a correct guess, and then the photo would be displayed for a full second to win $125.

Among the first *Tell It to Groucho* guests were the mother-daughter team of Beth and Betty, again asking for husbands who loved cats. This time they had only 13 felines and brought them all on stage. Groucho used some of the same lines he had used on *What Do You Want?* when interviewing them, like saying that if he had known there would be so many cats around, he would have taken a double allergy shot. This series lasted for only half a season.

Tell It to Groucho was Marx's final American TV series. However, late in his career, he attempted a TV comeback as a sitcom star and in other ventures. But without the support from his brothers and without the talented writers who had scripted many of their movies in the 1930s, Groucho was not successful.

Writer Sidney Sheldon, who created *The Patty Duke Show* and *I Dream of Jeannie*, developed a treatment for a 1965 Screen Gems comedy series to star Groucho as a ghost in a series called *That's the Spirit*.[9] The planned show bore some similarities to the Marx Brothers' *Deputy Seraph* pilot in that Groucho played an otherworldly character. The treatment dealt with reporter-photographer Scott Whitney being assigned by *World Magazine* to cover an archeological expedition to a 5000-year-old tomb uncovered by a shepherd in a small country in Asia. Scott, separated from the rest of the expedition, sees a man in Oriental costume smoking a large cigar. The man wants to help Scott get a better photo of a vase containing the alphabet of the lost Phonarian civilization. In the process, the man drops the vase, shattering it. When the rest of the expedition finds Scott, he is blamed for the vase's destruction since the native man has disappeared.

The man later appears to Scott in his hotel room with Scott concluding that he is seeing a ghost. The ghost, named Darius (Groucho), explains to Scott that he had been executed after being arrested while robbing a store and being caught by the owner whose wife was Darius' girlfriend. Reluctant to accept Darius into Heaven, God wants him to stick around on Earth to do some good deeds. Despite Scott's protests, Darius accompanies him back to the U.S. where he tries to help the reporter but usually gets Scott in more trouble. Darius asks Scott to be patient with him. The ghost writes down the lost civilization's alphabet which Scott gives to the expedition leader to help him translate the Phonarian language. The first translation that the professor is working on turns out to be a joke about a "farmer's daughter."

In an earlier draft of the treatment, the title for the proposed series was *Uncle Miracle* and the ghost's name was Ab. The character of Scott was previously named "Tom," and he could have been an archaeologist or a professor, before Sheldon decided on a magazine reporter. Early on, there was also a question of whether the ghost should be with the same family or haunt a different family every week. When the character of the reporter was finally decided upon, Sheldon considered giving him a buddy named Pete Whittington but settled on a girlfriend named Mary.

Sheldon developed the treatment for *That's the Spirit* into a script, *Just Call Me Julius*, changing the ghost's name to Groucho's real first name. The script follows the basic storyline described above with some changes.[10] The series was to open with an animated sequence showing the ghost Julius raising hell in Heaven and being tossed down to Hell. Julius escapes and sneaks to Earth. He explains to Scott that if he can show that he has reformed by assisting Scott, he can go back to Heaven. However, Julius only materializes when he wants to, usually just in Scott's presence. In the script, there are several scenes with Julius flirting with the ladies. For example, when Scott visits Mary at the modeling agency where she works, Julius, eyeing Mary, says that she makes Madame Pompadour look like an undernourished boy. Julius then poses as a photographer to take pictures of other models in bikinis.

At the end of the script, Sheldon describes other adventures that await Scott and Julius:

> They attend a performance of *Hamlet*, Julius appears on stage to show the other ghost how to do it. The actors and audience panic.... Scott covers a story on our space program, and Julius helps an astronaut out of trouble.... They go to a high school and Julius straightens out a class of juvenile delinquents.... They attend a séance, and Julius puts the medium into shock.... Julius traps a ring of spies ... takes care of an orphaned baby ... helps the President out of a jam ... foils a hold-up ... helps an ugly duckling win a beauty contest.[11]

Just Call Me Julius—That's the Spirit never became a pilot let alone a series. Groucho did appear on Sheldon's *I Dream of Jeannie* in its second season: He had a cameo at the end of the 1967 episode "The Greatest Invention in the World."

With no other offers coming from producers in the States for a TV series, Groucho returned to Britain in 1965 to host a 13-week reboot of *You Bet Your Life* titled *Groucho in Britain*. One of his biographers remarked, "From the opening shot *Groucho* looked cheap and the host discomfited. Reviewers were in no mood to cut anyone any slack. 'One big yawn,' said the *Daily Express*. 'Dismal beyond belief,' the *Observer* chimed in. The host seemed 'ill at ease, almost unable to roll his eyes. It was downright cruelty to present him this way.'"[12]

An animated version of the Marx Brothers was announced in 1966. The cartoon series, aimed at kids, was to be made by Filmation Associates and produced by Norman Prescott and Lou Scheimer. Groucho signed to be the technical adviser; he didn't do any voice work even though his character was to be the main one. Actor Pat Harrington, Jr., voiced the Groucho character. The pilot, "A Day at the Horse Opera," was set in the Old West; 156 shorts were planned but apparently no TV station expressed interest in the series probably because, unlike the comedy teams of Abbott and Costello and the Three Stooges (familiar to kids through TV reruns), children were not that familiar with the Marx Brothers.

In a 1967 pilot produced by Mark Goodson and Bill Todman, known mostly for their game show productions like *To Tell the Truth* and *I've Got a Secret*, Groucho starred as banker G. Paul Greedy in *Rhubarb*. Greedy, the richest man in the world, lived in Beverly Hills and for at least 20 years was said to be on his deathbed. In a role tailored to Groucho's persona, Greedy has lines like "I've made $1 million by doing what I could do, and $2 million doing what I can't do, and I had a lot more fun doing what I can't do."

In the pilot, young bank clerk Bill Cory (Sammy Jackson, who had starred in the situation comedy, *No Time for Sergeants*) visits Greedy to deliver his final will and testament. In front of his relatives, Greedy tears up the will and informs them that he's put the money he will not need into an irrevocable trust with Rhubarb, his cat, as the recipient. According to Greedy's lawyer, a trustee must be appointed when an animal is the recipient. Greedy lets the cat choose the trustee. Instead of one of his relatives, Rhubarb selects Mr. Cory. Cory becomes bank president with the cat as CEO. The character of Bill Cory was the lead in the series with Groucho billed as "permanent special guest star."

The rest of the pilot deals mainly with Cory and Rhubarb. After Greedy's relatives try to kidnap Rhubarb, Cory takes the cat with him to a party thrown by a woman, who wants to be Cory's girlfriend, and her mother. As might be predicted, the cat causes havoc and then escapes. Cory is jailed twice attempting to locate the feline, who finally comes to him in jail. Greedy is able to get the pair out of jail.

The unsold pilot, based on the H. Allen Smith book of the same name, was developed by Hunt Stromberg, Jr. Written by Norman Paul, the project was produced and directed by Arthur Lubin for ABC.

Even though he remained a popular guest on TV talk shows, Groucho's final acting appearance was in a 1968 episode of Diahann Carroll's comedy *Julia* in a small role as a cat lover. He died in 1977 at age 86.

Roddy McDowall

Child actors often have a very difficult time with their careers when they grow up. Many simply leave the entertainment business and pursue other endeavors. Those who continue acting usually have to try to adopt a new show business persona to find work. Roddy McDowall had a lengthy film and TV career by adapting his image as he grew older. As he matured, he became more of a character actor.

McDowall was born in England in 1928. As a child actor, he appeared in the classic films *How Green Was My Valley* (1941), *My Friend Flicka* (1943) and *Lassie Come Home* (1943). As an adult, his film appearances included *Cleopatra* (1963), *The Poseidon Adventure* (1972) and *Funny Lady* (1975). His most movie famous role as an adult was playing various chimpanzee characters in the original *Planet of the Apes* films between 1968 and 1973.

In 1950, McDowall became one of the first movie actors to have his own TV series, a local show on a Los Angeles TV station. He hosted a weekly amateur talent contest on KLAC-TV which featured local high school talent. About three months after the show debuted, he left the series because it was interfering with his movie career.

In 1954, McDowall and Peggy Ann Garner appeared in a TV pilot written by Norman Lear about a pair of newlyweds. The projected series was titled *I Take Thee Susan* to be produced by Lear and his writing partner Ed Simmons. According to Lear, the series concerned a boy and girl who grew up in the same New York apartment building but weren't close as kids.[1] They fall in love after college and are married. After their honeymoon, they find that both sets of parents have chipped in to buy them an apartment in the same building where their parents still live. Evidently, lack of a sponsor was the reason the pilot never became a series.

Beginning in the 1970s, McDowall's attempts at a TV series usually involved him playing some type of eccentric character. In the early '70s, the forever youthful-appearing (often described as "Dorian Gray ageless") McDowall filmed a half-hour sitcom pilot based on the 1930s *Topper* movies and the early 1950s TV show. He starred as uptight Cosmo Topper, Jr., along with Stefanie Powers and John Fink as the ghostly Kirbys. Written by A.J.

Carothers and directed by Hy Averback, the pilot was produced by Twentieth Century–Fox.

Cosmo Topper, Jr., was the fifth vice-president at a bank headed by H. Anson Jones, Thurston Abercrombie (John Randolph) and William C. Gibson. Topper, Jr., was the nephew of Cosmo Topper, the character from the *Topper* movies as well as the 1950s TV series. Since he was a nephew and not the son, one wonders why he used the "Jr." at the end of his name.

In a warehouse where his late uncle's possessions are stored, Topper discovers a beautiful antique car. When he gets in, the car begins to talk to him. He tries to rationalize the female voice by thinking that he is just tired, but the sound of the woman's laugh increases his anxiety. The hat that he had left sitting on the passenger seat suddenly levitates to reveal a beautiful woman. She asks how she looks, prompting responses from a male who suddenly appears next to her. The couple talks about Mr. Topper, unsure of the first impression they have made on him, and reveal that they knew Topper's uncle. The male ghost's name is George and the female is Marion. Cosmo admits to recognizing the ghosts from photos in the bank where he works.

The next day, the ghosts appear at the office and begin talking about their Kirby Foundation that they want Topper to manage. He seems reluctant, but they say that when he took possession of the antique car, he got their presence in the deal. The vehicle is apparently the one in which Marion and George had their fatal accident. They try to persuade Topper that the two of them can make his life better. Topper responds that he just wants to be left alone. Marion and George suggest they all go dancing.

The three go to a club where they drink a toast to Dreamland, the ballroom that the Kirbys want Topper to turn into a youth center but which Abercrombie wants to demolish. The two ghosts get Topper drunk so that he will say "yes" to everything.

The next day, Topper has a meeting with Mr. Abercrombie to make good on his promises to Marion and George. At the meeting, Topper attempts to sell Abercrombie on the idea of turning Dreamland into a recreation center. The ghosts move Abercrombie's pens around to keep him from signing a demolition notice for the place. Abercrombie's secretary enters, interrupting the conversation, and falls into Abercrombie's lap thanks to Marion. He seems delighted but embarrassed by the implication of a relationship between him and his secretary. Cosmo has Abercrombie agree to save Dreamland by promising his own discretion about the relationship between his boss and secretary. Marion and George reappear, congratulating Topper on his work.

Cosmo returns to his office. The Kirbys appear, celebrating him. Topper asks that they leave him alone now that he has helped them save Dreamland.

The ghosts disappear as Topper sits down at his desk. His secretary enters and sees a gloomy-looking Topper, who is clearly upset that George and Marion are no longer there. The two ghosts quickly reappear and lead him out of the office, which garners a lot of unwanted attention from his colleagues and Mr. Abercrombie.

John Fink, who played George Kirby, thought that the pilot was ill-conceived from the start. While McDowall and Powers were wonderful and fun to be around, he thought that the idea of having his character and Powers' character appear in 1930s attire as in the original movie and leaving McDowall in contemporary (1970s) dress was not a good one. "I thought mixing those two eras was like mixing oil and water.... For me, Roddy's comparable youth made it challenging to garner the same avuncular sympathetic qualities the older Roland Young (in the movie) and Leo G. Carroll (in the 1950s television series) had as the uncle."[2] Fink added that Stefanie Powers confided to him that it would be at least five years before any of them could get another series. Six years later, she starred in *Hart to Hart* with Robert Wagner. Fink left acting for a period of time due to a family health crisis but returned in the 1990s.

McDowall had a little better luck at playing eccentric characters on some short-lived series in the '70s and '80s. None of the shows lasted for more than a single season. He co-starred on the TV series *Planet of the Apes* playing Galen, a helpful chimpanzee who befriends two time-traveling astronauts who crashland on a future Earth ruled by apes. The show premiered in September 1974 but lasted only half a season. McDowall subsequently landed a featured role on the short-lived science fiction series *The Fantastic Journey* that debuted in February 1977. He appeared as Dr. Jonathan Willoway, a rather peculiar scientist from the 1960s who was caught in a time and space warp along with other scientists exploring uncharted land in the Bermuda Triangle. Dr. Willoway is introduced to the other characters as a person hungry for human contact since his only associates are androids which he has subjugated. In 1982, McDowall became a regular on *Tales of the Gold Monkey* starring Stephen Collins. Set in the South Pacific during the 1930s, the adventure show followed the exploits of Jake Cutter (Collins) who runs an inter-island air transport service. Impeccably dressed in a white suit and ascot and wearing a moustache, McDowall, assuming a French accent, played Bon Chance Louis, the French magistrate of Bora Gora and the owner of the Monkey Bar, a hangout for many of the island's shady characters.

The 1984 pilot *London and Davis in New York* starred Season Hubley as Claudia London, a photographer, and Richard Crenna as John Grayson Davis, a writer, McDowall appeared in a supporting role as Paul Fisk, Claudia's uptight butler and chef. The proposed series concerned a world-famous photojournalist team finding stories and solving crimes. Also in the pilot were Vernee Watson as Frances, Davis' cook and maid, and James Carroll Jordan as Brandon, a photographer friend of London and Davis.

McDowall's character in the pilot, which was written by Linda Bloodworth-Thomason (creator of *Designing Women*) and directed by Robert Day, always wore a suit and tie. He prepared healthy meals for Claudia and John; the latter despised them and waited for Frances to make heartier fare. London and Davis, while co-workers and lovers, still had separate apartments, which they alternated between, in the same building which is why they each had their own domestic help. Fisk, as he was called, occasionally helped London and Davis with their work.

Two years later, McDowall played a Fisk-like role in a series like *London and Davis*: *Bridges to Cross* starred Suzanne Pleshette as Bridges and Nicolas Surovy as Cross, reporters for a news magazine and former spouses. McDowall played Norman Parks, an efficient executive secretary. *Bridges to Cross* ran for only seven episodes.

McDowall attempted another television series with the 1988 pilot *Remo Williams,* based on the 1985 movie *Remo Williams: The Adventure Begins*. He had star billing as Chiun, a Korean master of Sinanja, a fictional martial art. Wearing a skull cap, moustache and glasses and looking very much like a little old man, McDowall's character trained Remo Williams (Jeffrey Meek) to battle the forces of evil. Stephen Elliott appeared as Harold W. Smith, who assigned missions to Williams.

The Chiun character, an aficionado of Barbra Streisand, introduced the pilot by announcing to viewers with an Oriental accent, "If you have chosen to watch my worthless pupil Remo Williams, switch please to another channel. Otherwise, you will be forced to watch humiliation of a grown man." The pilot, titled "The Prophecy," was written by Steven and J. Miyoko Hensley based on stories by Richard Sapir and Warren Murphy. Christian I. Nyby II was the director and it was produced by Dick Clark and Orion Television.

The unsold pilot had Chiun ready to return to Korea but being persuaded by Smith to stay and continue to teach Sinanja to Williams. Chiun is afraid that Remo is overconfident in his abilities to defeat evildoers so, to teach him a lesson, Chiun asks a hit man to give Remo a superficial injury. But the assassin decides to kill Williams, thinking that Chiun will then train him in the martial arts. Meanwhile, Smith has given Remo an assignment to destroy a bio-chemical lab. Chiun thinks that Williams is not ready for such a task. Remo goes ahead with the mission anyway, and Chiun has to help him escape after the lab explodes. Later, the hit man shoots and kills Remo,

Jeffrey Meek (left), a former cop who is brought back from the brink of death and trained by Zen master Roddy McDowall in the pilot for *Remo Williams*. Joel Grey had played the Zen master in the movie on which the pilot was based.

but Chiun brings him back to life with his mystical abilities. Chiun confesses that he hired the assassin but only to give Remo a superficial wound and that the prophecy, that one who is dead will become the greatest Sinanja master, will apply to Williams. After Remo recovers, he and Chiun visit the hit man. Remo gives the assassin the chance to shoot him; when he misses, Remo forces the man to shoot himself.

In his later years, McDowall did a lot of voice characterizations on animated series like *Batman: The Animated Adventures* and *Pinky and the Brain*. In 1994 he did voice work on a CBS pilot for a situation comedy called *Galaxy Beat*, written by Alan Spencer. The proposed series concerned a group of peacemakers patrolling the worst part of the galaxy. McDowall voiced the character of Corp. Cod, a large frog that was part of the team of peacemakers along with Comdr. Dack Steelbrow (Gregory Harrision), Lt. Sheila Fleckstein (Tracy Scoggins) and Larry Longspan (Alex Desert). Cod spoke English in between "rebbits," used his long tongue to retrieve objects, and liked to spend time in the spaceship's above-ground pool.

Roddy McDowall passed away at age 70 in 1998.

Ethel Merman

Ethel Merman is remembered mostly for her work on Broadway in musicals like *Roberta* and *Gypsy*. But she did appear in several iconic movies including *Call Me Madam* (1953), *There's No Business Like Show Business* (1954) and *It's a Mad Mad Mad Mad World* (1963). Merman made her first feature, *Follow the Leader* (1930), with Ed Wynn and Ginger Rogers and followed with eight other movies during that decade. The woman with the big voice, a belting mezzo-soprano, was so popular on Broadway during her career because, before sound amplification, she could project her voice to the back wall of a theater. Merman's persona on stage and in films was as a brassy female who usually got what she wanted.

As early as 1949, Ethel Merman did a pilot for a projected NBC comedy playing herself. In the late '50s, there were reports of Merman negotiating a deal with MCA, CBS and comic actor Phil Silvers to produce a situation comedy with her as the star. These negotiations never resulted in a TV series. In April 1958, Merman was set to make a pilot for Hal Roach, Jr., called *Carnival* which she hoped would be picked up as a series for the 1958–59 season, but then she was offered the role of Mama Rose in the musical *Gypsy* and asked to be released from this pilot commitment so she could begin preparations for the role.

After *Gypsy* closed in 1961, Merman again sought a TV vehicle to display her comedic talents, resisting the idea of doing a variety show. She opened discussions with Screen Gems for a series to be titled *Call Me Ethel*. While specifics remain unknown, one can speculate that Merman would be playing a character very similar to her star persona. However, in late 1961, Screen Gems dropped the proposed series earmarked for the 1962–63 season, blaming the actress for "temperamental problems." Merman had "no comment" in response to the Screen Gems announcement.[1]

Merman's next try at a sitcom, *Maggie Brown*, was initially called *The Ethel Merman Show* and then *Trader Brown*. In the 1963 pilot produced by Desilu, Merman played the title character, the larger-than-life owner of a bar on tropical Lobster Island that housed a Navy base with 1200 sailors. Commander John Farragut (Roy Roberts) headed the base. Maggie lived there with her teenage daughter Jeannie (Susan Watson) and her bartender-piano player. At the beginning of the pilot, Maggie sings "Friendship" to the sailors in her bar. McChesney (Walter Burke), the owner of a competing bar, complains to Farragut that Maggie is making illegal beer which indeed she is, in order to raise money to send her daughter to a private school in Connecticut.

The beer-making machine in her basement is broken, and the sailor who used to fix it has been transferred. Her brew master, Marv (Marvin Kaplan), finds a sailor named Joe Beckett (Mark Goddard), a machinist, who can repair the machine, but Joe demands 50 percent of her profits. He accepts 25 percent after he sees Maggie's cute daughter. To fix the equipment, Joe steals McChesney's bagpipes, the sounds from which are a dead giveaway to where the machine is located when the commander and McChesney make a surprise visit. The commander places the bar off-limits to his sailors. Learning of this, every patron of the bar pays their IOUs to raise the money so Maggie's daughter can attend school. But Maggie changes her mind and decides not to send Jeannie away. Mother and daughter sing "Mutual Admiration Society," and the bar is re-opened.

Cy Howard and Arthur Julian created the concept for the pilot; Bill Manhoff wrote the script, and David Alexander directed. This pilot was the first to be shot in color by Desilu. In discussing the project, Merman said, "There's nothing like it on TV now. It's a half-hour that's partly situation comedy and partly musical comedy. I'll be able to sing two songs each week."[2] Despite lobbying from Lucille Ball herself for the pilot to become a series, no network picked it up. ABC came the closest to turning it into a series, thinking of scheduling it at 9:30 p.m. on Fridays for the 1963–64 season, but ultimately decided to schedule *The Farmer's Daughter* with Inger Stevens in that slot.

Reminiscing about the project, Susan Watson, who played Ethel's daughter, recalls that Merman was always on time for their rehearsals "wanting to get the song ('Mutual Admiration Society') just right ... no nonsense, working our two-part harmonizing, letting me share the stage, when some other singers might have been wanting the stage all to themselves.... She was very particular about our number, and gave time for us both to look our best ... and we recorded it in 45 minutes."[3]

Merman's final attempt to star in a television series was *You're Gonna Love It Here* (originally called *Everything's Coming Up Roses*), written by Bruce Paltrow and directed by Paltrow and Gordin Rigsby. The projected series was about a three-generation family with Merman portraying Lolly Rogers, a Broadway star like herself, whose grandson Peter (Chris Barnes) needs a new home because his parents Marilyn and Arthur are in jail for income tax evasion. Since Lolly tours in various Broadway shows, she attempts to recruit her single son Harry (Austin Pendleton), a press agent, to take care of Peter. Harry reluctantly becomes Peter's guardian. He convinces his mother to talk with Peter in his apartment about living with him. Lolly ends up playing poker with Peter and his friends. When Harry discovers this, he argues with his mother and with Peter, who runs away to Lolly's place. Later, Harry brings Peter to his apartment and says that once he gets the hang of it, things will be pretty good. The pilot was filmed in front of a live audience in 1977 with Ethel singing the show's theme song.

The show was made for CBS, who liked it somewhat but thought it was too edgy. The network decided to make a second pilot, but not with Ethel Merman, perhaps thinking that her strong personality was too much for the projected series. The new pilot, with the same basic plot as the original but now titled *Big City Boys,* also featured Pendleton and Barnes. As a gentler, softer show, it was about to be turned into a series when *Soap* premiered on ABC and became a hit. The networks then all wanted edgier fare, and so *Big City Boys* never went beyond the pilot stage.

Merman's final TV acting appearance was as Gopher's mother in six episodes of *The Love Boat*. Her final episode aired in 1982, two years before her death.

Pat O'Brien

Pat O'Brien, one of the best-known screen actors during the '30s and '40s, often played characters of Irish descent. He is well-remembered for his roles in *Angels with Dirty Faces* (1938), *Knute Rockne, All American* (1940), *Fighting Father Dunne* (1948) and *The People Against O'Hara* (1951), many times appearing as a warm-hearted, sentimental character.

In the early 1950s, there were various reports of O'Brien tackling his own TV series. A great spinner of yarns, O'Brien was to be featured in *The Pat O'Brien Show* (aka *Pat O'Brien's Story Time*), an unrealized 1951 series which was supposed to have been filmed in color by Ade-Reid Productions. The 15-minute show, presumably slated for syndication, starred O'Brien in his role of storyteller. In 1952, *Your Neighborhood*, a series of human interest stories based on the short stories of William Cox, was also mentioned as a possible vehicle for O'Brien, but no series eventuated.

In a pilot the actor did make in 1952, *A Man's World*, he starred as a widower taking care of four sons. O'Brien described the proposed series as a "male *I Remember Mama*," adding: "I've got plenty of material of my own for a series like this because I've got four kids of my own—two boys and two girls—and almost any evening that the whole family is home would make another chapter for the TV show."[1] Broadcast July 25, 1952, as an episode of *Schlitz Playhouse of Stars*, "Dad Matson" had O'Brien in the title role, dealing with his son Buddy, apparently not the handsomest of the boys, overcoming his shyness to ask a girl out on a first date. This forerunner to *My Three Sons* never became a series.

Variety reported on March 23, 1953, that producer Leon Fromkess wanted O'Brien for a series about boxing to be called *Ringside*. O'Brien turned down the offer. Fromkess subsequently asked Barbara Stanwyck to star in the series.

The actor then appeared as Pat Duggan in *Parole Chief*, a 30-minute pilot about a caring parole officer trying to get his parolees on the straight and narrow. The projected series was based on a book by New York State Parole Chief David Dressier concerning case histories in that state. In the pilot, shot in 1954, that eventually aired on *Sneak Preview* as "The Way Back" in 1956, Duggan, head of the Parole Division, helps Roy Bennett (Robert

Arthur), a young man recently released from reform school and still attempting to find work. Duggan learns that Roy lives with his aunt and cousin Gene, who is not the best influence on Roy. Pat invites Roy home to have dinner with him and his wife Martha (Irene Hervey) and finds the boy a job as a mechanic. Roy soon quits his job, saying that the owner's family doted on him too much. Someone breaks into the garage, injures the owner and steals a car. Roy confesses that he quit the job because he knew what his cousin was going to do. Gene is arrested, and Roy goes back to work.

Directed by Erle C. Kenton and written by Richard Saunders and William P. Rosseau, the pilot was produced by Hal Roach, Jr. At the end, O'Brien makes an impassioned speech to potential sponsors about the importance of parole officers in the community and that his character of Pat Duggan will be similar to his iconic movie roles from the 1930s and '40s. He also mentions that the next episode will be about a female released from prison.

Roach had made a deal with Vitapix, a TV show distribution company owned by 42 stations, which would offer *Parole Chief* to national advertisers. Sponsors would pay to advertise on the series at a rate less than what they would pay to sponsor a network show. The idea was to have at least 60 stations involved in the deal. However, no advertisers signed on, and so the pilot never became a series.

In 1958, O'Brien filmed an untitled police anthology pilot (produced by California National Productions for syndication) which he hosted; he would have occasionally acted in the series. The anthology was to be based on real police files. O'Brien indicated that "every police chief in the country wanted to okay it."[2] In the same year, the actor became involved in a more concrete proposal for a series called *Savage Is the Name*. Created by Gwen and Irwin Gielgud, the show was to focus on the exploits of airline detectives with Barry Sullivan as Henry Savage, the lead detective. O'Brien would have played his sidekick. The pilot aired as an episode of the CBS anthology *Pursuit*. Titled "Ticket to Tangiers," the story dealt with Savage, who used to work for the FBI but is now a security officer for an airline, tracking a criminal who once shot him and left him for dead, halfway around the world. William Gargan appeared as Sullivan's partner in the pilot but would have been replaced by O'Brien if the pilot had become a series. Script problems apparently prevented this. If it had been picked up, *Savage Is the Name* would have been produced on videotape and not film—very rare for a dramatic series.

A potential series slated for production in Tokyo, *Assignment Tokyo*, announced in 1959, would have starred O'Brien as a retired detective. The series, to have been produced by Warner Toub, Jr.'s Viking Productions, never saw the light of day.

O'Brien did land his own TV show in 1960, *Harrigan and Son*. The actor, who had attended law school before launching his entertainment career, played Irish criminal attorney James Harrigan, Sr., working with Roger Perry as James Jr., a recent law school graduate who did everything by the book. His father, a practicing lawyer for years, knew how to just skirt the law when trying a case. Their differing approaches to the law resulted in personality clashes between the two. On ABC, Friday nights at 8:00 p.m., sandwiched between two cartoon shows (*Matty's Funday Funnies* and *The Flintstones*), the series lasted for only one season.

O'Brien said that he agreed to do the series on two conditions: one, that he would own a percentage of the production, and two, that there would be no laugh track.[3] About doing the show, he said, "I'd die without acting. I've been at it for 40 years. And what am I going to do now? Sure it's tough to be on every week—but it keeps you active, and it keeps you out of trouble."[4]

Roger Perry was under contract with Desilu Studios in 1960, and Desi Arnaz wanted him for the series. Perry had to turn down the role of Dr. Kildare in that MGM series which then went to Richard Chamberlain. As Perry recollects,

> Pat was a great "partner," and incredible storyteller, a loving family man, a good drinker, and extremely supporting.
>
> I do remember going to New York where we shot many exteriors (in and out of office buildings, on the streets, getting in taxi cabs, etc.). I think Pat seemingly knew everyone in New York. And he loved going to P.J. Clarke's and Moriarty's. In fact, when Georgine Darcy [who played Pat O'Brien's secretary on the series] and I would come home around midnight, hoping to get some sleep before our 7 a.m. call, Pat would still be out with "the boys" until the wee hours. He was 62 at the time but with the energy of a 22-year-old.
>
> The last time I saw Pat and wife Eloise was in Jacksonville, Florida ... doing a show at the local theater. My wife and I were following them

Actor Pat O'Brien in a promotional photograph for his ABC series *Harrigan and Son*. The Harrigans handled some quirky cases like changing the will for an eccentric, wealthy lady so that her cat and not her dog would receive her fortune.

and we were in rehearsal. We saw their show. Pat was terrific, as usual. He said afterward that he stayed on the stage during the act break. The dressing rooms were downstairs and he didn't like the walk because of arthritis. I asked him, "When did you get that?" He said: "When it first came out."[5]

In 1969, O'Brien starred in a potential pilot, *The Over-the-Hill Gang*, written by Jameson Brewer based on a story by Leonard Goldberg and produced by Aaron Spelling and Danny Thomas. O'Brien played Capt. Oren Hayes, a retired Texas Ranger who visits his daughter Hannah (Kris Nelson) and son-in-law Jeff (Rick Nelson) in a town with corrupt officials. Mayor Nard Lundy (Edward Andrews) is running for re-election and Jeff, owner of the local newspaper, is running against him. The mayor, the town's sheriff and the judge are all crooked, so Jeff doesn't stand a chance of winning the election. Hayes calls together his old buddies from the Rangers to clean up the town. Nash Crawford (Walter Brennan), once the quickest draw in the West, is not so fast nowadays; Jason Fitch (Edgar Buchanan) has poor eyesight, and George Agnew (Chill Wills) is a drunkard. Because they are all past their prime, they rely on trickery and deception to outwit Lundy. Although the movie's ratings justified a sequel, *The Over-the-Hill Gang Rides Again*, a series based on the films never materialized.

O'Brien's final appearance was on the television comedy *Happy Days* in the 1982 episode "Grandma Nussbaum," where he played Uncle Joe Cunningham. A year later, he died of a heart attack at age 83.

Maureen O'Hara

Sometimes called "The Queen of Technicolor" and known for playing strong, feisty characters, red-headed beauty Maureen O'Hara was discovered by actor Charles Laughton and first starred with him in Alfred Hitchcock's *Jamaica Inn* (1939) and subsequently as Esmeralda in *The Hunchback of Notre Dame* (1939). She went on to make many memorable movies in the 1940s including *How Green Was My Valley* (1941), the story of a Welsh mining family; the swashbuckling adventure *The Black Swan* (1942); and the Christmas classic *Miracle on 34th Street* (1947). In the '50s, she was paired with John Wayne in such iconic films as *The Quiet Man* (1952) and *The Wings of Eagles* (1957). In the following decade, she starred with Brian Keith and Hayley Mills in Walt Disney's *The Parent Trap* (1961) and with James Stewart in *The Rare Breed* (1966) among other features. She retired from the movie business in 1971. She made a comeback 20 years later as John Candy's possessive mother in *Only the Lonely*.

As long as her movie career was active, O'Hara essentially ignored television. In 1957, she remarked about a potential TV series, "It was very good, but I decided to stick to my guns and not do a series. I prefer doing movies."[1] The series to which she referred was *The Weaker Sex*, produced, directed and co-written by Kurt Neumann. The anthology show would have dealt with famous women of history, with scripts titled "Eve," "Madame Pompadour," "Lucreata Borgia," "Lillian Russell" and "Belle Starr." Twenty-six half-hour episodes were to be made with O'Hara hosting all and acting on some. The series never went into production.

In 1958, O'Hara considered a possible co-production involving CBS with the actress serving as the hostess and occasional star of an anthology series initially called *The Woman in the Case*. Although she would preside over each episode, she would act in only a third of them.

Based on the book by Edgar Lustgarten, *The Woman in the Case* dealt with women involved in some way in criminal cases. William Spier, husband of actress June Havoc, developed the series for his wife. Spier delineated a few storylines.[2] In one, a woman returns a Glendale Public Library book with two pages missing. She denies being the culprit, and complains that because of the missing pages, she was denied the opportunity to read a hot love scene. Librarian Jane Stanton finds strange razor cuts on the pages on each side of the missing ones. She compares the vandalized copy to a complete copy and finds that certain words have been cut out by the razor blade. Jane makes a list of the words and determines that, when placed in the right order, they are part of a ransom note.

Another storyline concerned out-of-work actress Pat Dodger, now a member of the Office of Special Services and Investigation, an undercover unit of the police department. Pat was likely to turn up anywhere there was a murder, missing person or a narcotics ring, and she would play a variety of undercover roles such as a cellist or a cigarette girl.

O'Hara and her brother Charles B. Fitzsimons formed a production company, Tarafilm Productions, to produce *The Woman in the Case* with CBS. William Self was executive producer, David Lewis producer and Fitzsimons associate producer. Reflecting on the proposed series, O'Hara stated that in the past she had refused TV work because she had not wanted to compete with the people financing movies. But, "now that those people have sold their movies to television and are competing with first-run movies, I see no reason why I shouldn't go on. My old movies are being seen on TV twice a week."[3] O'Hara starred with Tony Randall in the pilot for the show called "Open Windows," written by J.P. Miller and directed by Mitchell Leisen.

Based on the initial pilot script, apparently the concept of the proposed O'Hara series differed dramatically from the original book and the storylines conceived by Spier.[4] The script focused on Kate (O'Hara) and Bill Craig (Randall) who were in the process of divorcing. Kate, 32, is packing to leave her apartment in an upper-middle-class section of New York City when she sees her ex-husband Bill, a 35-year-old corporate lawyer, approaching the building. She had hoped to vacate the premises before he arrived. Bill is surprised that Kate is still there and is not taking all of her possessions, in particular the clothes Bill had bought for her which he thought she liked. Kate confesses that she never really liked the items Bill purchased and that she resented Bill for treating her like a possession. Bill divulges that he just quit his job with the family law firm and that he really always wanted to be a horticulturist but deferred that career when he met Kate in order to keep her in the style to which she had become accustomed. Bill then asks Kate to give their marriage a second chance, but Kate leaves. From the open apartment window, Bill yells down to her in the street about meeting some night. Kate relents and says "yes."

Apparently the O'Hara version of *The Woman in the Case* would have been less crime drama and more romantic dramedy which is no doubt why CBS, when trying to find sponsors, changed its title to *Men & Women*.

When the deal with CBS went nowhere, the concept for *The Woman in the Case* was passed around to several producers including Desi Arnaz and Quinn Martin, who was one of Desilu's producers at the time. Their take on *The Woman in the Case* was similar to the original concept of the psychology of the female mind involving criminal acts. The Desilu pilot script, "Ninth Commandment," written by David P. Harmon, focused on twentysomething Mary Smith, who worked in a sewing factory. Mary finds her neighbor Mrs. Rushmore dead.[5] The police and the D.A. manipulate her into identifying a suspect, but she is not certain the man is really the culprit. Her boss promotes her to receptionist just to garner publicity for the firm. When Mary refuses to positively identify the defendant at the trial, her boss sends her back to her previous job. But she is better at her job, and the murder suspect comes to thank her for telling the truth. This version of *The Woman in the Case* was intended for the 1959–60 television season but never became a series. In 1960, Paul Monash at MGM attempted to make a pilot deal with NBC for the show, but the network rejected the project because of excessive costs.

After O'Hara's version of *The Woman in the Case* failed to become a series and with her film career still burgeoning, O'Hara stated publicly that she would only do live TV.[6] She felt that she shouldn't hurt the box office potential of her movies by appearing on a weekly show. O'Hara added that if the time came when she wouldn't be making movies, then she would consider doing a series. That time apparently came in 1965.

Created by Charles Andrews and John Hese, the sitcom *Daphne!* starred O'Hara as Daphne Dunham, an "Auntie Mame–type" widow who leaves the jet set for a life in suburbia living with her brother Ben King, a conservative banker, and his two kids, Emmy, 15, and precocious Little Ben, ten.[7] Selma Diamond co-starred as Olive, the somewhat lazy and spoiled housekeeper, in the pilot produced and directed by Morton DaCosta for Belgrave Enterprises in association with CBS.

The storyline of the pilot "The Skin Game," written in September 1965, had Daphne arriving in Claremont to visit Ben and his children. After having been widowed a year earlier, she spent time traveling the world and arrives with 22 suitcases. Ben picks her up at the airport after meeting a new potential bank customer, Mr. Fellows, a manufacturer of electronic parts who wants to build a factory in Claremont. Ben's boss Milton Dwyer instructs Ben to make sure Fellows becomes a client of the bank.

At the King home, Daphne finds that Little Ben needs $20 to take his friend on a helicopter ride for his birthday, while Emmy, who is suffering from an allergy, is upset at having to have allergy tests on the day of her big dance. Daphne concocts a plan to solve both of the children's problems. She has Little Ben begin selling chances for the allergy patches on Emmy with the person who buys the chance on the patch that is causing the allergy being the winner. At the dance, attended by Daphne, the kids, Ben, Mr. Dwyer and Mr. Fellows, she confesses to her brother what the kids have been doing after Dwyer threatens to fire Ben over the stunt which he considers gambling and having a possible effect on Fellows' decision to be a bank customer. However, Daphne strikes up a conversation with Fellows, who remarks that she makes him feel 30 years younger and that selling chances on the patches was a cute idea. He thinks that Ben showed real style and decides to do his banking with Ben. In the end, Ben discovers that his daughter is allergic to his pipe tobacco.

CBS decided not to pick up the pilot for its 1966–67 season.

In 2014, a year before her death, O'Hara was presented with an honorary Oscar for her lifetime achievements in film.

Anthony Perkins

Anthony Perkins' most notable performance was that of psychotic Norman Bates in Alfred Hitchcock's *Psycho* (1960). The role colored his persona for the remainder of his acting career.

Perkins debuted in the film *The Actress* (1953) as the love interest of a teenage girl wanting to work in the theater. For his performance in *Friendly Persuasion* (1956), about a pacifist Quaker family during the Civil War, he earned an Academy Award nomination. The actor also starred as Boston Red Sox baseball player Jimmy Piersall in *Fear Strikes Out* (1957) and appeared in Eugene O'Neill's *Desire Under the Elms* (1958) with Sophia Loren.

With Broadway composer Stephen Sondheim, the multi-talented Perkins co-wrote the screenplay for the 1973 movie *The Last of Sheila*. In the 1980s, embracing his Norman Bates persona, he began appearing in sequels to *Psycho*: *Psycho II* (1983), *Psycho III* (1986) and *Psycho IV: The Beginning* (1990).

Also in 1990, Perkins made a sitcom pilot which started out as an ABC project titled *Haunted House* and then was shopped to Fox under the title *The Ghost Writer*. Hoping to capitalize on his *Psycho* fame, Perkins starred as Anthony Strack, a best-selling horror novelist who remarries (his first wife Judith died ten years earlier, breaking her neck in a fall down the stairs). Anthony brings his new wife Elizabeth (Leigh Taylor-Young) and her young daughter Cindy (Juliet Sorci) to live with him and his creepy son Edgar (Joshua John Miller) in an Addams Family-style house maintained by his Elvira-like housekeeper Miss Blasko (Pam Matheson).

Cindy is afraid of her stepfather and doesn't like her stepbrother who loves to be disciplined (spanked) by his father and who is infatuated with Miss Blasko. Elizabeth doesn't like living in the shadow of Anthony's first wife. When Elizabeth takes Judith's portrait down from the wall, the painting changes to show only an empty chair and no Judith. Elizabeth then thinks she hears the voice of Judith and falls down the stairs but recovers.

Edgar runs away to his mother's grave. After Anthony finds him, he explains to his son that he loved his mother but now loves Elizabeth. Returning home, Edgar apologizes for his behavior to Cindy and his new stepmother. Everyone goes to bed but Anthony. Ascending the stairs, he sees the skeletal ghost of Judith. He explains that he is now married to Elizabeth but dances with Judith's ghost one last time. He uses the experience for his latest book.

Perkins gave a restrained, expressionless performance as Anthony Strack, hoping viewers could see the dry humor in the story. The pilot, filmed before a live audience, was scripted by Alan Spencer and directed by Alan Rafkin. According to Spencer, "Anthony Perkins was a friend of mine and he asked if I'd create a sitcom for him. He was actually a light comedian in the theater long before Alfred Hitchcock ever turned him into a horror icon and mother's boy. Perkins' sole prerequisite was that it would be a live audience show, a multi-camera half-hour, but I wanted to keep it innovative so I made it more theatrical with live special effects and expansive Gothic sets."[1]

ABC thought *The Ghost Writer* was too dark. Fox passed on making it into a series because Spencer was working on a comedy for NBC called *The Nutt House* and couldn't devote himself full time to the Perkins project.

Perkins' final film appearance was in 1992's *In the Deep Woods* with Rosanna Arquette in which he played a private investigator who may be a serial killer. He passed away that same year.

Walter Pidgeon

Distinguished-looking, charming Walter Pidgeon began his film career in the silent movie *Mannequin* (1926) as the "other man." In the 1930s, he played second lead roles in movies like *Saratoga* (1937) with Jean Harlow and Clark Gable and was private detective Nick Carter in three crime thrillers. Pidgeon had a central role in the classic *How Green Was My Valley* (1941), and is well-remembered for his films as Greer Garson's husband including *Blossoms in the Dust* (1941), *Mrs. Miniver* (1942), *Madame Curie* (1943), and *That Forsyte Woman* (1949). The actor continued his movie career into the '50s with roles in *The Miniver Story* (1950), a sequel to *Mrs. Miniver,* and the science fiction classic *Forbidden Planet* (1956). In the '60s, he appeared in *Voyage to the Bottom of the Sea* (1961), *Advise and Consent* (1962) and *Funny Girl* (1968).

In the mid–50s, Pidgeon was one of two actors being considered to host and narrate NBC's anthology series *Lux Video Theatre* for the 1955–56 season (the other was Tyrone Power). Lux ended up settling for Otto Kruger. Because Pidgeon was under contract to MGM, he did become the host of *MGM Parade* on ABC beginning in March 1956, taking over for George Murphy for the series' final three months. Originally designed to be the MGM counterpart to the *Disneyland* series, *MGM Parade*, consisting mainly of promotional clips for the studio's new films as well as edited versions of existing MGM movies, lasted for only one season.

In 1959, Pidgeon was sought for a lead role in the syndicated British-made drama *Four Just Men*. It focused on the adventures of four men who had met in Italy while fighting in World War II. The men seek justice for individuals using money set aside by their late commanding officer. Vittorio De Sica, Dan Dailey and Jack Hawkins played three of the leads. Instead of Pidgeon, actor Richard Conte appeared as the fourth man. The show lasted 39 episodes.

Pidgeon's first attempt at a TV comedy, *Grandparents*, was produced in 1959 and '60 by Hal Roach Productions. It concerned two teens, recently orphaned, who go to live with their grandparents. Fittingly, because of his many father-figure roles in features, Pidgeon played the grandfather in the unsold pilot.

In 1962, Pidgeon made a pilot *Mr. Kingston*, written, directed and produced by Leslie Stevens. He appeared as Capt. Towers, in charge of the cruise ship S.S. *Atlantis*. His first officer was Mr. Kingston (Peter Graves). In the pilot, titled "Trouble in Paradise," Princess Alexandra (Ina Balin) is on a cruise to New York City. The opposition in her country wants to steal her royal jewels to finance their revolution against the current monarchy.

The leader of the group seeking the jewels, Stefan (Steven Hill), informs his henchman that the princess' cousin, Duchess Sophia, is allied with them. When Sophia and the princess see Stefan, the princess says he is a distant cousin who at one time was engaged to her and she still has feelings for him. While the princess watches a movie on the ship with other members of the royal family, Sophia tells her that a mysterious gentleman has slid a note under her door. The princess leaves for her room where Stefan says that he desires her. When Stefan locks the doors, she suspects that he is going to try to hurt her, but she doesn't do anything in protest. Meanwhile, Sophia and the henchman start multiple fires across the ship. Kingston and the captain figure out that the fires were set on purpose. Sophia tries to steal the princess' diamonds; when a guard refuses to turn them over, Stefan's henchman shoots him. The guard is able to pull an alarm and a different guard subsequently kills the henchman. In the princess' room, Stefan kisses her and then attempts to strangle her. At that moment, Kingston bursts in. Stefan is chased to a high point on the ship, while he shoots at different guards. Finally he is blinded by a light and falls off the vessel to his death.

As the *Atlantis* arrives in New York, a royal family member informs Sophia that the wounded guard on the ship has identified her. The princess thanks Kingston for saving her life and claims that she has started a new life.

Initially titled *Cruise Ship*, the pilot was produced by Daystar-United Artists for ABC. The potential series was conceived as "a *Wagon Train* at sea" with episodes to focus on the stories of the passengers, not on the crew. The show was shot in Seattle and earmarked for the 1963–64 TV season. ABC thought of turning the pilot into a series and considered scheduling it at 10:00 p.m. on Tuesdays. However, *The Fugitive* ended up being scheduled at that time.

Pidgeon was next considered for a starring role in another comedy pilot, *Conway and Company*. He would have again played a gregarious grandfather who lives with his daughter and her seven-year-old son. The pilot was developed by Joe Connelly and Bob Mosher, famous for creating *Leave It to Beaver* and other TV comedies. Pidgeon initially agreed to star in the pilot but then changed his mind. His role was taken over by Charlie Ruggles, who starred along with Joanna Moore as his daughter and Jimmy Mathers, brother of "the

Beaver," Jerry Mathers, as the grandson. At one time, *Conway and Company* was considered for inclusion in NBC's *90 Bristol Court*, a 90-minute comedy show consisting of three 30-minute sitcoms with the characters all living in the same apartment complex. *90 Bristol Court* premiered in fall 1964 with three segments, *Karen, Harris Against the World* and *Tom, Dick, and Mary*; the latter two were canceled in early 1965 and only the *Karen* segment continued to the end of the season.

In Mae West's last feature *Sextette* (1978), Pidgeon played *his* final movie role as the chairman of an international conference held in the same hotel where West's character was honeymooning with her newest husband. Pidgeon died in 1984 at age 87.

Jane Powell

Known as "the girl next door" because of her sweet, innocent movie roles, singer-actress Jane Powell was signed by MGM while still a teenager. The studio thought she would be the next Deanna Durbin, the popular young star of several movies who had retired from pictures when she was still young. For Powell's first film, MGM loaned her to United Artists for the musical *Song of the Open Road* (1944). The actress' real name was Suzanne Bruce; in the feature, she played a character named Jane Powell and adopted that name for her career. Powell subsequently starred in several classic MGM musicals: *Holiday in Mexico* (1946), *Royal Wedding* (1951) with Fred Astaire, and *Seven Brides for Seven Brothers* (1954). In November 1955, Powell left MGM. While she made a few movies after that, she mainly appeared on stage and on TV beginning in the late '50s.

In early 1957, Dick Powell (no relation to Jane), actor-producer and owner of Four Star Productions, was thinking of reviving the anthology series *Four Star Playhouse* which had run on CBS from 1952 to 1956. He, Charles Boyer, David Niven and Ida Lupino had hosted the original series. For the revival, he thought of having Jane Powell and Ginger Rogers host with Boyer and Niven. While the *Four Star Playhouse* reboot didn't happen, *Variety* reported on May 24, 1957, that Ms. Powell was one of five rotating hosts for a proposed Four Star Television series to be called *Gulliver's Travellers* (aka *Travel Agency*). The other hosts for this adventure-anthology were to be Niven, Boyer, Robert Ryan and Jack Lemmon. Originally *Gulliver's Travellers* was to be filmed in various locales around the world but that idea was abandoned because of the costs involved.

Gulliver's Travellers morphed into an anthology show called *Alcoa-Goodyear Theatre* produced by Four Star, who had been in competition with Screen Gems to make an anthology to be sponsored on alternating weeks by Alcoa Aluminum and by Goodyear Rubber and Tires. The series was scheduled at 9:30 p.m. Mondays on NBC with Jane Powell among the five rotating hosts who starred in the episode they hosted. Each host would also have an ownership interest in the series. Jane Powell said of this project,

> Every time I asked Metro ... for a straight dramatic part, they would turn me down. I was typed as a singer. And I still couldn't get a non-singing role after leaving Metro

two and a half years ago. Certain TV series were offered me, but I didn't want a weekly show; I didn't want to be identified with a character such as "My Little Margie." Then this series which gives me story and director approval came along, and it is the right thing, we hope.

I also didn't want a weekly series because I felt it would hurt my movies, and I don't feel movies are completely extinct. I'll only do five or six shows in this series, that's enough. Originally I was to have done 12, then they got Bob Ryan, and mine were cut. First I was hurt about it, but when I thought about it I was jumping for joy. People don't want to see you that much.

Sticking to the subject of over-exposure on TV, she added, "You have to fight to protect yourself against that. In our TV series, we will stress adventure and suspense, and I'm looking for such material, but I don't want it to get silly like a *Mr. and Mrs. North*."[1]

Powell starred in seven episodes of the *Alcoa-Goodyear Theatre* playing everything from a double role as a tourist who befriends a German girl who looks just like her (and wants to switch identities) to a policewoman who is not afraid of taking risks.

After a single season, Four Star stopped producing the series because the sponsors wanted to reduce the amount of money they were paying the production company for each episode. The sponsors also wanted to have Four Star make only half of the number of installments they did during the 1957–58 season with Screen Gems producing the other half. *Alcoa-Goodyear Theatre* continued for another two seasons but without Four Star making any of the episodes.

Dick Powell tried to sell the series to CBS under the title *Six Star Playhouse* by considering Joan Crawford and then Barbara Stanwyck as part of the roster of hosts, but CBS rejected the idea.

In 1961, Jane Powell changed her mind about appearing on a weekly series and made a pilot for her own sitcom, written by Michael Morris and Max Wilk from a story by Tom and Frank Waldman and directed by Rod Amateau. Powell played a singer-actress somewhat like her movie star image in the pilot "Short Course in Marriage." The actress appeared as K.C. McKay, who fell in love with a math professor named Jeffrey Edwards (Russell Johnson, later the Professor on *Gilligan's Island*). Jeffrey, who drove a Duesenberg, had met K.C. at a TV studio while she was rehearsing for a show and he was appearing on an educational program. They knew each other only for one weekend before deciding to marry. After the ceremony, the happy couple moved to a remodeled carriage house near Redwood College in California where K.C. became acquainted with Jeffrey's colleague and former housemate, Prof. Holly Harrigan (Al Checco).

In "Short Course in Marriage," K.C. meets the faculty of her new husband's college at a reception given by Dean Grover and his wife (Harriett

MacGibbon). After she sings "My Beloved" for the crowd, some of the faculty members engage in a discussion about what motivates entertainers, saying that performers are all exhibitionists. When Jeffrey agrees with them, K.C. becomes upset and makes him sleep on the couch. Compounding the marital difficulties, K.C. kills Jeffrey's queen bee Agnes when it tries to sting her.

K.C.'s agent Leslie (Elliott Reid) phones about resuming her show business career, but she reluctantly declines. Mrs. Grover stops by and says that K.C. should have spoken up during the faculty discussion about entertainers. Jeffrey realizes he should have supported his wife at the get-together. He brings her flowers, and she buys a new queen bee for him.

Four Star Television produced the pilot in association with Powell's company, Etoile Productions. Pepsi planned to sponsor *The Jane Powell Show*, which was initially shopped to NBC and then to CBS. Both networks passed on the series apparently thinking it was too sophisticated for an early time slot, and no later time period could be found.

Powell made two other attempts in the mid–60s for a sitcom of her own. In 1963, she was working with writer Robert Blees on a pilot variously titled *Cyn's for Me* or *Exclusively Connie*, to be produced by Desilu. Apparently nothing became of this endeavor. In 1968, writer Charles Isaacs was preparing a pilot called *Smile, Tiger* in which the actress would sing and act. Powell was to have portrayed a photographer on the series to be produced by Seymour Berns for the 1970–71 season.

Also in the early '60s, a treatment for another Jane Powell vehicle called *Calamity*, created by Jack Tellander, was considered by the actress. Set in the mid–1870s in a town in the West called Calamity, this proposal for a weekly musical comedy centered on a character named Jane who could do everything a man could.[2] Since everyone in the town could sing, each episode would have been a mini-musical mostly using popular songs with some original compositions in the mix. Also, each installment would have featured a special guest star in an unusual role such as singer Dean Martin as a preacher sermonizing on the evils of alcohol, Milton Berle as a Mississippi gambler or Bob Hope as a notorious gunslinger. No pilot resulted from this treatment.

Powell became a regular on the ABC daytime drama *Loving* from 1985 to 1986. She played troublemaking Rebeka Beecham, a member of a rich and powerful cattle-raising family. "I was tired of playing goody-two-shoes. This gives me a chance to do something which I seldom got to do in Hollywood— play a woman who goes after what she wants."[3] After *Loving*, Powell played the grandmother, Irma Seaver Overmier on several episodes of the comedy *Growing Pains* from 1988 to 1990.

Basil Rathbone

Before Benedict Cumberbatch, before Jonny Lee Miller, before Robert Downey, Jr., Basil Rathbone played Sherlock Holmes in a popular series of movies from 1939 to 1946 as well as on the radio. Rathbone was known for his portrayals of suave villains and swashbucklers in motion pictures like *David Copperfield* (1935) and *The Adventures of Robin Hood* (1938) before he portrayed the famous British detective which influenced his career from then on.

Rathbone's earliest TV appearances were on anthology series sponsored by automobile companies: *The Ford Theatre Hour, The Chevrolet Tele-Theatre* and the *Nash Airflyte Theatre*. Reportedly, before his first performance on TV, he called the medium "that bastard child of the dramatic arts, which borrows something from everything and contributes nothing to anything."[1] Despite that remark, in 1951 an announcement was made that Rathbone would recreate his iconic Sherlock Holmes role in a series of 26 half-hour episodes to be produced by Irving Allen, later to become famous for producing the *Matt Helm* films with Dean Martin, and by Albert "Cubby" Broccoli, who went on to make the James Bond movies.[2] However, no Holmes television series with Rathbone ever appeared. Ronald Howard, son of actor Leslie Howard, did play the famous detective in a mid–50s TV series, but it was not produced by Allen and Broccoli.

Being typecast as an "authority" figure based on his Holmes portrayal, Rathbone's attempts at TV series focused on this image. He became a game show host during the summer of 1952 on a CBS series called *Your Lucky Clue* on which real police detectives competed against amateur sleuths in solving fictional crimes. Rathbone gave the contestants clues and answered their questions. The actor was not entirely comfortable in his role as a TV personality. Commenting on the show, columnist Walter Winchell remarked that Rathbone "was as jittery as a bridegroom while presiding over the panel at *Your Lucky Clue*. Heranhiswordstogetherlike this. Oh, come now, Bahzil. Tizzent attawl like you, attawl. Rilly...."[3] The series lasted for eight episodes on Sunday evenings at 7:30 p.m.

One of Rathbone's first attempts at a drama series was in *War Birds*, a

1961 pilot produced by Filmways which centered on a World War I squadron commander and his unit of flyers in 1917 France. The script was written by Elliot Asinof and Sam Neuman. Actor Wayde Preston (*Colt .45*) played the squadron commander with William Wellman, Jr., son of movie director William Wellman, and Don Francks part of his unit. Rathbone had the role of the commandant and songwriter Hoagy Carmichael appeared as the owner of a Paris nightclub where the pilots often hung out. Tay Garnett directed the effort with famed stunt pilot Frank Tallman assisting with the aerial scenes. Wellman, Jr., remarked that he was so impressed to be working with Rathbone and found him "very professional, even personable."[4]

Describing the potential series, Rathbone said, "It will be a semi-documentary in nature. I will play an officer in charge of sending young pilots off to almost certain death. They took their lives in their hands just by climbing into those rickety old airplanes."[5]

After *War Birds* failed to become a series, Rathbone played the governor in a 1966 comedy pilot called *The Pirates of Flounder Bay,* set in the 1880s.[6] The project starred William Cort as Barnaby Kidd, the grandson of the infamous Captain Kidd. Whereas his grandfather was evil and nasty, Barnaby was kind and bumbling. However, he wanted to become as famous as his grandfather.

The governor, a tall, crafty-looking gentleman, visits Flounder Bay to announce that pirate Jack Slash (Keenan Wynn) has escaped from prison. He tells Mayor Abner Bunker (Hal Peary) that he thinks Slash is headed to his town. What the governor doesn't know is that the mayor and Barnaby Kidd are in cahoots involving Kidd stealing booty for the town's mayor so the mayor can sell it.

The governor decides to stay in Flounder Bay for a while because he thinks pirates are near. When Slash comes to town, unbeknownst to the governor, Mayor Bunker wants Slash to work for him instead of Kidd, thinking Slash will be more effective in finding loot. Slash asks the mayor to turn Kidd over to the governor so that the governor will be satisfied that he captured a pirate. However, the mayor's daughter Molly (Brigette Hanley), who likes Kidd, suggests to Barnaby that he turn the tables and hand Slash over to the governor. Kidd convinces Slash to rob the guests at the dinner the mayor is having for the governor that evening. When Slash and his gang attempt to steal the dinner guests' valuables, Kidd and his crew capture them.

The pilot, written by Maurice Richlin, was produced for ABC by Selmar Productions. The network broadcast it on August 2, 1966. In July 1967, less than a year after *The Pirates of Flounder Bay* aired, Rathbone died of a heart attack in New York City at the age of 75.

Edward G. Robinson

Edward G. Robinson made his movie debut in a 1923 silent film, *The Bright Shawl*. Best known for his bad-guy roles in movies like *Little Caesar* (1930), Robinson also played good guys such as in *Double Indemnity* (1944) where he had the role of an insurance claims manager pursuing Fred MacMurray, an insurance agent who kills Barbara Stanwyck's husband because he is in love with Stanwyck. During the late 1940s and early '50s, because of his support of liberal causes, Robinson became caught up in the political witch-hunting to ferret out Communists in the entertainment business. Although he was never blacklisted, controversies surrounding his membership in certain groups led to fewer offers to star in pictures. He became a character actor, generally still playing tough guys, and attempted his own TV series.

Robinson was proposed as the lead in a 1952 project called *Secrets of the French Police* which would be filmed in Paris. He turned it down, and it went to Akim Tamiroff. Robinson was then offered the chance to recreate his role as Captain Barnaby of the Los Angeles Police Department that he had originally played in a 1953 movie called *Vice Squad*. This film was one of the first B pictures Robinson starred in after his career was sidetracked because of the Communist association controversies. To be produced by Sol Lesser, Arthur Gardner and Jules Levy, the same team that had produced the movie, the TV series was never made.

Robinson starred as Matthew Considine, a former police captain, now a defense attorney, in a pilot titled *For the Defense,* written by Donn Mullally and directed by James Neilson. Robinson and Sam Bischoff produced the pilot. Bischoff, a long-time movie producer, had helped make movies like *Kid Galahad* (1937) with Robinson, Bette Davis and Humphrey Bogart.

The actor attempted this TV project not only because of lack of work in movies for a star of his age and the blowback from his liberal political associations but also because he simply needed the money with his wife and him continually spending more than he was earning.

The 1955 pilot began with the tough-talking Robinson character taking the case of Kenny Jason, who has been arrested for murdering Al Russell in his hotel room. Russell's room was subsequently set on fire in an effort to cover up the killing. During the trial, the hotel desk clerk testifies that he saw Jason accompany Russell to his room but that he never saw him leave. Considine reveals that the clerk is also a bookmaker. In his defense, Jason says that Russell gave him money to purchase liquor and that another man, named Skipper, took the money and slugged him while he was out of the hotel when the murder occurred. The police have been unable to locate Skipper. In his summation to the jury, Considine pretends to point out the real murderer in the courtroom with everyone watching in order to show that there is reasonable doubt that Jason committed the crime. The jury finds Jason not guilty, but Considine receives some bad press for his courtroom antics. When the man called Skipper is discovered dead, the police arrest Jason. Jason tells Considine that a man named Duke told him where Skipper was, and that Skipper was dead when he found him. Duke, the man behind the hotel clerk's bookmaking, had murdered both Russell and Skipper.

At the end of the pilot, Robinson addresses the camera directly, saying that each week a new episode will be presented featuring a different criminal case. Had the pilot gone to series, other scripts had been prepared by David Dortort, who later created the hit Western *Bonanza*, and by George Bricker, who had written screenplays for films like *She-Wolf of London* (1946) and *The Corpse Came C.O.D.* (1947).

Late in his career, Robinson was offered roles on two different CBS series. He starred as Dr. Lee Forestman, a physician needing a heart transplant, in *U.M.C.*, the 1969 pilot for the drama *Medical Center*. The actor was to make occasional appearances on the series but never did. CBS also wanted Robinson for the role of senior partner on the 1970–71 drama *Storefront Lawyers* but he declined the role.

Robinson always preferred to act in films instead of on television. His final TV acting appearance was in a segment of Rod Serling's *Night Gallery* titled "Messiah on Mott Street" in 1971, two years before his death.

Jane Russell

Singer-actress Jane Russell's first starring role was in a 1943 Western produced and directed by Howard Hughes, *The Outlaw*. It's perhaps most famous for showing Russell's ample bosom using a special underwire bra designed by Hughes. The actress later starred in many other features, most notably as Calamity Jane with Bob Hope as dentist Painless Potter in *The Paleface* (1948) and with Marilyn Monroe in *Gentlemen Prefer Blondes* (1953). Russell made several crime dramas with Robert Mitchum such as *His Kind of Woman* (1951) and *Macao* (1952). The actress' highly sexualized screen image, however, always seemed to overshadow her singing and acting talents.

CBS was dickering with Russell to appear in a 30-minute comedy, *Guestward Ho,* in 1957. The network had earlier sought Nanette Fabray for the sitcom based on the book by Dennis Patrick, who wrote *Auntie Mame*, but could not reach an agreement with her. CBS was unsuccessful in signing Russell for the pilot; Vivian Vance from *I Love Lucy* eventually got the role of Babs Hooten who, with her husband and son, buys a New Mexico dude ranch sight unseen. Vance did not feel comfortable as the lead on her own series, and so the role ultimately went to Joanne Dru. *Guestward Ho* premiered on ABC in 1960 and lasted one season.

The following year, Dick Powell's Four Star Productions produced a pilot for Russell called *MacCreedy's Woman*. Directed by Allen H. Miner, it was written by Gloria Saunders and Dick Carr. Russell had a participation interest in this effort if it had become a series. In the pilot, the actress appeared as Brandy MacCreedy, the singing hostess-owner of a nightclub her late husband had left her. Helping her run the establishment were Aristotle (Sean McClory) the bartender and Felix (Jonathan Harris) the maitre d.'

Nicky Weston (Don Durant) comes to MacCreedy's establishment to claim that the late Mr. MacCreedy owed him $500 (a gambling debt) and produces an IOU to that effect. Mrs. MacCreedy refuses to pay but offers the man a job in the club playing piano. Nicky, wanting the money to continue his gambling habit, asks a friend to rob MacCreedy's to get the $500, but the friend refuses and informs Brandy. Eventually, she does pay Weston. Brandy explains that she had kept the $500 originally because she knew he needed a job more than the money and that her late husband always would have given a person another chance.

Discussing *MacCreedy's Woman*, Russell said, "A lot of people liked it, but none of them would buy it. They were just looking for westerns last fall and weren't in the mood for anything else."[1]

In late 1958, newspapers reported that the actress was interested in another TV project, *Don't Blame Jane*. The series would have focused on a former showgirl (Russell) who marries a college professor and has to adjust to small town life. No pilot appears to have resulted from this proposal which sounds very close to the central theme of *The Jane Powell Show* profiled above.

In 1959, Russell starred in "Ballad for a Bad Man" (originally titled "Guns and Guitar") that aired as an episode of the *Westinghouse Desilu Playhouse*.[2] Written by Bob Barbash from a story suggested by Desi Arnaz and directed by Jerry Hopper, the show also featured Steve Forrest as bounty hunter Chris Hody. Russell played Lilli Travers, a singer with the traveling entertainment troupe known as the Barnaby Tibbs Bandwagon.

Lilli was described as an attractive woman of about 30 who has a tough exterior but a sincere desire to help others. Lilli knows men but blames herself for the kind of life she led before becoming a Bandwagon singer. Her sister Amy (Karen Sharpe), also a member of the troupe, is in love with Danny Cash (Roger Perry), who is wanted for bank robbery and the murder of a bank teller. Chris Hody (Forrest) has been shadowing the troupe hoping to capture Cash.

One night Danny comes to the troupe's wagons to see Amy. He tells Lilli he's not guilty of the crimes for which he is wanted. Members of the troupe create a diversion so Cash can escape capture by Hody and the town's sheriff. Hody then volunteers to guide the troupe as they travel through Indian Territory to their next town. Chris becomes infatuated with Lilli, who discovers a wanted poster for Cash in his shirt and realizes why he wants to be with the troupe. Lilli and Barnaby Tibbs (Jack Haley) confront Hody about his plans to capture Danny Cash. Although they say that Danny never robbed the bank, Hody is not convinced. One night, when Hody sees Danny come to the wagons to meet Amy, he realizes that he no longer has the heart to capture him. After Amy and Danny go off together, Lilli thanks Hody for letting them go.

Danny returns to the troupe late at night to remove sideboards from a wagon to retrieve a canvas money bag. When he is discovered by a troupe member, Danny shoots him and flees with the bag. Chris tracks him down. Danny admits to the robbery and the murder as well as the shooting of a member of the Bandwagon. Chris and Danny have a shootout and Danny dies. Chris decides to join the Bandwagon as its permanent guide.

After "Ballad for a Bad Man" was filmed, Desi Arnaz asked Russell to make another pilot playing the same character. Russell wasn't thrilled with the idea: "I don't know if I want to or not. It's another western."[3] At the time, Russell didn't really care if she had her own series. She was still under contract to Howard Hughes, who was paying her $1000 a week for the next 20 years. So a Western series starring Jane Russell as a voluptuous singer never became a reality.

However, one of Russell's final TV appearances was on the 1983–84 prime time, modern-day Western soap opera *The Yellow Rose* starring Cybil Shepherd, David Soul, Sam Elliott and Edward Albert running a 200,000-acre cattle and oil ranch in Texas. Russell played Rose Hollister in three episodes. The actress liked the fact that her character appeared infrequently on the show: "I've always been lazy. I never had any ambition to do a television series, not with the hours they work. You've got to be on the set at 7:45 in the morning and you don't quit until 8:30 in the evening. Too much."[4]

Jane Russell starring as Rose Hollister in the NBC series *The Yellow Rose*. Her first appearance was in the episode "Divide and Conquer," broadcast on January 7, 1984, in which the Sam Elliott character meets his long-lost mother (Russell).

Her final TV appearance was in a 1986 episode of the Fred Dryer crime drama *Hunter*. Russell passed away at age 89 in 2011.

George Sanders

Sometimes playing a hero and sometimes a scoundrel but always a sophisticate, actor George Sanders was also a composer, singer and author in a career that lasted more than 40 years. He appeared in such classic features as *Rebecca* (1940) with Joan Fontaine and Laurence Olivier and *Foreign Correspondent* (1940) with Joel McCrea, both directed by Alfred Hitchcock, and as Simon Templar in the *Saint* movie series from 1939 to 1941. Sanders won an Oscar for Best Supporting Actor for his performance as theater critic Addison DeWitt in *All about Eve* (1950). He married two of the Gabor sisters, Zsa Zsa (1949 to 1954) and Magda in 1970. The latter marriage lasted a little over a month.

In October 1955, Sanders considered a TV pilot, *The Ringmaster*, which he would host and narrate. The series was to be about circus life; it never saw the light of day.

In the summer of 1957, Sanders hosted of a short-lived anthology series originally titled *Mystery Writer's Theatre* and then called *George Sanders Mystery Theater*. Based on properties of the Mystery Writers of America, the 13-episode series was produced for Screen Gems by David Diamond and Sam Bischoff. Sanders acted in two episodes. In "Broker's Special," he played a man who is cleared of charges in the motor vehicle death of a child, but later, suspecting his wife of cheating on him, he decides to duplicate the accident. In another installment, "Morning Boat to Africa," he appeared as a businessman who double-crosses his partner and plans to leave on a trip to Africa with his wife, unaware that she is trying to poison him.

When the series was not renewed, Sanders appeared in a 1958 pilot called *The Fabulous Oliver Chantry* playing a character almost identical to the critic he portrayed in *All About Eve*. Doris Singleton played Chantry's secretary, Steven Geray his butler. The unsold pilot, directed by Roy Del Ruth, was produced by Hal Roach Studios. In the story, Rachel (Ellen Corby), a wardrobe mistress, is upset that her niece Lois (Ann Baker from the *Meet Corliss Archer* TV show) wants to give up acting and marry Bob (Doug McClure, who went on to star in TV's *Checkmate* and *The Virginian*), a farmer from upstate New York. Oliver thinks he has a part lined up for Lois in a play being directed by George Richmond. But Richmond wants the play to star an acting couple, Alfred (Ian Keith) and Lynn Barry (Cicely Browne), who had previously appeared in the work. Chantry convinces Lois to not give up the stage and throws a party for the Barrys in order to pit the couple against each other. He spreads the rumor that Alfred and Lynn don't intend to act together any more. At the party, Alfred talks with Lois about her playing opposite him. Lynn and Alfred argue. She says that she will not be in the play and accuses Alfred of starting the rumors. After Lois gets the female lead in the revival, Chantry learns that she is doing a terrible acting job. He thinks this is because she is still in love with Bob. Later, Lois admits to loving Bob and being distraught over his return home. Bob and Lois reunite, and Chantry goes to see Lynn to convince her to work with Alfred. Lynn reconciles with her husband, and they both star in the revival.

The pilot was promoted this way: "The fabulous Oliver Chantry muddles his way into the affairs of the heart and marital bliss; breaking people up and putting them back together, all while maintaining his absolute fabulousness."

After *Chantry* failed to become a series, Sanders appeared in several movies and TV shows until his suicide in 1972. In 1966, he appeared as Mr. Freeze on the *Batman* TV show. His final television role was as an arms dealer on *Mission: Impossible* (the 1971 episode "The Merchant").

Randolph Scott

Randolph Scott began acting in the late 1920s. At the start of his career, his physical features—tall and handsome—out-shined his acting talents. He became well-known for his Westerns. Some of his notable non–Western films were *Go West Young Man* (1936) with Mae West in which Scott played a mechanic whom West wants to seduce, *My Favorite Wife* (1940) with Cary Grant and Irene Dunne, and *Home Sweet Homicide* (1946) where Scott appeared as a police detective trying to solve a murder. Of his 100-plus movie appearances, 60 were Westerns including his final film *Ride the High Country* (1962) where he and Joel McCrea guarded a gold shipment.

Billboard reported in February 1957 that Scott would play a U.S. marshal in an ABC series for fall 1957. That never happened, but Scott did make one TV pilot in the late '50s. Like other movie stars of the '50s, Scott invested in a production company, Federal Telefilms; his partners were producers Harry Joe Brown, who had helped make several of Scott's Western films, Buster Collier and Bernard Schubert. However, unlike some other actors such as Dick Powell, Scott appears not to have been that involved in the operation of the company, particularly in developing possible TV pilots. Federal Telefilms was responsible for at least three shows that made it to the air: *Crossroads*, an anthology series which dramatized the experiences of clergymen, *The Adventures of the Falcon* with Charles McGraw, based on the movie series of the same name, and *Mr. and Mrs. North*, about a husband-and-wife team of amateur detectives.

Scott's company made one anthology pilot hosted by the actor that was similar in concept to *Dick Powell's Zane Grey Theater*. Ralph Murphy directed, and Murphy and V.D. Portianko wrote the pilot from a story by Ernest Haycox. It was titled *Randolph Scott's Theater of the West*.

The actor, dressed in Western garb, introduced the episode about a small town (Lost Eagle, population 462) in 1890 whose sheriff, Cliff McClain (Scott Brady), dressed all in black. The episode was called "Officer's Choice." U.S. Ranger William Young (Paul Kelly) arrives in town looking for a man who helped hold up a train five years earlier. Young's description of the suspect matches Sheriff McClain. McClain, now married with a young daughter, arrived in town about five years ago. At his home, Cliff tells his wife that he does not want to run away again, making it obvious that he is the robbery suspect. Young observes how McClain performs his duties and admires him for standing up against the leader of a gang terrorizing a Lost Eagle citizen (a former gang member who now wants to go straight). McClain kills the gang leader in a gunfight, and Young, who knows that McClain is really the person he has been seeking, decides to file a report stating that the gang leader was the train robbery suspect.

Bernard Schubert tried to get General Foods to sponsor the series, apparently with no luck. Scott commented, "If General Foods doesn't buy it, then scrap it. I don't like the idea of being offered around."[1]

Scott retired from films in 1964, very wealthy from wise investments. He passed away in 1987 at the age of 89.

Zachary Scott

"Suave," "sophisticated" and "sinister" were some of the adjectives used to describe the screen characters portrayed by Zachary Scott. He appeared first in 1944's *The Mask of Dimitrios* as the title character Dimitrios Makropoulos. His most memorable screen roles were in Joan Crawford films: In *Mildred Pierce* (1945) he played Crawford's cheating husband and in *Flamingo Road* (1949) he was Crawford's suicidal lover. The actor made several film noirs with titles such as *Danger Signal* (1945), *Ruthless* (1948), *Guilty Bystander* (1950), *Shadow on the Wall* (1950) and *Born to be Bad* (1950). In each, his character was either victimizing others or the victim of others' cruel intentions.

In a 1954 pilot produced by Lee Blevins for Kling Studios, Scott played Reno English, a lawyer with a reputation for always being successful in defending his clients. Fast-talking Reno was suave and sophisticated, but not sinister. Penned by Geoffrey Homes (aka Daniel Mainwaring) and directed by Jus Addiss, the pilot was titled "The Lady with the Scales."[1]

Reno has just won a case for Mary West, who was found to have shot her husband in self-defense. Meanwhile, in his house, Paul Payne (Charles Chaplin, Jr., son of the famous comic actor) tells his sister Deborah (Frances Rafferty) that he is going gambling, and that he has trick dice from Red Bailey's that have led to him losing money at that gambling establishment. Paul walks with a severe limp. Early that morning, Deborah is staring out her office window at Reno Highland Estates and hears two gunshots. She sees a limping man roar out of the parking lot in his car only to get into a fender bender with another car. The car hits Mr. and Mrs. Ferguson's vehicle, leading to fender damage for both. The car then takes off. When police arrive, they are notified of a murder at Red Bailey's. Deborah finds that Bailey has been killed and his safe has been looted. Her boss J. Harold Burns claims that the world is a better place without Red.

That day on the news she hears that a paroled ex-convict named Marty Ryan has been identified by the Fergusons and charged with the murder. Meanwhile, Deborah encounters her brother fixing the fender of his car. Paul claims that he drank too much after winning $300 at Bailey's. While the D.A. questions Marty Ryan, Reno arrives and decides to represent him. News reports claim that the police are looking for a gun and the stolen money along the highway. Deborah watches Paul wipe his gun down as she hears this report. A scene reveals a bag from Paul's bed and a gun being tossed along the side of the highway. Deborah soon finds that she has been picked for jury duty, only to come home to Paul moving out. She tells her brother that she is not sure what he has done but doesn't want him to run. Paul angrily says she should go to the police if she wants to and that they won't convict an innocent man if she is on the jury.

Reno comes to Deborah's office to ask her if she has seen anything. He suspects that she knows more than she is saying. He advises that he may subpoena her and argues that even though people have identified Marty, mistakes are easy to make. When Deborah is picked for jury duty, Reno challenges her and has her excused, claiming she would have led to a hung jury. At the trial, the prosecution goes through Marty's long and violent criminal record, but Marty still claims that he has never touched a gun. Outside of the courtroom, Deborah tells Reno that her brother has gone for an operation on his legs. Reno says that he wants her to sit in the courtroom and that Marty is "crippled in the head." Reno argues that Marty is assumed to be a bad kid and that everyone would prefer to see him executed. The judge orders the eager jury to give the death penalty if they find Marty guilty, but to ignore his past crimes. At the last minute, Deborah speaks up and asks Reno to save Paul and then asks Marty to forgive her for waiting so long to testify.

Re-titled "The Unwilling Witness," the pilot aired as part of *General Electric Summer Originals* on ABC on July 24, 1956. According to the producers, *Reno English* had a sponsor, but no time slot could be found for it.

As noted in the section dealing with Myrna Loy's TV pilots, Scott appeared as her boss and potential love interest in the unsold comedy pilot *It Gives Me Great Pleasure*. The closest Scott came to starring on a regular series was as co-host of a 1959 summer replacement show for Red Skelton, *Spotlight Playhouse*. He hosted this anthology series on alternating weeks with actress-spokesperson Julia Meade. The show consisted of reruns of episodes from other anthology series.

Scott continued to appear in episodic television, on the stage, and in features up until his death from cancer in 1965 at the age of 51. His last TV role was in "Bow to a Master," an episode of *The Rogues* in which Scott played a thief nicknamed "the Cat."

Ann Sheridan

> Having been saddled with the earthy title of "oomph" girl, attractive, sexy Annie had played various roles in B pictures, then graduated to small parts in A pictures, all the while learning her craft. She became one of the most skilled comediennes in Hollywood.... She knew how to toss away a line, underplay it with a wry quality, and get the full measure of the laugh therein. She could also play a dramatic role with the best of them. But because she came up from the ranks, her skill was underestimated.[1]
>
> —director Vincent Sherman on Ann Sheridan

Ann Sheridan appeared in such films as *Angels with Dirty Faces* (1938) with James Cagney and Humphrey Bogart, *The Man Who Came to Dinner* (1942) with Bette Davis and Monty Woolley in which she played actress Lorraine Sheldon, and *I Was a Male War Bride* (1949), a film about an American lieutenant (Sheridan) and a French Army captain (Cary Grant). With film roles becoming scarce in the 1950s, Sheridan turned her attention to television. Her attempts at a series were sitcoms which allowed her to display her classic comedy timing, sometimes with a hint of impudence.

In the 30-minute pilot *Calling Terry Conway* (1956), originally titled *Las Vegas Woman*, Sheridan starred as the publicity and public relations director of the Paradise Hotel in Las Vegas. Exteriors for the pilot were filmed at the Flamingo Hotel in the city. Also appearing were Una Merkel as Pearl McGrath, Conway's secretary, and Philip Ober as Harry Garvey, a member of the hotel's board of directors who didn't like women in positions of authority. Jacques Mapes of Jack Chertok Productions produced the pilot, written by Tom Seller and directed by Walter J. Thiele.

The storyline dealt with a prince and his mother from the mideastern country of Karestan staying at the Paradise Hotel. Garvey wants to impress the visitors so that they will permit his company to build a hotel in their country. Terry decides to hold a reception for the prince, which his mother refuses to attend. His mother hates antelope meat (a staple in Karestan), which Terry has ordered for the dinner. When Terry takes the mother out to sample American food, she confides that she is worried about her son being spoiled in America. Terry speaks with the prince about his mother's concerns. Bud, a bellboy, punches the prince in the face for flirting with Bud's girlfriend and then saying that he is tired of the girl and prefers Terry. The prince's mother approves of what happened to her son and gives the go-ahead for building a hotel in her country.

Calling Terry Conway never sold, evidently because sponsors were wary about being associated with a show that indirectly related to gambling.

Columnist Erskine Johnson reported in October 1956 that Sheridan was to star in a pilot titled *Assignment Mexico* produced by Harry Ackerman's Ticonderoga Productions for CBS.[2] The projected adventure-romance series concerned a female travel agent working in Mexico City and dating a Mexican police detective. She becomes involved in various stories involving her clients and the police. A pilot was filmed but with Peggie Castle playing the travel agent instead of Sheridan.

Writer Norman Lessing created a comedy pilot script for Sheridan in which she would have starred as Ann Norton, a widowed mother whose husband was killed in the war.[3] Ann had two boys: Tommy, age ten and a half, who liked to invent things, and Steve, 12 and a half, who was the "promoter" in the family. Ann's mother Bertha Fell lived with her daughter and took care of the household duties. Ann managed the Norton Garage whose tenant Chuck Samson, 40 and husky, maintained his fleet of cabs.

When Chuck asks Ann out, she rejects him. However, she watches a TV show about an overbearing mother whose son is angry because she didn't remarry and give him a father. Ann feels guilty that she is not providing her two sons with a dad. And so, much to his surprise, Ann invites Chuck over for dinner with her sons. After dinner, Tommy asks Chuck how much he makes a year since he says he needs braces that will cost $1500. Steve questions his mom about how much it will cost to send him to Harvard. When Steve goes upstairs to bed, he says to Chuck, "Good night, Dad." Chuck is panic-stricken, thinking he is being roped into marriage. After the boys go to bed, Chuck says that he is "willing to go through with it." To which Ann replies, "Go through with what?" Ann goads him to say he loves her, but Chuck is stubborn. Ann ends up slugging him.

After Chuck leaves, Ann talks with Steve and Tommy, who say that they don't mind if she marries because she loves the man, but they don't want her to marry just for them. The next day at the garage, Ann asks Chuck to take a cab down off the rack so a handsome and charming man named Mr. Hadley can get a quick grease job for his car. Apparently, Hadley may have become a love interest for Ann if the script had been filmed and become a series.

Sheridan commented on her efforts to find a TV vehicle:

> I've looked for a series for years. Lots have been offered, and have been just plain bad. A lot had some halfway decent writing, but the minute an agent or producer tells me "This is like *The Lucy Show*," I don't want it. I don't want to compete with Lucy—I would be an idiot. I don't want to be like someone else.[4]

Left to right are Douglas Fowley as Grandpa, Ann Sheridan as Henrietta Hanks and Ruth McDevitt as Grandma in *Pistols 'n' Petticoats*. Initially, the comedy was up against the hit sitcom NBC's *Get Smart* and ABC's *The Lawrence Welk Show*, and it did not do well in the ratings.

After joining the cast of the NBC daytime drama *Another World*, Sheridan finally got her own prime-time series on CBS in 1966. On *Pistols 'n' Petticoats*, she played Henrietta Hanks, a woman living with her grandparents in the West during the 1870s and raising a young, beautiful daughter, Lucy (Carole Wells). Henrietta and her grandparents all knew how to handle a gun, which was a good thing since the town of Wretched, Colorado, had a somewhat inept young sheriff, Harold Sikes (Gary Vinson). Sheridan described her character and those of her grandma and grandpa as "do-gooders. We teach people manners. Grandma always says 'don't hurt them, just teach them manners.' Guns can be persuasive. We always run into somebody in trouble, and we always help. All of us are crack shots except my daughter, and she is a delicate thing who has been sent east for school."[5]

In a typical episode, "A Wagonload of Women," Henrietta has sent for five single women as possible brides for the men of Wretched, but the women are kidnapped by marauders from Sorrywater. When Henrietta goes to Sorrywater to free the women, she is kidnapped as well. The women including Henrietta are about to be married when Grandma and Lucy appear, pretending that Lucy is part of a group of more attractive women wanting husbands. The single men from Sorrywater leave to find the other women.

After filming five episodes of the series, Sheridan had to reduce her workload because she was diagnosed with lung cancer. She worked as much as possible but doubles had to be used for many scenes and script adjustments had to be made to accommodate her absences. As Carole Wells recalled,

> She was very ill during the shooting of the series. She never complained. I would ask her, "How do you feel today?" She would respond, "Wish I felt as good as you do, sweetie." She was always kind and respectful and I adored her. She kept to herself since she wasn't well. She smoked constantly even though she was dying from cancer.[6]

Sheridan passed away in January 1967. Her role on *Pistols 'n' Petticoats* was not recast; the series was canceled after a single season.

Alexis Smith

Alexis Smith's movie career blossomed in the 1940s with roles in the Errol Flynn films *Dive Bomber* (1941), *Gentleman Jim* (1942) and *San Antonio* (1944). Tall and chic, the actress appeared in many films with other iconic leading men such as Fredric March in *The Adventures of Mark Twain*, *Night and Day* with Cary Grant and *The Two Mrs. Carrolls* with Humphrey Bogart. In the 1950s, she made *The Turning Point* with William Holden, *Beau James* with Bob Hope and *The Young Philadelphians* with Paul Newman, among others. Smith frequently played the (often very wealthy) wife or love interest of the male character in her pictures.

In 1957, the actress tried to launch her own sitcom by appearing in a pilot for Twentieth Century–Fox called *Mother Is a Freshman* (based on the 1949 movie of the same name). Written by Seaman Jacobs and directed by Erle C. Kenton, the comedy was produced by Peter Packer. *Mother Is a Freshman* focused on a widow who enrolls in the college her daughter is attending. The comedy was to be syndicated by National Telefilm Associates to local TV stations, but evidently not enough stations expressed interest in airing the potential series.

Finding fewer roles in movies and on television, Smith plied her trade in the theater, oftentimes with her actor-husband Craig Stevens, best known for the TV series *Peter Gunn*. In 1972, she won the Tony for Best Actress in a Musical for her performance in Stephen Sondheim's *Follies*. Her theater performances resurrected her film career. In the 1970s, she had parts in *Once Is Not Enough* (1975) with Kirk Douglas and *Casey's Shadow* (1978) with Walter Matthau.

Also, in the '70s, she tried again for her own TV series: She played Smitty, a nightclub owner, in a failed 1973 pilot titled *Nightside* that starred John Cassavetes as press agent Carmine Kelly and Mike Kellin as Aram Bessoyggian, a private detective who sometimes worked for Kelly. Smith replaced actress Lee Remick in the role of Smitty. The pilot, filmed entirely on location in New York City at night, was written by journalist-novelist Pete Hamill, who had begun his newspaper career as a night side reporter for *The New York Post*. Titled "A Very Special Place," the show, directed by Richard Donner, was produced by Herbert B. Leonard, who had made ABC's New York–based

Naked City series. The following description of the storyline is from the revised third draft script[1]:

> While Smitty is frantically trying to order more meat for her club after a delivery fails to arrive, an earth-mover plows into the side of Smitty's building. The police arrive, and the foreman doing construction work claims that it was an accident. Smitty believes that Mike Gable (Richard Jordan), of Mike Gable Construction Company, is at fault and that he wants to force her out of her property in order to buy it. The next day the health inspector stops by after an anonymous tip and discovers a rat in the bathroom. Aram investigates, and several patrons remember seeing a suspicious man who may have brought the rat. Carmine visits Mike Gable and accuses him of the failed meat delivery, the earth-mover crash, and the rat. Gable declares that he will take the building from Smitty but that he does not break the law. Carmine threatens to go to the police and prove his guilt.
>
> Meanwhile, after showing mug shots to different patrons of Smitty's club, Aram has been able to identify the man who planted the rat as Acky (F. Murray Abraham). Carmine and Smitty visit wealthy Al Grudin (Joseph Wiseman), who had previously invested in a play starring Smitty's late husband. He also has a past in the Builder's Association. Grudin tells Smitty to sell and that she cannot beat Gable. He relates a story about Gable's late father being a tough man who fought in several wars. However, later Carmine and Grudin develop a plan to prevent Gable from closing the night club.
>
> Carmine convinces Gable to take a ride with him and Grudin. They take Gable to the roof of a building to view some of the structures that Grudin and Gable's father built. Grudin explains to Gable about how it is important to build for people and make relationships with them the focus, just like Gable's father did. Grudin subsequently takes Gable to a social club and introduces him to a room full of people who are honored to meet him and who loved his father. Gable cries after seeing the legacy his father left. Back at Smitty's, business is booming thanks to TV publicity about the restaurant, and the vandals have all been taken to jail. Smitty decides to not follow up with charges against Gable and just wants to run her "saloon."

Later in her career, Smith often played supporting roles as troublemakers on various TV dra-

A photograph promoting Alexis Smith's appearance on *Dallas* as Clayton Farlow's sister. Smith appeared in seven episodes of the series in 1984 and returned in 1990 for four additional installments.

mas. The actress began a recurring role on the nighttime drama *Dallas* as Clay Farlow's (Howard Keel) sister, Lady Jessica Montford. This being a soap opera, she was up to no good. Jessica first appeared in a March 1984 episode when she was invited to the wedding of her brother to Miss Ellie (Barbara Bel Geddes). Asked to describe her character, Smith remarked, "Well, she's this very rich lady. Then it occurred to me that all my life, whenever I was asked that question, my answer was: 'Well, she's this very rich lady…' Oh my God, I simply never have been poor." Commenting on TV series work, she indicated that she never really wanted to do a series in which she was the main star. "The responsibility of a series when you're the leading character and are practically in every shot, day in and day out, is just too strenuous."[2]

In 1988, Smith starred on the short-lived ABC series *Hothouse*, originally called *The Clinic*. The drama concerned a family-owned psychiatric hospital in New England. The head man is Dr. Sam Garrison (Josef Sommer), whose former wife Lily (Smith) is now married to a millionaire, in keeping with Smith's self-described screen image. Lily became frustrated with Sam's devotion to his work, and so divorced him. After marrying a wealthy man, the new couple bought a horse farm next door to the clinic. The series aired for seven episodes during the summer of 1988.

Smith was nominated for an Emmy for her guest star appearance on the comedy *Cheers* in 1990. In "Sam and the Professor," Smith played Alice Anne Volkman, Rebecca's former college professor, who ends up sleeping with Sam. The actress passed away in 1993.

Barbara Stanwyck

Barbara Stanwyck had a long and storied career in movies and some success in television. She was one of the most versatile actresses ever, able to perform exquisitely in films noir like *Double Indemnity* (1944), dramas such as *Stella Dallas* (1937), Westerns like *Cattle Queen of Montana* (1954) and comedies including *Christmas in Connecticut* (1945). She appeared in 85 movies. Although Oscar-nominated four times, she never won the award but was presented with an Honorary Oscar at the 1982 Academy Awards ceremony.

Stanwyck's image was that of a self-reliant, self-assured but down-to-earth woman—cool on the outside but with a warm heart. In her TV roles, she often played the matriarch or the "boss" lady. The actress was particularly fond of appearing in Westerns. As early as 1952, NBC was negotiating with the actress for her own dramatic series, but the talks were never completed. Also that year, producer Hal Roach wanted Stanwyck and Montgomery Clift as leads in *The Dramatic Hour,* a never-produced series to be syndicated to local stations.

In 1953, producer Leon Fromkess offered Stanwyck the lead in a TV series called *Ringside* in which she would play a fight trainer. Actor Mike Mazurki had been signed to appear as a boxer. Fifty-two episodes were to be made and syndicated and the actress would have had profit participation. She rejected the deal, and the series idea was shelved.

Stanwyck told Hollywood columnist Vernon Scott, "I don't want to sell soap, cigarets [sic], candy bars or any other product. I know TV programs have to increase the sales of the sponsors' products, otherwise there wouldn't be much television. But it's not for me."[1] Like other film stars flirting with TV, the actress also didn't think one could appear in 39 quality episodes of a series in a season. "I don't think it's possible to come up with 39 good scripts, especially for a straight, dramatic actress.... Besides that, why should I disappoint my fans by appearing in things on television that I wouldn't do for the movies?"[2]

By the mid–50s, Stanwyck's opinion about doing a TV series changed. In late 1955 it was announced that she would host an anthology series and star in one out of every four episodes. A pilot was made titled *Barbara Stanwyck Presents* [the sponsor's] *Theatre* with the belief that a sponsor would be found, which never happened. Stanwyck introduced a pilot episode scripted by Larry Marcus based on a story by William Heuman. The actress played Irene Frazier, wife of an Old West town's sheriff, Tom Frazier (Jeff Morrow). The Fraziers had a young son who was ill with an undiagnosed malady.

Since the family lived outside of town, Tom would leave his house in the evenings to handle his duties. He learns that old man Jordan (Trevor Bardette), the father of a man whom he had arrested and who was subsequently hanged, is in town looking to avenge his son's death. He goes looking for Jordan, leaving his deputy to guard Irene and their son. When the boy becomes sicker, Irene asks the deputy to find a doctor. She then leaves the house to take care of a sick neighbor. When she returns, Jordan is waiting for her. However, when he sees her son is seriously ill from scarlet fever, he has a change of heart and, instead of seeking revenge, he helps take care of the boy. When her husband returns from town, he confronts Jordan, but Irene tells him to thank the man for helping their son. Screen Gems purchased the unsold pilot (directed by Lewis Allen and produced by Jack Denove), deleted Stanwyck's introduction and closing remarks about "next week's episode," and aired it as an installment of *Ford Theatre* in 1956.

In 1957, there was a brief mention in the show business trade papers that Stanwyck was in talks with Peter Godfrey, who had directed the actress in *Christmas in Connecticut* and *The Two Mrs. Carrolls*, to star on a series called *Love Story*. No details of the project appear to exist, but it was no doubt another anthology-type show that never materialized.

Keeping in the Western vein, the actress next made a pilot for a series to be called *Lady Law* which aired as an installment of *Dick Powell's Zane Grey Theater* on January 17, 1958. In the episode, "The Freighter," she had the role of Belle Garrison, a tough woman and an expert at using a bullwhip. She took over her grandfather's (James Bell) freight line which was being terrorized by Rufus Murdock and his three sons. Murdock wanted to merge his freight line with the Garrison line, but Belle would have no part of it. The Murdocks try to steal Belle's customers. She disguises her wagon to look like Murdock's and so is able to evade him. He mistakenly blows up his own wagon as it is being driven by two of his sons. This dissuades him from pursuing his takeover of her freight line. John Archer played Belle's assistant Ad Masters in the pilot which was written by Fred Freiberger and directed by Christian Nyby.

Commenting on the fact that Westerns at the time always featured a male actor in the lead, Stanwyck remarked, "For a nominal fee, I'll switch to playing male roles. I can ride as well as any actor in the business, shoot as well and use a whip as well. What's more, I have a very deep voice."³

After *Lady Law* failed to become a series, Stanwyck was interested in starring on another anthology series called *Inside Story,* developed by Aaron Spelling, who at the time produced *Dick Powell's Zane Grey Theater.* Stanwyck had met Spelling while working on the Powell series. Spelling would influence her TV career for much of the 1960s and through the 1980s. Around this time, Stanwyck was under consideration as one of six rotating hosts of Four Star Productions' proposed *Six Star Playhouse* which failed to become a series.

Stanwyck finally succeeded in getting her own anthology series in 1959. Before its premiere, she observed, "Television is a snake pit, It's an octopus. It's a wonder to me there are as many good things on TV as they have. This small box consumes material 24 hours a day. It's frightening. It's remarkable it's as good as it is."

About her own upcoming series which was packaged by the William Morris Agency, the actress remarked:

> We go into production in April [1959] at Desilu Gower. I have formed a company with Lou Edelman, who will be executive producer, and William Wright, the producer of the series. We will make a minimum of 26 pictures, which I will host. I will star in 19 of them. It's an anthology series. I'm looking for good, dramatic gutsy stories.
> No, it won't be like Loretta Young's. She does her series extremely well, but I'm more hard-hitting.... That doesn't mean I'll go around poisoning people or kicking hell out of them. I prefer the meaty, dramatic stories. I don't want to be left at the log cabin with the kids, waving as the men ride off. I always want to go where the fellows go. It's much more fun.⁴

The Barbara Stanwyck Show ran on NBC during the 1960–61 season. In developing the series, producers were thinking of making it either a continuing character show with Stanwyck as a Hong Kong adventuress or an anthology series which the actress would host as well as act in most of the episodes. In the end, the producers tried to combine both concepts. Stanwyck starred in most of the installments and introduced all. However, during the run of the series, she played the same character on three separate episodes: Josephine Little, owner of a Hong Kong export-import. In a November 1960 installment, Little attempts to help a young boy who wants to visit the U.S. A January 1961 episode had the character teaming up with U.S. Intelligence to uncover a dangerous spy, and in a March 1961 story she helps a doctor get needed medical supplies. Apparently, if the character had been popular enough with viewers, *The Barbara Stanwyck Show* may have become a continuing character drama instead of an anthology series.

Despite Stanwyck's remarks that her show would not be like Loretta

Young's, NBC apparently had other ideas. Initially, the network slotted the Stanwyck show at 10:30 on Sunday nights after *The Loretta Young Show*. But before it premiered, the network changed the time period to Mondays at 10:00 p.m., the same time slot that Young had on Sunday nights. Also, like Young, Stanwyck made glamorous entrances dressed in evening gowns to introduce each female-centric story.

In a very rare occurrence for the lead in a canceled series, Stanwyck received an Emmy in 1961 as best dramatic actress for her acting on the show. Her producer Lou Edelman thought that maybe the series was not a success because the producers did not use Stanwyck correctly. He thought that he "should have surrounded her with young people."5

After the demise of *The Barbara Stanwyck Show*, the actress was considered for the lead in an MGM pilot based on the Katharine Hepburn-Spencer Tracy movie *Woman of the Year*, a film about the relationship between an international affairs correspondent who had been named "Woman of the Year" and a sports writer. Both worked for the same newspaper. Gary Merrill was reported to be the main contender for the sports writer role. However, no pilot was ever developed.

In Stanwyck's next attempt at a series, *The Seekers*, she played Lt. Agatha Stewart of the Chicago Police Department's Missing Persons Bureau in the 1930s. Two episodes of ABC's *The Untouchables*, produced by Desilu, served as pilots for the drama. The first, "Elegy" (November 20, 1962), concerned a racketeer, Charley Radick (John Larch), dying of cancer, who wants to see his long-lost daughter. Eliot Ness (Robert Stack), the Federal agent fighting Chicago gangsters and *The Untouchables*' main character, fears that Radick's death will prompt a gang war over control of the gangster's rackets and so makes a deal with Radick that he will find his daughter if the racketeer turns over his books to him. Ness asks Aggie to locate the daughter. Aggie is assisted by Detective Frank Benson (Ed Asner). Her secretary is June played by African-American actress Virginia Capers.

Tough, no-nonsense Stewart eventually finds Margaret Radick (Peggy Ann Garner) and reunites her with her father, who is in a hospital. Radick turns over his records to Ness. Robert Butler directed the episode which was scripted by Herman Groves.

The second episode featuring Aggie Stewart, "Search for a Bad Man," aired on January 1, 1963. In that episode, Stewart attempts to learn the identity of a dead man found floating in Lake Michigan. Meanwhile, Ness investigates a $1 million shipment of illegal liquor from Canada to Chicago. Stewart discovers that the dead man was gangster Jake Portuguese, who was behind the illegal liquor smuggling. His brother Rudy dumped the body in the lake after Jake had a heart attack. He wanted to keep his brother's death a secret until he got the liquor and sold it for $1 million. In the end, Rudy is killed in a shoot-out with Ness and his men.

Stanwyck's next unsuccessful pilot, *Calhoun* was filmed in Las Cruces, New Mexico, in 1963. For the first time in one of her TV pilots, she was not the star. Jackie Cooper played Everett Calhoun, the county agricultural agent in Calhoun County, named for his grandfather. Stanwyck appeared as Abby Rayner, a home agent who teaches 4-H Club members how to grow plants and instructs women on cooking, sewing and homemaking tasks. Merle Miller, who wrote the initial script for the pilot, said that he asked Cooper how old he could make the Stanwyck character. Cooper discussed it with the actress, who responded, "I don't care. He can say I'm 50, if he wants to. Let him make me whatever age fits the part and that's how old I'll be." The actress was 56 at the time the pilot was made.

Also in the proposed series were Ken Berry as Dr. Otis Sorenson, Robert Lansing as Eric Sloane, owner of a large citrus company, Beverly Garland as his wife Nan, and Barbara Luna as Felicia del Valle, Calhoun's secretary.

In the storyline, Calhoun discovers diseased trees in a citrus grove and attempts to find a cure for the blight before Sloane destroys the trees on a tenant's property. When Calhoun can't treat the blight, the tenant himself decides to bulldoze and burn the infected trees. Stanwyck's character was featured prominently in a subplot dealing with her estranged husband Ray (Howard Duff) paying her a visit. They had been separated for eight years after he had left her for another woman. She confides that she invited Ray to the county and is seriously considering reconciling with him and dropping plans for divorce. Abby suggests that he stay with her, but Ray doesn't like the idea and so leaves.

According to Cooper's autobiography, the storyline about Abby and her estranged husband was inspired to a certain degree by Stanwyck's relationship with her former spouse, actor Robert Taylor.[6] While conversing with Stanwyck about the pilot, the actress began telling Cooper about her life with Taylor. Cooper added lines to the scene between the actress and Duff discussing a possible reconciliation based on what she had told him.

Stuart Rosenberg directed the pilot for Jackie Cooper Productions in association with United Artists and CBS. The making of *Calhoun* resulted in Merle Miller publishing a book, *Only You, Dick Daring!*, about his efforts to develop the pilot script.

After the failure of *Calhoun* to become a series, Stanwyck returned to the genre she liked the best. ABC's *The Big Valley*, a Western that has often been described as a matriarchal *Bonanza*, became the actress' most successful

The cast of *The Big Valley*. Back row, left to right: Lee Majors, Peter Breck and Richard Long; front, left to right: Linda Evans and Barbara Stanwyck. Not pictured is actor Charles Briles who played son Eugene Barkley, a student attending medical school, on eight episodes of the series.

series. About the comparison to the hit NBC Western *Bonanza*, Stanwyck commented, "You've got to be compared to something, so why not *Bonanza*? I'll tell you this, though. We get mad at each other in our show, and make mistakes. Lorne Greene [the patriarch on *Bonanza*] is the Loretta Young of the West. That's not for me."[7]

In *The Big Valley*, which premiered in September 1965, Stanwyck played Victoria Barkley, the widowed matriarch of the family that included her sons Jarrod (Richard Long), Nick (Peter Breck) and seldom-seen Eugene (Charles Briles), her daughter Audra (Linda Evans) and her deceased husband's illegitimate son Heath (Lee Majors). Stanwyck thought that the Heath character should have been her illegitimate son instead of her husband's, but producers believed that that would spoil her mother image on the show. The series ran for four seasons.

The Big Valley was a rare adult Western with a female as its lead. (The only other TV Western with a heroine as the main character, *Annie Oakley*, was aimed at juveniles.) Created by Lou Edelman, the producer of *The Barbara Stanwyck Show*, and one of its writers A.I. Bezzerides, Stanwyck's character was originally conceived as a tougher female but potential advertisers were leery of women in Westerns. Edelman sold the show to producers Levy, Gardner and Laven, who had produced the successful *The Rifleman* for ABC. They made a deal with Four Star Productions and ABC to make and air the series.

Stanwyck won her second Emmy in 1966 for *The Big Valley* and was also nominated as best lead actress for the series in 1967 and 1968. She won a third Emmy in 1977 for her performance in the mini-series *The Thorn Birds*.

According to Christopher Knopf, who wrote the *Big Valley* pilot, Stanwyck was the ultimate professional on the set:

> We had a bunch of first-time would be "stars" assigned, who spent their off-camera moments wondering the lot to see who had air conditioning, TVs, refrigerators, etc., in their Winnebagos. Barbara would have none of it, setting a style and professional behavior the others had to follow. She was on the set early every day, knew her lines which brought the newbies quickly in line.

Knopf added that Stanwyck was superb in handling talent.

> Each episode, in the beginning of the series, ended with Barbara emoting a homily before her family. I'd written one at midnight, anxious to get the script in on time. She called me to the set. Barbara was a poker, always poking you in the stomach when she had something important to say, so you were forever bracing against it.
>
> "Christopher," she said, poking away, "these words you've written for me are so beautiful, I wonder if you could take me through them so I won't get them wrong." ... As I went through them, I realized I didn't have a clue what they were about, they were simply blah, blah, blah. In doing so, however, I began to rethink what it was I wanted to say, coming up with something totally different, to which she poked my stomach and said, "I wonder if you could write them just the way you said them to me." Point? Instead of saying, "What's this crap all about?" she saved my ego and got me to rethink what I'd written rather than stupidly defending a bad scene out of pique. That was Barbara.[8]

The Big Valley never ranked among the top 30 series during its four-season run but performed respectably for ABC on Monday nights at 10:00. *The Big Valley* has flourished in reruns and is still seen today on "nostalgia" channels.

Saying "I like the idea," Stanwyck was set to star in a 1969 legal drama called *Until Proven Guilty* written by Richard DeRoy and produced by William Dozier and Stan Sheptner for Universal.[9] The pilot, intended for ABC, was to be made as a two-hour TV movie. According to a first draft of the pilot script, Stanwyck would have appeared as widow Kate Dodds, a lawyer in a firm headed by Arthur Conover, with whom she was intimately involved.[10] Arthur, separated from his wife Marian, was being considered for an appointment to the Supreme Court but was thinking of refusing the offer. He refused to confide to Kate his reasons for rejecting the offer. Arthur leaves the lakeside lodge where he and Kate have been staying, intending to fly back to Los Angeles in a small plane owned by neighbor Sidney Burns. The plane crashes on take-off, and Arthur eventually succumbs to his injuries. The police inform Kate that the crash was not an accident and arrest Sidney's son-in-law, an ex-football player who had served time in jail for involuntary manslaughter and whom Arthur had gotten kicked out of professional sports. Kate has doubts that the son-in-law is the culprit and decides to defend him. But before the trial begins, the son-in-law escapes from jail. That is where the script ends without any resolution as to who was really responsible for Arthur's death.

A few years after *Until Proven Guilty* failed to get off the ground, Stanwyck considered taking on another TV series playing a lawyer. In *Fitzgerald and Pride*, Stanwyck would play a role similar to that of Kate Dodds, but emergency kidney surgery forced her to give up the part, which went to Susan Hayward. There's more about this pilot in the section on Susan Hayward.

In 1972, Metromedia had a number of pilot projects for CBS including a pilot for Stanwyck somewhat based on *The Kingdom and the Power*, a Gay Talese book about *The New York Times*. Scripted by Robert E. Thompson and produced by Dick Berg, *American Eagle* was to be about a family that owns a newspaper and is deeply involved in public works. Stanwyck was to play the matriarch of the family, a character similar to that of the late Katherine Graham, owner of *The Washington Post*. According to an August 1972 newspaper article by Kay Gardella (shared with this author by Talese), in the proposed series, set in the Great Lakes region, Stanwyck's character would have had a daughter on the brink of divorce from the newspaper's managing editor and a 26-year-old son named Christopher who was apprenticing at the paper. In an ongoing storyline, the prestigious publication would have been struggling for survival.

Talese met with the actress about the project, but no pilot was ever made.

As he commented, "I was (and remain) committed to books and articles (*print*), never caring about writing for TV or film. What a horrible life for a writer: trying to please actors and directors and producers! Not for me."[11]

In 1980, Stanwyck tried her luck at another venture into weekly TV, starring in a *Charlie's Angels* spin-off called *Toni's Boys*. In this male version of the hit ABC series, Stanwyck headed a detective agency inherited from her late husband that had three handsome employees: Cotton Harper (Stephen Shortridge), a former rodeo rider, roper and tracker; Matt Parrish (Bruce Bauer), a master of disguise and weapons; and Bob Sorensen (Olympic star Bob Seagren), a former U.S. Olympic champion. Toni, making her initial appearance dressed all in red, had been contacted by Charlie Townsend to work on a case involving murder attempts against his Angels.

"I swore I'd never do another series, but here I am," remarked the 72-year-old actress. "Aaron [Spelling] did a little bit of arm-twisting, and I was attracted by the role. Hopefully, it'll have a lot of action, which I like."[12]

Unlike the character of Charlie Townsend, who was heard but never seen, Antoni (Toni for short) was more active in the cases her detectives worked. She thinks that Michael Durano (Robert Loggia) is behind the murder attempts since the Angels had testified against him, resulting in him going to prison. Now that Durano is out of jail, Toni and her boys (and the Angels) attend a wine-tasting event to meet Durano. Toni instigates a fight involving Durano's men and her detectives, but Durano's men get away and kidnap the Angels. She comes up with a plan to free the Angels before Durano traps them behind a brick wall. The Angels are freed and Durano is captured.

Airing on April 2, 1980, as an episode of *Charlie's Angels*, the pilot was directed by Ron Satlof from a teleplay by Kathryn Powers, based on a story by Powers and Robert Janes. Commenting on the pilot, producer Aaron Spelling referred to Stanwyck as "the female John Wayne.... I think anything with Barbara Stanwyck should be put on the air."[13] But ABC decided not to proceed with a series.

Stanwyck's final role as a regular on a TV series was as Constance Colby on the first season of *The Colbys*, a 1985 prime-time soap opera (a spin-off from *Dynasty*) produced by Spelling. Constance was the sister of Jason Colby (Charlton Heston), the head of a multinational conglomerate, and owned half-interest in the enterprise. Her character was written out of the series after its first season.

The Colbys was Stanwyck's last acting appearance. She passed away in 1990 at the age of 82.

Gloria Swanson

Gloria Swanson began her career in silent movies in the 1910s and '20s, usually playing a woman of the world dressed in extravagant fashions. She was one of the few silent stars to continue making movies after the transition to sound. In 1950, Swanson made a major comeback playing silent movie actress Norma Desmond in *Sunset Blvd.*, a performance for which she received an Academy Award nomination. In addition to acting, she also produced some of her own films. Expanding her career beyond show business, Swanson became involved in fashion design, health food and nutrition.

She was married six times; her first husband was legendary movie actor Wallace Beery. While she was not the first female movie star to make over $1 million in a year, she was probably the first to spend that amount in a year. She lavished money on homes and fashions. Swanson had to continue to work to keep her head above water financially.

As Swanson starred in movies in the early days of the film industry, so she became a television personality at the beginning of TV. In New York in 1948, she had her own show on WPIX when it first began broadcasting. Aimed at female viewers, *The Gloria Swanson Hour* had segments dealing with fashion, cooking, beauty and glamour with Swanson interviewing actors, designers and others involved with lifestyle trends. The series began in June and lasted until December.

In 1951, the actress tried to revive the show at ABC. Focusing mainly on her personality, the proposed series would have also included film star Erik Rhodes as her butler (he had appeared in the same role on her WPIX show), her press agent Clip, her real-life youngest daughter Michelle Farmer, and her secretary Ms. Tracy with everything taking place in a facsimile of Swanson's Fifth Avenue apartment. Geared for a Sunday afternoon time slot, the different elements of *The Gloria Swanson Show* were to include[1]:

- "The Swanson Week": a filmed account of the glamorous star's eventful week
- "Thought for Sunday": inspirational human interest stories with guests such as Dale Carnegie and Bishop Fulton Sheen
- "Yesterday's Films": Swanson commenting on silent movies

- "Fashions by Swanson": Swanson, a self-taught fashion designer, would show off her designs
- "Understudy and Star": well-known theater actors would introduce their understudies or their protégés
- "A Star Is Interviewed": famous columnists would interview stars with the results later appearing in the newspaper
- "The Living Book": Swanson would profile a best-selling book with parts dramatized by actors and with the author being interviewed
- "Star of Tomorrow": new talents, endorsed by Swanson, from the Met or from schools like Juilliard would be presented
- "Sports in Season": something for potential male viewers, a segment centered on sports personalities and their special talents
- "Things to Come": a preview of coming events of national and international importance

Of course, everything would be scripted to avoid anything going wrong during the hour.

Each show was to have a common storyline throughout. For example, in the pilot, Swanson pretended to be under the impression that it was just a dress rehearsal. Ethel Merman and her *Call Me Madam* understudy Nancy Andrews come by Swanson's apartment. The actress shows them a silent movie and discusses the book *The Foundling* by Cardinal Spellman. She then mentions that all the fashions she wears on the show are made by the Puritan Dress Company (she had a contract to design and advertise their clothes). Swanson dictates responses to some letters from her fans, and Paul Richards, then manager of the Chicago White Sox, stops by to talk about baseball. At the end, the actress reveals to her daughter and Clip that she knew the actual show was being aired but played along with the idea that it was just a dress rehearsal.

The second show's proposed storyline concerned Swanson appearing in a TV drama in place of one of her friends who had suddenly become ill. Swanson rehearses her role with the leading actor. Clip and her daughter play other parts. Swanson interviews her protégé. In the end, her actress friend appears at Swanson's doorway to say she had a bout of laryngitis but is now feeling better. However, as she is about to leave, Clip trips her. She injures her foot, and Swanson has to go on for her after all.

In the third proposed episode, Swanson and a movie producer discuss her taking a role in a movie about the 1920s. The producer is having *Life* magazine do an article about Swanson still living as if she is in the '20s, and so Gloria redoes her apartment in a '20s motif. When *Life* photographers arrive, she performs an impromptu Charleston number for them. After they leave, the producer phones to tell her that the period of the movie is being changed to the early English restoration period.

Swanson's "larger-than-life" persona did not exactly make her a TV personality that audiences could relate to and so perhaps it is not surprising that no sponsor picked up *The Gloria Swanson Show*. By the end of 1951, ABC terminated its contract with the actress.

In 1952, Swanson was being courted by various producers and agents presenting ideas for different series. The Jerry Rosen Agency proposed a nostalgia series, *Gloria Swanson Reminisces*, on which she would discuss various events relating to show business along with her own viewpoints and experiences. Swanson would interview stars with whom she had worked, show filmclips and play music that was popular during the particular time frame. She responded to the offer by saying that time would not permit her to appear on live TV at the moment.

Also in 1952, Swanson and producer Irving Salkow were in discussions to have her star in a series similar to *Gloria Swanson Reminisces*. It would consist of commentaries on various motion pictures.[2] The idea was to produce 26 episodes of 15 minutes each with Swanson talking about movies and showing clips. Nothing appears to have come from this proposal.

During the same year, Swanson came up with her own idea for a TV panel show in which a cartoonist would present one of his drawings and a panel would guess the caption.[3] A charitable contribution would be made in the name of the cartoonist or panel member depending on whether the panel correctly guessed the caption or the artist stumped the panel. This proposal also went nowhere.

Swanson did begin hosting her own anthology series in 1952, *Crown Theatre*. Swanson acted in four of the 26 episodes that were made, several of which were filmed in Mexico. In "My Last Duchess," she appeared as Eleanor Hallam, a once-famous actress seeking the lead in a movie version of a play she once starred in. Her second *Crown Theatre*, "If Speech Be Silvern," concerned a salesman who no longer wants to live when an accident causes him to lose his voice. His wife (Swanson) attempts to restore his faith in himself. In a "Choice of Weapons," the actress portrayed an adventuress who falls in love with a stranger. The last episode in which Swanson acted, "Short Story," dealt with a famous female novelist searching for a short story idea to complete a collection of such. The novelist comes up with the tale of her falling in love with an aging busboy.

In the 1960s, Swanson attempted some other TV series projects. The first in 1963 was a pilot for a science show called *Attention for Invention* to be hosted by the actress. (Apparently, she had always been interested in science and inventions: In the late 1930s with the rise of Hitler and Mussolini, Swanson had created Multiprises, Inc., a business that brought talented inventors, facing Fascist threats, from Europe to the U.S. where they could patent their inventions and attempt to market them.[4]) Like her many other ideas, this proposal never became a series.

Larry Gelbart, creator of the TV series *M*A*S*H*, and Charles Peck came up with a script for Swanson in 1965: *Remember Mona Faye*, a sitcom. A pilot was to be produced by Goodson & Todman along with Peck Productions for CBS in November 1965 and Swanson was to play the title character, an aging former movie star from the 1930s who still lived in her mansion, somewhat rundown, named Casa Mona. Gerald Lang, who supposedly had been one of the great silent film comedians, acted as Mona's gardener, butler and chauffeur.

The script had Mona's nephew and niece, Kenny and Linda Davis, wanting to visit. Kenny worked for a newspaper and thought he could do a feature article about his once-famous aunt. Gerald announces their visit with the lights dimming in Mona's house, Mona descending the staircase, and Gerald playing a fanfare on the organ. The siblings haven't seen Mona for 20 years, and she is surprised that they are no longer babies. Kenny says that "People do get older," and is promptly rebuked by his aunt. Mona is in deep denial about her age and suggests that they tell her friends to whom she wants to introduce them that they are each 15 years old. Mona decides that they should spend the night with her. The next day Linda discovers piles of unopened mail and unpaid bills and thinks that she and her brother should stay to help their aunt get her affairs in order. The script ends with Mona in her bedroom where Gerald has rolled down a movie screen so she can view one of her old films. "Mona smiles contentedly, then props her head comfortably against her silk pillows, and prepares for an hour or so with her favorite person in the whole, wide world."[5]

Remember Mona Faye was intended for the 1966–67 season on CBS. I could find no evidence that a pilot was ever made; Swanson probably disliked satirizing her star persona.

In 1967, Swanson became involved with another potential series about the arts and sciences: A five-minute daily show titled *What's New?* was designed to follow a local TV station's newscasts, with Swanson interviewing directors, writers, fashion designers, scientists and other individuals.[6] Like *Attention for Invention*, this proposed syndicated series never sold.

Swanson's attempts at becoming a TV personality were no doubt unsuccessful because her radiant presence on the silver screen could never be translated into a more ordinary TV presence with which viewers could feel comfortable. Her final TV appearance was as a woman who had a strange hold over the bees in her vineyard in an *ABC Movie of the Week*, *Killer Bees* (1974). She died in 1984.

Shirley Temple

The #1 box office star in the mid–1930s, Shirley Temple began her movie career when she was three years old. For Twentieth Century–Fox, the child actress appeared in *Bright Eyes* (1934) where she sang "On the Good Ship Lollipop," *Little Miss Marker* (1934) as a child held as a "marker" (collateral) by gangsters, *Heidi* (1937) and others. She continued her career as a teenager in films including *Since You Went Away* (1944) with Claudette Colbert, *The Bachelor and the Bobby-Soxer* (1947) with Cary Grant and Myrna Loy, and *Fort Apache* (1948) with John Wayne, Henry Fonda and her husband John Agar.

As early as 1951, Temple was receiving offers to star in her own TV show, but she decided to retire from show business. Then in 1958 she staged a comeback as the host and narrator of NBC's hour-long *Shirley Temple's Storybook,* which presented dramatizations of fairy tales ranging from "Beauty and the Beast" to "Rip Van Winkle" to "The Emperor's New Clothes." Who better to present classic fairy tales than the actress whom many TV viewers remembered growing up with and to whom they could introduce their children? The first season of 16 episodes ran from January to December 1958 with a new story appearing once or twice a month. During 1959, these episodes were repeated on ABC. Temple appeared on 11 episodes over the series run playing various roles from Katrina Van Tassel in "The Legend of Sleepy Hollow" to the Little Mermaid in the tale of the same name.

The series was brought back to NBC in 1960 and titled *The Shirley Temple Show.* Twenty-five episodes were made ranging from "The Land of Oz" to "The House of the Seven Gables." The show was expensive to produce and because of diminished ratings, it was not renewed at the end of the 1960–61 season.

Temple then made a few guest star appearances on variety shows like *Red Skelton* in 1963, playing a society debutante who, dressed like a hobo, becomes the love interest of Skelton's Freddie the Freeloader. In 1965, her original movie studio Twentieth Century–Fox signed a deal with the actress to appear in a situation comedy for ABC for the 1965–66 season. Perhaps producers thought that Temple's sweet, innocent persona as a child star would transfer well to the small screen as a friendly character who liked to help others. However, the script for the comedy was not tailored to her talents but instead had been written for another actress.

Bill Hayes, best known for his role as Doug Williams on the daytime drama *Days of Our Lives*, co-starred with Temple in the pilot. He said that the teleplay was originally written for blonde actress Judy Holliday, who passed away before the project could be filmed. "They didn't change the script to fit Shirley; they just went ahead and used the script as written. The 'dumb blonde' character fought for justice."[1]

The pilot, originally titled *Go Fight City Hall* and then *The Shirley Temple Show*, had the actress playing social worker Susan Pepperdine, a single working girl at the San Francisco Bureau of Public Aid, who tended to come up with solutions to one social welfare problem after another. Cloris Leachman portrayed her roommate and co-worker; Jack Kruschen appeared as her supervisor. Hayes had the role of David, an attorney who was also Temple's boyfriend. The pilot was produced and directed by Vincent Sherman.

The show begins with Susan Pepperdine visiting an elderly gentleman, Mr. Levington, who says he is dying but is really in love with Susan. He jumps out of his "deathbed" and chases her around his room promising to build settlement houses for the poor if she marries him. Next Susan sees a harried mother who has locked herself into her apartment for a respite from her three young kids. Susan woos her out and comes up with the idea of having public servants babysit children in the park to give their mothers a break. When funds are not available for this project, she proposes that her fiancé David, who represents Globe Department Stores, make an appointment for her with the head of the store chain. She wants the store to create a supervised play area for children while their mothers shop. All the department stores in the city create child care centers but then find that the mothers leave their kids at the centers to relax and not buy anything. The stores decide to close down the centers. Later, Susan visits an elderly couple who had sent for their uncle to immigrate to this country but a total stranger arrives instead of the uncle. The couple needs money to send the man back. Ultimately the pair decides that they like the stranger and don't send him packing. In the end, Susan again meets Mr. Levington, who vows to fund playgrounds in the city but still wants to marry her.

William Self, executive producer for Twentieth Century–Fox, said that the pilot was "not funny enough," and so it never became a series.[2] After this project, Temple permanently retired from show business.

Shirley Temple Black later became involved in Republican politics. She was appointed ambassador to Ghana in 1974 by President Ford and then became Chief of Protocol of the United States. In 1989, President Bush appointed her ambassador to Czechoslovakia. She died at age 85 in 2014.

Orson Welles

Orson Welles, producer, director, writer and actor, liked to make fiction seem like real life and real life appear as fiction. In his memorable Mercury Theatre radio drama "The War of the Worlds" (1938), he presented the H.G. Wells classic as a simulated news broadcast; some listeners actually believed that Earth was really being invaded by Martians. Welles' 1941 cinema classic *Citizen Kane*, which shows the life and legacy of publisher Charles Foster Kane, was based at least in part on the real life of newspaper entrepreneur William Randolph Hearst. In his unfinished picture *It's All True* (1941), that ultimately was to focus on Central and South America, Welles sought to combine real events with staged ones.

Welles' forays into television were a very mixed bag, consisting of a blend of fact and fiction. Welles once remarked that he had a weakness for doing a lot of different things more or less at the same time. As he was attempting to write, direct and produce different TV series, he was also making movies and appearing on a variety of TV shows.

Welles produced, directed, wrote and starred on two British TV series in the mid–1950s. The first, *Orson Welles' Sketch Book*, consisted of six 15-minute episodes with Welles commenting on various subjects such as how he became an actor and the 1938 "War of the Worlds" radio broadcast. Then Welles wrote and directed *Around the World with Orson Welles*, a travelogue featuring various people and sites in Europe. Supposedly, Welles was to make 26 episodes, but only six were filmed with a seventh left incomplete.

In July 1955, *Variety* reported that CBS signed a contract with the filmmaker to direct and star in a series of 90-minute color specials based on contemporary and classical plays and novels with George du Maurier's *Trilby* as the first. Set in Paris, *Trilby* was about a half–Irish girl named Trilby O'Ferrall working as an artists' model who comes under the spell of Svengali. Three months later, the show business paper stated that the negotiations over these specials had broken down and the deal had been called off.

In 1956, Welles made his sitcom debut on an episode of *I Love Lucy* playing himself with Lucy becoming his assistant in his magic act. The first consequence of appearing on *I Love Lucy* was that Desilu commissioned Welles to do a pilot for his own anthology series, *The Orson Welles Show*. For the Desilu show, Welles, the master storyteller, wrote, directed, produced and served as the on-camera host and narrator. Sometimes he even mouthed the characters' words while still photos of them appeared, giving the pilot the feel of a documentary. Desi Arnaz claimed that he was the one who suggested to Welles that he wanted a different type of setting for the host of an anthology series. Instead of the host being on the same set each week to introduce an episode, he wanted Welles to appear as though he were "in front of the television set in the viewer's living room, telling them what is happening or about to happen…"[1]

The 1956 pilot, "The Fountain of Youth," set in the 1920s, was based on the John Collier short story "Youth from Vienna." The stars were Dan Tobin as Dr. Humphrey Baxter, an endocrinologist involved in developing an experimental youth serum, Joi Lansing as the beautiful blonde actress Caroline Coates, and Rick Jason as handsome tennis pro Alan Brodie. As Welles explains at the outset, "Eternal triangle plus eternal youth equals a wacky little romance."

The story begins with Baxter attending a play starring 23-year-old Caroline. He meets and falls in love with her but, before they marry, he has to return to Vienna to resume his experiments with renowned Dr. Vingleberg in developing a serum that stops the aging process. After three years abroad, he returns and learns that Caroline has fallen in love with and wants to marry tennis star Alan Brodie.

Humphrey tells a magazine reporter that he has isolated a glandular secretion that controls aging. Upon returning from her honeymoon with Brodie, Caroline and her new husband visit Baxter and want him to stop their aging. He explains that the anti-aging formula is not yet available but that he has one sample that he could give them as a wedding gift but that they cannot each simply take half. For it to work, a full dose must be administered. The couple goes home and discusses who should take the serum. Each wants the other to take it. Brodie finally swallows the dose and fills the empty bottle with a liquid that tastes bitter. Not knowing this, Caroline later consumes the contents of the bottle and refills it with water and quinine.

After some time, Caroline leaves her husband and confesses to Humphrey that she took the dose and no longer loves Brodie. When she says that the dose tasted bitter, Baxter responds that he just put salt in some water to fool the couple into thinking he had found the Fountain of Youth.

At the end of the story, Welles says that next week's episode "Green Thoughts" would be about a man-eating tiger orchid, a spook story with a seasoning of giggles. While that episode description may have sounded like some Wellesian humor, Welles did want to film another John Collier short story about a unique orchid received by a Mr. Mannering. Initially, the blossoms on the orchid resemble flies' heads. But then strange happenings occur in the Mannering house: His cousin's cat disappears, and then the cousin herself is nowhere to be found. The orchid flourishes with blossoms that unmistakably resemble the cat and the cousin. Readers can probably guess who disappears next. Dann Cahn, who edited "The Fountain of Youth," recalled Welles saying about this next episode, "I got it all in my head, Danny. I'm going to take that short story and that'll be our second show."[2]

Originally, Welles wanted to do a one-hour anthology series, but the network demanded a 30-minute show. Desilu's Martin Leeds had a luncheon date with Welles to tell him what the network wanted. Welles questioned why not an hour series. Leeds responded. "Because an hour is not commercial—you can't sell it in syndication."[3] Welles then bellowed for all to hear, "How dare you talk to me about crass commercialism!"[4]

In his online autobiography, Rick Jason, who played Alan Brodie in the pilot, recalled working with Welles:

> Inventive is a word that doesn't come close to what this genius could do. He used a technique I'd never heard of, and one that I don't believe has ever been used since. Rather than shooting scenes on Hollywood sets, he photographed still pictures of the exteriors and interiors he needed. What he couldn't find for interiors, he had built, photographed, then tore down.
>
> To shoot a scene, there was a slide projector 60 feet or so away from the camera that projected the still onto a huge opaque screen (which more than filled the camera lens) in front of which we worked. A few pieces of furniture, or whatever were required in the foreground to dress the set, completed the arrangement. Most scenes were in either medium or close shots and, rather than cut from one scene to the other, Welles had the actor stand in place while the opaque screen behind him dissolved to the new scene. If the actor was going from an exterior to an interior, the lights on him would go dark, leaving him in silhouette during the backscreen dissolve. As the background changed to the interior, the lights came up on his face and he removed his hat and coat as the camera pulled back revealing the new interior set.
>
> Everything had to work with exactness, which was extremely time-consuming. Welles was doing a lot of the cutting in the camera. The effect was astounding, though subtle, and Welles settled for nothing less than perfection. In his usual manner, money meant nothing to him. Desi had given him a five-day schedule to shoot the half-hour pilot. Welles managed to bring it in in eight and a half days. By the third day of shooting, a somewhat hyper, and very nervous, Desi would pop onto the stage in a spiffy sport jacket and black-and-white wing-tipped shoes, every two or three hours, smiling as broadly as he could, and call out, "How's it going, Orson?"
>
> Welles, without looking up from whatever he was doing, would dismiss him in an offhand way, "Fine, Desi, I'll see you later."[5]

Arnaz indicated that CBS liked the pilot but wasn't sure if the average viewer would understand it. General Foods wanted to sponsor the series but then trouble began with Welles about whether he was going to make 38 episodes, 30 or even less. Also, at the time the show was made, Arnaz told *Variety*, "We made the Orson Welles pilot too late for the regular season, but were offered a 10:30 Saturday night time slot. Not a good time; we wouldn't take it."[6] And so, given issues about Welles' ability to deliver a sufficient number of episodes on time and concerns about a suitable time slot, the Welles anthology project never became a series.

According to Welles, the networks thought the show was too different to be a success with viewers. "It's a drama based on a story published in a popular magazine. Too different? It just looks different. TV doesn't yet realize the importance of something offbeat."[7]

"The Fountain of Youth" was televised once on September 16, 1958, as part of NBC's *Colgate Theatre*, a series of unsold TV pilots. It subsequently won a special Peabody Award for being one of the most irreverent half-hour broadcasts that year.

Another consequence of Welles' *I Love Lucy* appearance was that he used his $5000 compensation to film a pilot for a proposed series to be called *Orson Welles and People*, a documentary profiling famous individuals. The pilot "Camille, the Naked Lady and the Musketeers," presenting a portrait of Alexandre Dumas, was filmed on one day in October 1956. The actor-producer wanted to do other episodes about Winston Churchill and P.T. Barnum. However, the series was never picked up by a network, and the film itself has been lost.

Also in 1956, Welles partnered with former CBS production executive (and one of the men responsible for bringing *I Love Lucy* to the network) Harry Ackerman on an idea for an adventure series. In that year, Ackerman had left CBS and formed his own production company, Ticonderoga Productions. Welles and Ackerman came up with the concept for a TV program to be called *This Family Robinson*, a modern-day version of the classic *Swiss Family Robinson*.[8] Taking into account the popularity of avocations like skin diving, mountain-climbing and other activities pitting man against nature, Welles and Ackerman thought that a series about a well-to-do family stranded on a deserted South Pacific atoll would appeal to viewers. The cast would consist of a mother, father and four kids (a seven-year-old girl, a ten-year-old boy, a girl, 15 and a boy, 17) who, on an extended vacation, find themselves marooned. Storylines would range from the family fighting off dangerous animals and sea creatures to the misadventures of building a house and battling typhoons and tidal waves. While all six family members would be involved in every episode, each adventure would be seen through the eyes of a different member of the family based on a particular problem or endeavor of that individual. In the treatment for this potential series, there was the suggestion that the family could be rescued at some point in the future with episodes then dealing with how the members re-adapt to the civilized world.

For the 1957–58 television season, NBC contemplated broadcasting a 90-minute dramatic anthology like CBS's *Playhouse 90*. The network thought of scheduling the series for Tuesday nights. NBC had talks with Welles to produce this ambitious series but nothing came of the negotiations or the series. At the same time, NBC and Orson Welles were discussing a half-hour live and filmed series featuring Welles as a storyteller. He would narrate a story with the aid of film, artwork and other devices. This unrealized and untitled show would have been scheduled for an early Sunday time slot to be sponsored possibly by an insurance company such as Prudential. Also in 1957, CBS discussed with Welles the idea of doing a 15-minute talk show similar to *Orson Welles' Sketch Book* that he had done in Britain.

In that same year, former NBC executive Nat Wolff came up with a unique idea to have Welles star on his own series. Welles would be featured in an undetermined type of series which would be sold in only one TV market and slotted against the highest-rated programs of the three networks at the time where the show's sponsor was not making any headway. Welles and Wolff's theory was that the master storyteller's star power could stand up against anything the networks had to offer. Production costs for the 13-week series would be low. Welles proclaimed that he could do with a table, lamp and chair anything the networks could do with elaborate sets. Wolff and Welles were confident that, after the 13-week trial, the networks would clamor for the series. This idea never got off the ground.

In 1958, Welles' next attempt at a TV series was a documentary about Italy called a "Portrait of Gina" or "Viva Italia!" The actor-producer apparently wanted to resurrect the series he had done for British television profiling different people and places. Using the music from *The Third Man* as the theme, Welles illustrated this essay on Italian cinema with still photos, snippets of conversations and film of the Italian countryside focusing on the career of Gina Lollobrigida.

Before interviewing the actress, Welles first talked with Rossano Brazzi about why he is more popular abroad than in Italy. He then converses with actor-director Vittorio De Sica, who says that he has had five comebacks in Italy as an actor. Finally, Welles looks at the career of Lollobrigida as somewhat of a Cinderella story showing her humble beginnings in a small rural community where some of the townspeople are jealous of her success. He speaks with Gina's longtime friend Anna Gruber, who says that the actress had few friends when growing up and that she (Lollobrigida) has doubts about her success. Welles then visits the actress' fashionable residence outside Rome where Gina complains about the income taxes in the country and the Italian newspaper reporters. The actress says that if she wasn't an actress, she would have been a snake charmer and states that Italians only appreciate actors after they achieve fame outside of their country. She ends the interview by remarking that Italy is an adorable country but very strange. Reportedly, Lollobrigida was displeased with the way her interview came off, showing her as an ambitious young actress.

The pilot was financed by ABC; the network's head of entertainment was Jim Aubrey. The concept was that Welles would host each episode of the magazine-style program but only perform on some of the installments. The network even considered a time slot for the series on its 1958–59 schedule, thinking of placing it after the hit Western *Maverick* on Sundays at 8:30 p.m. or after the other Warner Brothers Western *Lawman* at 9:00 p.m.

Upon learning that ABC had negotiated a deal with Welles for the pilot, Desi Arnaz, miffed that his production company was left out of the project, told Aubrey, "I hope you are going to lose a bundle with Orson. In fact, I know you will because he doesn't care how much of the Establishment's money he spends."[9] Arnaz asked Aubrey, when he had to postpone a meeting with Desi about the Desilu series *The Untouchables* and go to Italy to see what Welles was filming, how much Orson had spent thus far. Aubrey responded that Welles had expended over $200,000, and the network hadn't seen any film yet.[10] When Welles submitted the pilot to ABC, the network deemed it unwatchable, and it was never broadcast. What was thought to be the only copy of the pilot was mistakenly left in Welles' hotel room in Paris. A copy surfaced in 1986, but Lollobrigida saw it and took legal action to have it banned. It is currently available for viewing on YouTube.

The proposed teleseries *The Unexplained* was created by Julian Lesser, who had developed the travelogue series *Bold Journey*. *The Unexplained* would focus on historical mysteries such as "Did Francis Bacon actually write Shakespeare's plays?" "Whatever happened to Amelia Earhart?" etc. To reduce production costs, the show would be shot without sound, relying on Welles' narration to give each episode its shock value. *The Unexplained* was to be produced by Lesser and Welles with Welles' narration filmed in Rome where he was currently residing. Ben Hecht and Norman Corwin were doing the scripts. The first one was to be about King Tut. Earmarked for the 1960–61 season, the series never saw the light of day.

In the 1960s, Welles remained in-demand to host possible anthology series. At one point, CBS considered him as a candidate to host the iconic fantasy series *The Twilight Zone* for the 1960–61 season. For its initial season, creator-writer Rod Serling had presided over the series, but the network and the show's sponsor General Foods thought that Welles as host would bring in a bigger audience. Welles was interested in the job provided arrangements could be made for him to film the introductions in Europe where he lived. Serling was against the idea, and CBS, concerned over the costs of hiring Welles, dropped the idea.

Welles' name also surfaced as a possible host of three other anthology pilots in the early '60s. *The Dark Side* was a proposed series of half-hour psychological dramas written by Ben Roberts and Ivan Goff, to be produced by Company of Writers in association with Screen Gems. *The House of Riddle* was a projected series for the BBC written by Sam Marx and Lewis Meltzer. *Terror* was to be made by ITC in Britain; set in the 1880s, the show would have focused on gothic stories. None of these became a weekly series.

Welles did make a series for Italian TV, *In the Land of Don Quixote*, in 1961. At the time, Welles was filming a movie titled *Don Quixote*. Doing a travelogue series about Spain was a way of raising money for his film. Co-starring with Welles, as he traveled around Spain, were his wife Paola Mori and his daughter Beatrice Welles. Filming began in 1961, but the nine episodes were not broadcast on RAI-TV until 1964. RAI added narration for each episode written by Gian Paolo Callegari and voiced by Arnoldo Foa.

During the 1967–68 season, Welles made his first appearance on Dean Martin's hit variety hour. Greg Garrison produced and directed the Martin show, and he and Welles proposed a series of specials and a possible weekly half-hour variety program starring the actor-producer. Initially, Garrison planned ten installments a year of the Welles series using the same title as Orson's 1955 British series, *Around the World with Orson Welles*. Garrison wanted both Charlie Chaplin and Laurence Olivier to guest on the first show. The Chaplin segment was to be shot in Switzerland with Welles interviewing the comic legend. Olivier and Welles were to be shown in rehearsals at the Old Vic in England. NBC turned down the idea, but CBS gave it the go-ahead.

Shot in Europe, Asia and the U.S. between 1968 and 1969 with Welles narrating and also starring in a variety of roles, the special could be termed a "pre-pilot" in the sense that if it (and succeeding specials) scored good ratings, a weekly series could have followed. The program was to combine comedy, magic and drama. While no special, let alone a weekly series, was ever completed, there are bits and pieces of different segments of what Welles had in mind—both fragments of film that were shot and written notes of what Welles intended the TV spectacular to be.

Somewhere along the way, Greg Garrison's participation in the project ended and it became known as *Orson's Bag*, written, directed and produced by Welles. "Bag" was a popular term in the late '60s and early '70s, used to describe something that one did well. Based on documents in the Orson Welles-Oja Kodar Papers at the University of Michigan, the special had three main segments focusing on the cities of London, Vienna and Venice.[11]

Welles opens the program: "During the next 90 minutes there'll be very few magic tricks, I promise you. But if you've got a show, what do you do for an opening? We could have given you a line of dancing girls—you've seen that often. But have you ever seen the mystical levitation of a duck?"[12] Welles then performs the trick and goes to a commercial. After the commercial, he introduces his "Uncle Harry," a spry old gentleman talking like a young person in the 1960s. Welles delights in satirizing the youth movement by making fun of their hair, dress and music. Eighty-nine-year-old Uncle Harry greets Orson with a "Hi there, Orson baby!" and describes himself as a psychedelic senior citizen drop-out.

The next part deals with Orson's London tour. Welles plays Winston Churchill in silhouette, responding to questions from various individuals with Churchillian witticisms. For example, in reply to a question about the desirable qualifications to become a politician, Welles (as Churchill) responds "The ability to foretell what is going to happen tomorrow and next week, next month and next year. And to have the ability afterwards to explain why it didn't happen." Replying to a question about what he thinks of America, Churchill remarks, "Toilet paper too thin, newspapers too thick." Then a young guide giving a tour of London and trying to find Carnaby Street, encounters Welles as a variety of characters: a bobby, an old lady selling flowers as well as "dirty" postcards, an Oriental man enticing customers into a strip club, and a one-man band. When the guide finally gets to Carnaby Street, he removes his bowler, revealing shoulder-length blonde hair. There is then a bit with Orson playing elderly English men at a club, drinking whiskey and talking about the young generation. Part of the conversation goes as follows:

> Gentleman One: "If we were bored, we didn't stand around listening to gramophones, waiting for our hair to grow."
> Gentleman Two: "We went off and fought in France."
> Gentleman One: "We didn't have any gramophones."
> Gentleman Two: "There weren't any."
> Gentleman One: "No gramophones. Had to play our records on the sewing machine."

Welles next takes the viewer on a tour of a stately English manor that is open to the public. After Lord Plumfield (Welles) introduces his son, wife and butler, he says that he would like to sell the manor house since his family currently resides in the guard house in front of the manor.

In the final part of the London tour, Welles enters a tailor shop to be measured for a new suit. Tailors Johnson and Mapleton make caustic comments about Welles' size. Welles remarks to the audience that our English cousins do have a knack of giving us a bit of an inferiority complex.

The program's second segment involves a tour of Vienna, the setting for the Welles-starring film *The Third Man*. He describes Vienna as the grand capital of sweetness—sweet things to listen to, sweet things to look at (i.e., women) and sweet things to eat (a variety of pastries is shown). In part of the script for this segment, Welles reflects on *The Third Man* with a Ferris wheel in the background like the one from the film:

> Once upon a time an actor was somebody who mattered—in show business, where else. This was before the pop singers came down upon us in their ravening hordes, when you could make it as a star without hooking yourself up to an electric guitar. Actors like Garbo and Gable were superstars for years.
>
> I was a superstar myself for about twelve and a half minutes. Not quite as long as it takes you to ride on that Ferris wheel.
>
> My theme song ... that was what did it. *The Third Man*, I didn't sing or dance it or whistle. They just played it on the soundtrack while I lurked about ... the Viennese sewers. No success story was ever more richly underserved.

Welles then explores the idea that spies are still operating in Vienna and becomes part of a spy spoof with the *Mission: Impossible* theme playing in the background as Mickey Rooney kidnaps beautiful Senta Berger with Welles rescuing her from a sack and comedian Arte Johnson saying his *Laugh-In* catchphrase: "Very interesting."

In the third segment, which deals with Venice, Welles plays Shylock from *The Merchant of Venice*. He introduces this part as follows:

> I'll tell you why we've come here to Venice—it's to fulfill a lifelong ambition.... Each man, according to Shakespeare, in his time plays many parts. Well, every actor likes to play as many of the great Shakespeare parts as he can manage.... What we're going to do for you now is our own special adaptation for TV of the most important scenes featuring that character. We call it "The Shylock Story."

The segment would have run between 30 and 40 minutes but was never completed because the negatives went missing. In 1969, CBS withdrew their funding for *Orson's Bag* over his long-running dispute with the IRS concerning his tax status. Welles did try to complete his version of *The Merchant of Venice* with his own money.

In 1978, Welles' final attempt at producing his own weekly series was a 90-minute pilot titled *The Orson Welles Show*, a combination talk-variety show with guests Burt Reynolds, the Muppets and Angie Dickinson. For most of the show, Welles had the studio audience interview Reynolds based on questions the actor-producer had scripted for them. During these segments, Welles mainly smokes his cigar, introduces commercial breaks and occasionally comments on the questions asked Reynolds. Both stars are dressed in black suits and red shirts. Following the Reynolds segments, Welles engages in patter with the Muppets, primarily Kermit the Frog and Fonzie Bear. He then performs a magic trick called "The Legend of the Mummy's Curse" where a woman is placed in a gilded mummy case with metal plates inserted into the case. Her midsection disappears, but she is intact when she is extracted from the case. In the next segment, Welles talks with Frank Oz and Jim Henson, the creator of the Muppets, about how they became puppeteers. In the final part, Angie Dickinson assists Welles with a card trick and then helps him with a feat of legerdemain, holding a revolver and playing Russian roulette. As Dickinson fires the gun at him, Welles, dressed as a Chinese magician and blindfolded, says he is able to foretell which bullet in the handgun is live ammunition. Of course, he predicts correctly or else the pilot would have had the most morbid ending in the history of television. He ends the show reciting a poem titled "Jenny." G.G. Spelvin directed the pilot, which was produced by Idiom Productions.

Welles tried to sell his show to one of the networks. According to him, the networks said the talk show "was too strange for the May sweeps..."[13]

In early 1978, *Variety* indicated that Welles would host a one-hour dramatic adventure series called *Great American Short Stories*, created and produced by Robert Halmi. The prime time show would be syndicated to local stations through the Hughes TV network and sponsored by the Liberty Mutual Insurance Company. Filmed on location in Northern California, the initial show was titled "Calloway's Climb" with Patrick O'Neal and Mariette Hartley. Mort Fine wrote the script with Paul Stanley directing. The pilot, about husband and wife (O'Neal and Hartley) having marital problems, helping to rescue young climbers in trouble, and eventually reconciling after the wife saves the husband from a difficult situation on the mountains, did eventually air on local stations in August and September 1978. However, Welles did not host, and no episodes were made beyond the pilot.

Resuming his association with producer Greg Garrison in 1978, Welles was to preside over a series profiling various performers to be called *A Closer Look*. This initiative seems to have been an outgrowth of Welles hosting a special produced by Garrison about NBC's 50th anniversary which aired on November 21, 1976. The 90-minute pilot for this first-run syndicated series was evidently never made.

In the late '70s, Paramount purchased the rights to Rex Stout's *Nero*

Wolfe novels hoping to have Welles star as the cranky, overweight, agoraphobic detective. Welles initially turned down the offer, and actor Thayer David starred in a pilot for the proposed ABC series. ABC did not pick up the pilot. Paramount subsequently sold NBC a mystery series based on the *Nero Wolfe* stories. The show was a midseason replacement beginning January 16, 1981, starring William Conrad as the rotund, reclusive sleuth. However, again NBC and Paramount had wanted Welles for the lead. NBC entertainment head Brandon Tartikoff indicated that Welles would play the detective if the scripts met his approval. However, by the end of 1980, it was clear that Welles had no interest in playing that character on a weekly basis.

In the 1970s and 1980s, Welles did star on three television series as host or narrator, but he wasn't involved in the production of any of these shows. He took the jobs to raise money for his own personal projects. The first of these series was *Orson Welles' Great Mysteries* (1973–74), originally titled *The Clock*, for the British ITV network. He hosted 26 episodes produced by Anglia TV. In 1981, Welles narrated a six-part, one-hour series for the Canadian Broadcasting Corporation, *Jack London's Tales of the Klondike*. The premiere episode "The One Thousand Dozen" concerned a man who carries 1000 dozen eggs to the Klondike Gold Rush thinking that he'll make a small fortune. After weeks of travel, he arrives and finds that the eggs have gone rotten. *Variety* said that the Klondike scenes were riveting and the acting good but the narration by Orson Welles, "while topnotch, was too much—leaving the performers not all that much to do."[14]

In 1984, Welles hosted *Scene of the Crime,* which NBC said would be TV's first interactive mystery show. In this whodunit, Welles introduced suspects, summarized the clues and then invited the audience to solve the murder before he revealed the true culprit. Hosting this series did not take much of his time since he could film his introductions and endings wherever he happened to be. As he commented, "I'm really just a small part of the show. But I hope it sells."[15] The series lasted for five episodes and was his final appearance as a regular on a TV series. Welles passed away in 1985.

Mae West

There was no one quite like Mae West. In the 1930s, her bawdiness and sensuality on the big screen made most women blush, men fantasize, and the "protectors of the moral order" irate. Her show business career started in burlesque, went on to vaudeville, and then Broadway where she wrote and starred in her big hit play, *Diamond Lil*. Her movie career began in 1932 with a supporting role in *Night After Night* with George Raft as the owner of a speakeasy. The following year she was the lead in *She Done Him Wrong* with Cary Grant, a reworking of *Diamond Lil*. In *I'm No Angel* (1933), West again appeared with Grant, this time playing a burlesque performer who falls in love with a wealthy man. Other iconic movies from her heyday include *Klondike Annie* (1936) playing a kept woman who kills her keeper in self-defense and flees to Alaska, and *My Little Chickadee* (1940) with W.C. Fields, a comedy-western where her character was a Chicago singer traveling to the wild West to meet relatives.

Few actresses have created and lived their movie image throughout their lifetime as thoroughly as Mae West did. She became the quintessential vamp both on and off screen. A female character, irresistible to men, who freely admitted that she liked sex, West never changed this persona even through her "golden" years.

West was the queen of the double entendre with such aphorisms as "A hard man is good to find" and "Is that a gun in your pocket, or are you just glad to see me?" Her 1930s movies were all heavily censored by the Production Code in effect at the time.

By today's standards, West was not a typical sex symbol. She was small in stature—about 5'5"—with ample breasts and somewhat plump. However, special costumes and photography made her appear more glamorous than she really was. Her works, be they stage productions or movies, were usually censored in some form, and so it is perhaps not surprising that she never had her own TV series despite numerous attempts.

West also caused a furor on radio in the 1930s when she guest starred on NBC's *The Chase and Sanborn Hour* with ventriloquist Edgar Bergen and his wooden dummy Charlie McCarthy. Here is an excerpt:

West: "I like a man that takes his time. Why don't you come home with me? I'll let you play in my woodpile... You're all wood and a yard long. You weren't so nervous and backward when you came up to see me at my apartment. In fact, you didn't need much encouragement to kiss me."

Charlie: "Did I do that?"

West: "You certainly did and I got marks to prove it, and splinters too..."[1]

On the same show, there was a sketch set in the Garden of Eden with Mae playing Eve, Don Ameche as Adam and Charlie McCarthy as the snake, with the idea that it was Eve who tempted the snake to give her the forbidden apple rather than the other way around. That Sunday, December 12, 1937, broadcast caused an uproar in the country with an official FCC investigation and a demand for a Congressional probe. In the end, no official action was taken.

In the 1950s, West attempted to become a TV star. Commenting about a possible series, she remarked, "It will keep Dad home at least once a week."[2] Several proposals were made, but evidently none resulted in a pilot being produced. Given that most of these proposals occurred during the conservative 1950s, one can probably understand why they never resulted in a series. While West took credit for developing most of these proposals, as others have pointed out, she never liked to attribute her screenplays or other ideas to anyone else such as ghostwriters or script doctors.[3]

One of her ideas was to adapt *Diamond Lil* as a television special. The play had been filmed as *She Done Him Wrong*, but to get past the censors the characters were modified. For example, some of the characters were changed from Hispanic to Russian, and a white slavery storyline in the play was changed to a counterfeiting ring for the film. Mae's undated teleplay resurrects the Hispanic characters and white slavery plot.[4]

Diamond Lil (West) performs at Gus Jordan's Bowery Place in New York City and lives in an apartment upstairs. Jordan, who is running for county sheriff, is the boss of the Bowery and a power in the city's politics. Dan Flynn, Gus' rival for political power and for Lil's affections, tells Spider Kane, who works for Jordan and is loyal to Lil, about Rita Christina, a Latino who has shady business dealings with Gus involving white slavery. A distraught woman named Sally comes into Jordan's place. At Jordan's urging, Lil talks to Sally and learns that she has been taken advantage of by a married man. Lil convinces Sally to go with Rita to South America, not knowing that Rita and Jordan are white slavers.

Lil is attracted to tall, handsome Capt. Cummings, who works for the

Salvation Army trying to improve the lives of Bowery residents. He asks about Sally. Eventually, Lil tells him that she went to Rio. Cummings admits that he might be attracted to Lil.

Cummings is revealed to actually be an undercover police officer investigating Jordan and arrests him for white slavery. In the end, Cummings confesses that he is mad about Lil. The teleplay probably had too much sex and violence for it to be broadcast on 1950s network TV.

Famous Women of History, also known as *Great Romances of History*, was another idea that West developed, along with movie director Paul H. Sloane, for TV in 1953. It was to be a half-hour comedy anthology series to be produced by William LeBaron with West playing her own version of famous historical characters. Of course, all of the characters she would have portrayed would simply have been variations on her legendary Diamond Lil. LeBaron had helped to produce, among other movies, West's *She Done Him Wrong*. Each show would begin with a travelogue describing the setting and background for the episode with a narrator giving a straight version of the story and Mae saying: "History is a fake! I'll show you what really happened."[5]

One of the episodes would have had West playing Catherine the Great of Russia. West participates in an introduction with a man playing a travel guide showing the Winter Palace and discussing the men surrounding Czarina Catherine after the death of her husband Peter the Great. As Mae says in an outline of the proposed episode, "Catherine would never have been called great if she hadn't told the men what to do."[6] The episode then transitions to Catherine's antechamber with characters talking about the recent demise of Peter. In her bedroom, Catherine is having her hair styled by a French hairdresser, Maurice. She asks Maurice what people are saying about her at Court.

> Maurice: "The men talk of nothing but the best way to be noticed by you—they make wagers on who is next."
> Catherine (West): "Oh, my! I should hate to think I am the cause of gambling."
> Maurice: "And the ladies, your majesty—oh, they are jealous. They say you take all the men."
> Catherine: "All the men! Ridiculous! I haven't that much time."[7]

Other famous women West would have played in this TV effort were Cleopatra, Ann of Cleaves, Fatima, Bluebeard's eighth wife and Lady Godiva.

As reported in the August 21, 1958, issue of *Variety*, a Mae West TV series titled *Klondike Lil* was proposed by Robert Alexander Productions, the company owned by actor Steve Cochran, a friend of Mae's. Robert Schwartz would co-produce and Robert Stevens was to write the pilot script with Cochran directing. The actress would play an adventuress in the Alaskan gold country. Segments were to be filmed in Dawson, Alaska, including meetings of the International Yukon Order of Pioneers and the International Sourdough Association. In December 1958, this project was described as a movie and not a TV series for West where her character becomes involved romantically and politically with the English and Russian ambassadors who visit Dawson in 1896. Supposedly, Cary Grant and Randolph Scott would make cameo appearances in the feature, but nothing appears to have ever been filmed.

Another proposed TV series focused on a character, much like the ones she played in her movies, named Glory Carter, a blonde singer and sex goddess who leaves New York for the Wild West. Three treatments were developed for this comedy-drama. Of particular note is that they were "written for" West by "Dahl Lee Lyons" and not by West herself. And so who is Ms. Lyons? Dahl Lee Lyons appears to be the pen name of Dolly Lyons Dempsey, a longtime fan of Mae West's and the first president of her fan club.

In the first treatment, Glory is on a train headed to Gold City where she will live and perform at the Golden Bar saloon run by handsome Brandt Callahan.[8] Also on the train are wholesome-looking Jim Hall and a good-looking Latino named Jose Gonzales. The train is held up by a gang, and the conductor thinks someone on the train was in on the robbery since the bandits knew about a safe full of cash in the baggage car. When the train finally arrives in Gold City, Brandt Callahan is waiting for Glory along with the local sheriff, Jeb Winters. Upon meeting the sheriff, Glory remarks, "Mmmm, any more like you at home!" The sheriff responds, "Yes ma'm, six brothers, and we're really just about alike." To which Glory says, "Mmmm, one for every day of the week!"

Some time after her arrival, Jim Hall, who is enamored with Glory, gives her a diamond bracelet. Later, Glory invites the sheriff to her room and tells him to hide when Hall arrives for a visit. Hall gives Glory another gift, a necklace. Glory says that her maid had been carrying her jewelry bag on the train when it was stolen and the necklace is hers. The sheriff then appears and arrests Hall as head of the gang of thieves. As the sheriff leaves, Glory says, "Come up and see me some time!"

If this treatment of the Glory Carter character had become a series, later episodes would have revealed that Glory came to Gold City with a map of a fabulous gold-digging area given to her by her boyfriend in New York right before he was murdered to obtain the document.

The second treatment for the Glory character was called "Portrait of a Lady" dated September 16, 1958.[9] In this treatment, Glory is appearing at the

Golden Bar saloon, owned by Brandt Callahan but located in the Klondike. She had left New York after Mike Morelli, a Tammany Hall boss with whom she had been involved, was murdered. Other characters in this treatment were Capt. Fitzgerald, in charge of the local Royal Canadian Mounted Police detachment, and Bridgie, Glory's maid.

One night, Big Jim Dyer enters the bar drunk, asking to see Glory. The patrons say that Jim has never been the same since his son Tim, an artist, was paralyzed in an accident. Jim leaves the bar after being told that Glory will not be performing until later that night. A few minutes later, Bridgie bursts into the bar saying that Glory has been kidnapped by a large man. Brandt, Fitzgerald and others go after Jim and Glory. At Jim's cabin, Dyer threatens to shoot anyone who enters his house. After about 20 minutes, Jim opens the door and says he kidnapped Glory for his son. His son had painted Glory when he was in New York and yearned to see her again. Glory promises Tim that she will come back when the weather is warmer and pose for him on a bear rug, saying, "I had a picture of me once, when I was a kid, lying on a bear rug.... I think I could do a lot more for that rug now!" Eventually, the portrait of the Mae West character "in all her glory" is hung above the bar in the saloon.

The final treatment featuring Glory Carter, "The Lady and the Lawman," dated October 14, 1958, is set in Seattle, the jumping-off point for those going to the Klondike gold fields.[10] We see a newspaper with the headline, "Police Still Seek Morelli Killers," and the sub-headline, "Glory Carter, Blonde Actress Friend of Slain Man, Also Sought as Possible Witness to Killing."

Joe Keene and Mack Wilson, who killed Morelli, are in Seattle looking to do the same to Glory because she witnessed Morelli's murder. Mack and Joe want to be on the same ship as Glory, who is going to the Klondike. Also on the ship is Capt. Jeffrey St. John, a Royal Canadian Northwest Mounted Police officer who, like all of West's heroes naturally, is handsome. Commenting on their Klondike destination, Carter's maid Bridgie says that, according to Capt. St. John, "the nights are six months long!" Glory replies, "Mmmm, a girl would certainly have to think twice before invitin' a gent over for the evening!"

Bridgie says that she has seen two men shadowing Glory. Glory asks Bridgie to find Capt. St. John. When Bridgie exits the cabin, she is knocked unconscious by Mack and Joe, and the two take Glory at gunpoint to the deserted deck. They then happen to encounter Capt. St. John. Glory surreptitiously gives St. John a copy of a wanted poster for the two killers. St. John tackles Joe, while Glory hits Mack over the head with a marlin spike.

There were no pilots, let alone a series, with Mae West as Glory Carter.

Other proposed TV projects among the Mae West collection at the Margaret Herrick Library include a list of episode titles for what appears to be a possible Mae West comedy series.¹¹ The titles for proposed installments were "Mae West Meets Hercules," "Mae West Meets Mark Anthony," "Mae West and Santa Claus" (which if made may have ruined Santa Claus's image for millions of children), "Mae West and Paladin" (Paladin was the main character in the Richard Boone TV Western *Have Gun, Will Travel*) and, the best title, or worst, depending on one's perspective, "Mae West and Matt Drillem" (a take-off on the Matt Dillon character from *Gunsmoke*).

In 1958, West attempted to make a deal for a show with Los Angeles TV station KCOP. *Mae West Tells All About Love* was to be a daily ten-minute segment with the actress responding to letters sent to her concerning love, sex and relationships in her unique style. The show was to be syndicated to other stations across the country, but ultimately KCOP rejected the project. West shopped the series to CBS which also passed on it.

Two years later, in 1960, newspapers reported that West was going to appear on a syndicated TV series, *At Home with Mae West*. While there is no documentation in the Margaret Herrick Library's Mae West collection about a series with that title, there is information about a proposed show called *Come Up and See Me Sometime* which would supposedly emanate from the actress' home or at least a TV studio facsimile of it. Trying to become a TV personality, West proposed co-hosting a series with a Dr. Phil–type psychologist named Dr. Harry Hoffman.¹²

The projected 30-minute show would find answers to the problems of everyday life based on the experiences of West and the knowledge of Dr. Hoffman. The setting was a room in West's home that she called the "consultatorium"—a room outfitted with several couches and chairs designed to make the subject feel relaxed. West's Filipino servant, Wellington, introduced the guest subject who, in the treatment for the series, was a shy, sensitive young man named Bob whose problem is that he is nervous around women. Bob begins discussing his relationship with Betty, a girl he likes. Bob's interaction with Betty is then dramatized, showing how tentative he is in talking with her. Their conversation is interrupted when Betty's friend Andy stops by. Andy is much more forthcoming with his thoughts around her, and, instead of Bob and Betty doing something together as a couple, Andy invites both of them to go to a café with him. While Bob is sitting in a booth by himself, Andy and Betty dance.

Back in the "consultatorium," West says that Bob has an inferiority complex, while Dr. Hoffman advises Bob on how he should change his behavior. The doctor explains that Bob needs to visualize himself meeting any situation with positive action, to see himself behaving confidently. There is then a dramatization of the "new" Bob being more assured in situations with Betty.

In the closing, West and Hoffman mention the types of common neuroses that will be demonstrated on future shows. West ends the program with the signature line, "Come up and see me sometime—anytime. The sooner, the better." As with her other TV proposals, this one never resulted in a series.

In May 1963, West tried to sell an animated TV series based on her character which she would voice. The show was to be called *Pretty Mae*. Former long-time Disney animator Jack Kinney received a call from West's agent asking if he would like to animate the proposed series. According to Kinney's book,

> we had story meetings with her at our studio, and even dropped in to see her in her penthouse atop her Ravenswood apartments, in her white-and-gold bedroom complete with circular bed, mirrored ceiling and pet spider monkeys. She indeed was a real lady. She believed in proper diet, exercise, and no booze or tobacco. She had a delightful personality and a great gag and story sense, very clean dialogue and speech, only innuendo, a real pleasure to work with.
>
> But, alas, as happens so often in Hollywood, a contract couldn't be negotiated and the deal fell through.[13]

Mae West made very few TV appearances during her career. In 1959 she was supposed to be a guest on the CBS interview show *Person to Person*, but it was never broadcast. West's responses to questions were deemed too bawdy. Probably her most memorable TV appearance was on the comedy *Mister Ed* where she played herself in the March 15, 1964, episode "Mae West Meets Ed." The talking horse overhears his owner, architect Wilbur Post, say how posh West's horse stables are, and goes to her house wanting to be adopted. She gives the horse a bubble bath.

West was to star on another episode of *Mister Ed*, "Mae Goes West," but that appearance never happened. However, a script was written for her second guest shot during the 1964–65 season in which West would first appear in modern dress when she calls Wilbur to approve his designs for an addition to her stables. Ed then relates the story of how a horse was responsible for the 1849 California gold rush. In the story, West would have played Lady Belle, owner of a high-class gambling casino near Sutter's Mill, California, where gold had been discovered. (The name Lady Belle was reminiscent of West's *My Little Chickadee* character name, Flower Belle Lee.) It appears that health problems prevented the 71-year-old actress from making her second *Mister Ed* appearance.

West starred in two last movies, *Myra Breckinridge* (1970) and *Sextette* (1978), neither of which was well-received by either audiences or critics. Sometimes, movie legends should leave fans with their memories and not attempt a comeback. Reportedly, while filming *Sextette*, "Mae was crotchety, snappy with her designers, uncomfortable with the gowns and immense wigs,

Mae West's only appearance on a TV sitcom was in an episode of *Mister Ed*. To the right of West are Mister Ed and his owner Wilbur Post (Alan Young). *Mister Ed* producer-director Arthur Lubin, a longtime friend of West, convinced her to guest star on the series.

unable to remember her lines, unable to carry out simple movements like hitting an elevator button. Lines had to be fed to her via a concealed radio headphone..."[14] Not willing to wear eyeglasses on-camera, West had to follow a crew member crawling on the floor in front of her, out of sight, to hit her marks during the filming. She was 85 at the time. West passed away on November 22, 1980, at age 87.

Esther Williams

Very few movie stars can be credited with introducing their own genre or subgenre of films. One who did is Esther Williams. During her movie career, she acted in a few standard comedies and dramas such as *Andy Hardy's Double Life* and *A Guy Named Joe*, but she is best remembered for her aquamusicals. *Neptune's Daughter* (1949), *Pagan Love Song* (1950), *Million Dollar Mermaid* (1952) and *Dangerous When Wet* (1953) featured elaborate swimming and diving performances. After all, Williams had been a champion swimmer as a teenager in the 1930s. Her film performances brought about the introduction of synchronized swimming as an Olympic event. Her persona as a female athlete and actress influenced her attempted television series.

Describing her planned venture into series TV in 1958, Williams explained, "I don't want to be a fad—on for a year or two. You don't get a chance for a second series as a rule. Losing a series must be like losing a baby—you lose heart." Williams actually hired a research firm to survey people on what type of series they wanted her to star in.

> They talked to from 6000 to 8000 people in this survey. They tell me I'm identified with a happy, wholesome type of entertainment, and on the basis of what we learned in the survey I'm almost transposing what my picture career was to TV. ... Sponsors want a show with strong sponsorship identification, and we've already been approached by sponsors who want a show which has a natural wholesome, athletic background, as ours will have.[1]

The actress also thought that having a weekly series might boost sales of the International Swimming Pool Company which marketed her pools. Williams was president of the firm.

A weekly outdoorsy comedy-drama anthology series was created for Williams. The actress would host each episode and act in every other episode. In describing the potential NBC series, she indicated that she would play three different roles in the episodes on which she would appear:

> The entire series will be thematic—it will all be based on outdoor life, whether I'm in them or not. I'll play a Lake Arrowhead social director, a city playground supervisor and a third Americana role that hasn't been developed yet. We go into full production in February and will be on the air in September. I've already seen to the writing of the first 17 scripts, by which I mean I've provided them with the springboard for 17 stories.[2]

Herbert B. Swope, Jr., was the executive producer for Twentieth Century-Fox, and the pilot, to be filmed in February 1959, would be written by Robert and Edith Soderberg. But in March 1959, Williams canceled her deal with Fox, saying that other production companies were interested in her TV series ideas. At the time, she related that she and Martin Manulis, head of Fox's TV division, had agreed on a series format, but that when the contract was drawn, the approach that had been proposed was missing. "They're still acting like a big picture studio," she remarked, "little knowing or caring that flexibility is the key to TV. Their terms were so rigid that I would have been hampered in everything I wanted to do."[3]

In 1960, the actress, still pursuing a TV series, indicated that she was interested in doing a 30-minute show in Europe where she would operate a health club. Evidently, nothing came of this idea. Also in that year, her swimming pool company declared bankruptcy after four years in operation. Williams claimed that she was just a figurehead and did not really run the company.

In the early '60s, Williams tried again with a comedy series where she would portray Ellen Barnes, a physical education instructor at Porter College.[4] Her responsibilities included training a swimming team. Ellen lived with her bother Bert, who owned a profitable real estate and insurance business, and his wife Sally, who frequently arranged dates for Ellen. The Barneses had three kids, eight-year-old Ronnie, 14-year-old Penny and 18-year-old Tommy, who was in the Air Force.

Ellen's friends included Dr. Frank Cole, a dedicated orthopedic physician, Barry Longstreet, a Porter College professor who taught Ancient History, and Harriet Wallace, an Associate Home Economics professor and Ellen's best friend. There was discussion of airing the pilot as an episode of *Mrs. C Goes to College* which starred Gertrude Berg, but that never happened.

Williams' final appearance as an actress on a TV series was on a 1960 installment of *Dick Powell's Zane Grey Theater*. Her devotion to physical fitness paid off: She lived to be 91, passing away in 2013.

Shelley Winters

Regarded as a "blonde bombshell" when she started in films, Shelley Winters quickly became a respected dramatic actress. Her breakout role was that of a victim of an insane stage actor (Ronald Colman) in 1947's *A Double Life*. She went on to appear in *The Great Gatsby* (1949), *Winchester '73* (1950) and *A Place in the Sun* (1951). Winters won Best Supporting Actress Oscars for *The Diary of Anne Frank* (1959) and *A Patch of Blue* (1965). The actress' movie career extended into the 1990s. To later generations, she was probably best remembered for her role in 1972's *The Poseidon Adventure,* playing a former Olympic swimmer, and for her 1990s appearances on TV's *Roseanne*, as Roseanne's grandmother.

The actress thought of becoming a TV series regular in the 1970s, as she matured and as movie roles for her dwindled. One of her first potential vehicles was the comedy *The Shelley Winters Show*, with Winters as the head of a cosmetics company. It was written by Bob Kaufman and Steve Pritzker and to be produced by Kaufman. Winters wanted the pilot to be shot before a studio audience. A script was written but no pilot was ever filmed. Reflecting on this endeavor, Pritzker said, "I don't recall much about the project other than meeting Shelley Winters somewhere she was performing a play so we could decide if we wanted to work together on the pilot. She was a very big personality, used to being the center of attention."[1]

In the script, Winters would have played Shelley Redford, in charge of the St. Louis Cosmetics Company.[2] Her recently married 21-year-old daughter Stephanie wrote newspaper horoscopes, and her 19-year-old son Joshua studied at Washington University. At the firm, her secretary Diane Fertig was romantically linked with plant manager Tom Cunningham. Herb Waterman was the company's accountant. Shelley's husband Max had divorced her and left for Australia to pursue his dream of a music career.

Mike Pelligrini, a Trousdale Wax salesman, is visiting the company and asks Shelley to have dinner with him to discuss business. The next day, Shelley tells Diane that she and Mike had dinner but didn't talk about business, and so Shelley invites him to dine at her place. She hasn't had a date in 23 years and is concerned that Mike will make a pass at her. At dinner, Shelley informs

Mike that he is not going to be the supplier of the wax for her company. He realizes that she thinks his intentions toward her are all about making a sale and insists that she doesn't understand that he is a lonely salesman on the road all the time and just grateful that she invited him into her home. He says that the night before, he was more interested in her as a woman than as a buyer. Shelley softens her attitude toward him, and they agree that she will show him St. Louis over the weekend.

Winters' next attempt at a TV series was a pilot, *Big Rose: Double Trouble*, a CBS movie broadcast March 26, 1974. She starred as Rose Winters, a Los Angeles private eye. Like other movie stars contemplating series, Winters had mixed feelings. She wanted to remain active in her profession but was concerned about the commitment of time to a series. "The money is nice, and there's so little going on elsewhere. The movies aren't very much nowadays.... And there isn't much left of the Broadway stage. That only leaves TV. But, still, when you think about the work involved, it's scary."[3]

In a typical character role for her, Winters played a slightly overweight widow whose husband had passed away ten years ago. She does needlepoint, has a dog named Poukie, uses a camera concealed in her handbag to take photos of suspects, and has a secretary named Marian (Peggy Walton).

In the movie, originally titled *Winters & Mills*, Rose and her associate Ed Mills (Barry Primus), partners in the Winters-Mills Detective Agency, attempt to expose a team of con artists blackmailing wealthy contractor Mr. Gunther (Michael Constantine). Gunther was discovered with a woman named Nina (Joan Van Ark) when her husband Troy (Paul Mantee) and a friend unexpectedly returned home. The contractor witnesses Nina shoot Troy and has thus far paid $25,000, supposedly for Troy's hospital bills. Mills poses as a state legislator staying at the same hotel where Nina had met Gunther, while Rose tries to track down the swindlers. Rose and Mills discover that the con artists are using vacant houses to stage their cons and that Nina is really a flight attendant and her husband Troy a realtor. Troy's friend Blass (Paul Picerni) works at the hotel where Mills resides, identifying potential marks. Rose's police lieutenant friend (Lonny Chapman) locates the house that the swindlers will use, to set up Mills. However, this time when Troy comes home to find his wife with Mills, the gun Nina uses to shoot Troy contains real bullets. Nina is arrested for Troy's murder, but Mills finds that Gunther had put live ammunition in the gun after he found the real estate office where Troy worked.

The characters in the pilot, written by Andy Lewis and directed by Paul Krasny, were based on ones created by famed mystery writer Erle Stanley

Gardner of *Perry Mason* fame. Under the pseudonym A.A. Fair, Gardner wrote a series of crime novels about a widowed, overweight private detective Bertha Cool and her partner Donald Lam. Writer Andy Lewis recalls writing "a pretty good pilot, but that as things continued it was rewritten (as often happens) by someone or other at Universal and that everything I felt was sharp or distinctive in my script was carefully smoothed into mediocrity."[4] Despite this or maybe because of it, CBS ordered additional scripts for *Big Rose* as a possible midseason replacement series for 1974–75, but no additional episodes were ever made.

Reminiscing about *Big Rose*, co-star Barry Primus indicated that he knew Winters from the Actors Studio where she was one of his teachers.

> She suggested and got me the part opposite her in *Big Rose*…. It was dramatic but had a comic side to it. It was kind of in the style of those '30s and '40s movies of detectives that would be played by someone like Myrna Loy. A lot of it was shot in a hotel in Century City over a period of two weeks. I arrived to meet the producers, got cast, and didn't go home for the first week until we started shooting at Twentieth Century. Shelley was wonderful to work with and I don't think that she was up to doing a television series, which would have meant keeping a real schedule. Shelley, I believe, turned down the offer to make a series of it, so it only showed as a two-hour movie. She was a great colorful character and kind of an emotional genius.[5]

During the 1980s, Winters explored other opportunities for her own series. She thought of having the Neil Simon play *Gingerbread Lady* turned into a series with her in the lead role. Having successfully starred in the play on the road, she thought that it could serve as the basis for a television show. In 1983, Winters contemplated becoming a talk show host on a series to be called *Shelley's Place* to be produced by Imeno Fiorentino Associates. (Imeno Fiorentino was a lighting designer who sought to expand his business into TV production.)

In Winters' final endeavor at a series, she returned to comedy. *Shelley* (1986) was a comedy pilot written by Michael and Jake Weinberger and directed by Peter Bonerz. Winters took on the role of a wife and grandmother who had retired and, with her husband Mike (Harry Guardino), adopted three children. Lee Garlington played Paula, the couple's biological daughter; the children they adopted were Margie (Laura Jacoby), Nick (Christian Hoff) and Danny (Brandon Cal). The Landsburg Company produced the pilot for CBS.

According to Bonerz, Winters had some difficulty working with the multi-camera set-up for sitcoms. However, he recalls that she was a dedicated and talented actress who, when the pilot was completed, gave him a copy of her autobiography with very kind and generous words of thanks. "She also gave me the shirt off her back. Literally, she took the Actors Studio T-shirt off and gave it to me."[6]

Winters' last film role was in the 1999 Italian picture *La Bomba,* about three actors attending the Actors Studio who decide to set up an extortion plan playing real mobsters. The actress appeared in the feature with one of her former husbands, Vittorio Gassman. Winters died at age 85 in 2006.

Chapter Notes

Preface

1. Philip K. Scheuer, "Moviedom's Top Stars Tell Why They Shun Television Parts," *Los Angeles Times*, March 20, 1960.
2. Dave Kaufman, "On All Channels," *Variety*, October 15, 1957.
3. Scheuer, "Moviedom's Top Stars," *Los Angeles Times*.

Introduction

1. Lloyd Shearer, "Why So Few Women Stars on TV?" *Independent Star-News* (Pasadena, CA), November 11, 1962.

Fred Astaire and Ginger Rogers

1. Dave Kaufman, "On All Channels," *Variety*, December 13, 1961.
2. Army Archerd, "Just for Variety," *Variety*, May 24, 1961.
3. "Astaire's 1st TV Situation Comedy Series, for Revue," *Variety*, December 3, 1963.
4. Roger Perry, private communication with author, May 10, 2016.
5. Quoted in Peter J. Levinson, *Puttin' on The Ritz: Fred Astaire and the Fine Art of Panache* (New York: St. Martin's Press, 2009), 337.
6. Ron Friedman, "*The Fred Astaire Show*: Presentation for a New TV Series," undated, TV Script Collection, Popular Culture Library, Bowling Green State University.
7. Rick Du Brow, "Fred Astaire to Be in Television Series," *Redlands Daily Press*, October 16, 1969.
8. Dave Kaufman, "On All Channels," *Variety*, April 5, 1955.
9. Dave Kaufman, "On All Channels," *Variety*, May 14, 1957.

Joan Blondell

1. Matthew Kennedy, *Joan Blondell: A Life Between Takes* (Jackson: University Press of Mississippi, 2007), 5.
2. Ibid., 194.
3. Ron Hussman, private communication with author, September 29, 2015.
4. Matthew Kennedy, *Joan Blondell*, 196.
5. Bill Persky, private communication with author, September 28, 2015.

Stephen Boyd

1. Joe Cushman, *Stephen Boyd: From Belfast to Hollywood*, FeedaRead.com Publishing, 2013, 150.

Claudette Colbert

1. "Claudette Colbert Just as Glad She Didn't Get TV Contract," *Newport Daily News*, September 2, 1954.
2. Ibid.
3. Ibid.
4. "Claudette Colbert Vows Never Again to Sign an Exclusive TV Pact," *Variety*, January 6, 1956.

Gary Cooper

1. Dave Glickman, "Hollywood Talent," *Broadcasting*, August 13, 1951.
2. Charles Mercer, "Gary Cooper to Turn Down Show," *Lubbock Avalanche-Journal*, July 21, 1957.

Joan Crawford

1. "Makes TV Offer," *Broadcasting*, February 11, 1952.
2. "Joan Crawford Leery of Full Pierce Series," *Variety*, May 5, 1953.
3. Dave Kaufman, "On All Channels," *Variety*, November 13, 1953.
4. "Crawford Eyes Telepix Re-Runs for Future Cushion; Says Bing Wrong," *Variety*, February 10, 1954.

5. Dave Kaufman, "On All Channels," *Variety*, August 13, 1954.
6. Dave Kaufman, "On All Channels," *Variety*, June 26, 1956.
7. "Joan Crawford Up for Own Vidseries," *Variety*, October 8, 1958.
8. Dave Kaufman, "On All Channels," *Variety*, July 3, 1962.
9. Connie Bruck, *When Hollywood Had a King: The Reign of Lew Wasserman, Who Leveraged Talent into Power and Influence* (New York: Random House, 2003), 471.

Bette Davis

1. Whitney Stine, *Mother Goddam: The Story of the Career of Bette Davis* (New York: Hawthorn Books, 1974), 7.
2. Christine Becker, *It's the Pictures That Got Small* (Middletown, CT: Wesleyan University Press, 2008), 67.
3. Whitney Stine, *Mother Goddam*, 267.
4. Marie Torre, "Out of the Air," *The Evening Review* (East Liverpool, OH), March 25, 1958.
5. Davey Davison Silverman, private communication with author, September 14, 2015.
6. Ibid.
7. Barry Oringer, private communication with author, September 8, 2015.
8. Joan van Ark, private communication with author, October 18, 2015.
9. Whitney Stine, *Mother Goddam*, 335.
10. Dick Kleiner, "Young Actors Lose, Bette Says," *The Wheeling Herald* (Wheeling, IL), 1973.
11. James Brolin, "Perfectionism and Beauty of the Spirit Make Bette Davis a Legend," *Detroit Free Press*, August 27, 1983.

Irene Dunne

1. "Irene Dunne Says Filming TV Is Exciting as Movies," *Herald and News* (Klamath Falls, OR), April 15, 1952.
2. Frank Galen, "*Vanity and Mrs. Fair* TV Script," undated, Ann Morrison Chapin Papers 1922–1980s, UCLA Library Special Collections.
3. Hal Humphrey, "Viewing TV," *Oakland Tribune*, January 28, 1962.

Nelson Eddy and Jeanette MacDonald

1. Edward Baron Turk, *Hollywood Diva: A Biography of Jeanette MacDonald* (Berkeley: University of California Press, 1998), 301.

Douglas Fairbanks, Jr.

1. "Fairbanks Mulls 'Gaucho,' Flock of Other TV Entries," *Variety*, October 31, 1956.

Jose Ferrer

1. "Royal Performance Program Idea," undated, Gloria Swanson Papers, Harry Ransom Humanities Research Center, University of Texas at Austin.
2. Bernard Slade, "*Everything Money Can't Buy* TV Script," Revised Third Draft, February 15, 1974, TV Script Collection, Popular Culture Library, Bowling Green State University.
3. Jose Ferrer, "Out of ABC's 'Money' Show," *Variety*, June 4, 1974.
4. Tom Hallick, private communication with author, May 25, 2016.

Geraldine Fitzgerald

1. Sidney Carroll, "*The Quinns* Revised TV Script," February 2, 1976, Sidney Carroll Papers 1957–1981, UCLA Library Special Collections.
2. John Pasquin, private communication with author, May 9, 2016.
3. Pat H. Broeske, "Full Circle," *The Los Angeles Times*, May 3, 1987.

Joan Fontaine

1. Dave Kaufman, "On All Channels," *Variety*, May 10, 1955.
2. Robert McCullough, "Hollywood 'Stunt' Casting and TV Movies with Aaron Spelling," Where Hollywood Hides podcast, May 5, 2013.

Janet Gaynor

1. Ted Key, "*Emma's First National Bank*: A TV Comedy Series," undated, Ted Key Papers, Syracuse University Libraries.
2. Paul Gregory, private communication with author, September 8, 2015.
3. Helen Hayes, letter to Ted Key, March 11, 1965, provided by Peter Key.

Stewart Granger

1. Don Shiach, *Stewart Granger: The Last of the Swashbucklers* (London: Aurum Press, 2005), 227.

Kathryn Grayson

1. Peter H. Brown, "Lights, Cameras, Embrace! The Hollywood Love Scene," *Los Angeles Times*, December 23, 1979.
2. Erskine Johnson, "Hollywood Today," *Park City Daily News*, September 27, 1957.

Susan Hayward

1. "Doin' Television's More Fun than Makin' Movies," *The Robesonian* (Lumberton, NC), June 25, 1972.
2. Christopher P. Andersen, *A Star Is a Star, IS A STAR!* (Garden City, NY: Doubleday, 1980), 244–245.

Betty Hutton

1. George Rosen, "Liebman—Hutton's 300G Spec Bow Needed Spurs for Those Satins," *Variety*, September 15, 1954.
2. "Betty Hutton Quitting Show Biz at 33," *Variety*, September 28, 1954.
3. "TV Review: The Chevy Show," *Variety*, November 2, 1955.
4. Bert Granet, "Cassidy Collins and Complexes," undated, Bert Granet Papers, Margaret Herrick Library, Academy of Motion Picture Arts and Sciences.
5. Dave Kaufman, "On All Channels," *Variety*, September 26, 1956.
6. Steve Stevens, private communication with author, October 6, 2015.
7. Ibid.
8. Dave Kaufman, "On All Channels," *Variety*, July 19, 1957.
9. Mike Connolly, "Notes from Hollywood," *Pasadena Independent*, September 30, 1963.
10. Steve Stevens, private communication.

Van Johnson

1. Army Archerd, "Just for Variety," *Variety*, June 23, 1960.
2. John Fink, private communication with author, March 11, 2016.
3. Army Archerd, "Just for Variety," *Variety*, January 7, 1972.
4. Gail Parent, private communication with author, September 22, 2015.
5. Chris Thompson, "*The President of Love* (Pilot)," Second Draft, March 23, 1983, University of Illinois, Urbana-Champaign Script Collection.
6. Robert Peirce, private communication with author, September 4, 2015.

Buster Keaton

1. "Television Review: Buster Keaton Show," *Variety*, December 23, 1949.
2. Buster Keaton, "Format of T.V. Show (Comedy) entitled 'School of Acting,'" undated, Buster Keaton Papers, Margaret Herrick Library, Academy of Motion Picture Arts and Sciences.
3. "New Sales Approach," *Broadcasting*, February 8, 1960.
4. Ray Allen, *Medicine Man* Script Ideas, undated, Harry Ackerman Collection, American Heritage Center, University of Wyoming.

Alan Ladd

1. John L. Scott, "Alan Ladd Balances Three-Cornered Career," *Los Angeles Times,* July 21, 1957.
2. Vernon Scott, "Actor Alan Ladd Is Empire Building," *Pampa Daily News* (Pampa, TX), October 5, 1958.
3. Dave Kaufman, "On All Channels," *Variety*, January 2, 1959.
4. "Ladd Strictly Pix Man, Denies He'll Act in TV 'Saddle,'" *Variety*, January 6, 1960.

Hedy Lamarr

1. Stephen Michael Shearer, *Beautiful: The Life of Hedy Lamarr* (New York: St. Martin's Press, 2010), 1–2.
2. "TV Filming Abroad," *Broadcasting*, October 27, 1952.
3. John Fraser, *Close Up: An Actor Telling Tales* (London: Oberon Books, 2004), 106.
4. Dave Kaufman, "On All Channels," *Variety*, October 8, 1957.

Janet Leigh

1. Michelangelo Capua, *Janet Leigh: A Biography* (Jefferson, NC: McFarland, 2013), 122.
2. Leonard Gershe, "*The Janet Leigh Show* TV Script*,*" 1967, Leonard Gershe Papers 1944–2000, UCLA Library Special Collections.
3. Larry Gelbart, "*My Wives Jane* Final Draft TV Script," December 11, 1970, Larry Gelbart Papers, UCLA Library Special Collections.
4. Stephen Rebello, "Janet Leigh on Surviving Hollywood with Style and Grace," *Movieline*, January 1, 1991, 86.
5. Dave Kaufman, "On All Channels," *Variety*, September 9, 1976.

Peter Lorre

1. Quoted in Stephen D. Youngkin, *The Lost One: A Life of Peter Lorre* (Lexington: University Press of Kentucky, 2005), 20.
2. Morton Fine and David Friedkin, "Giver and Taker Pilot Script," undated, Mort Fine Papers 1950–1968, UCLA Special Collections Library.
3. Youngkin, *The Lost One*, 386.

Myrna Loy

1. James Devane, "Look & Listen," *The Cincinnati Enquirer*, August 4, 1953.
2. Dave Kaufman, "On All Channels," *Variety*, August 27, 1957.
3. George Oppenheimer, "*Myrna Loy Show*: 'The Boltons Go to Brackton,'" Second Revised Draft, January 16, 1958, George Oppenheimer Papers 1943–1977, Billy Rose Theatre Division, New York Public Library.
4. David Everitt, *King of the Half Hour: Nat Hiken and the Golden Age of TV Comedy* (Syracuse: Syracuse University Press, 2001), 178.

Chico, Groucho, and Harpo Marx

1. Christine Becker, *It's the Pictures That Got Small*, 74.
2. Ted Newsom, "Deputy Seraph," *Filmfax*, March/April, 1989, 54–55.
3. Philip Rapp, *The Television Scripts of Philip Rapp: From the Marx Brothers to Joan Davis*, Albany, GA: Bear Manor Media, 2007, 3–60.
4. Newsom, "Deputy Seraph."
5. Jack Hellman, "Light and Airy," *Variety*, June 22, 1959.
6. Gore Vidal, "The Magical Monarch of Mo Script," Norman Lessing Papers 1943–1982, UCLA Library Special Collections.
7. "Jaffe and Groucho Spec May Become Series on NBC-TV," *Variety*, August 26, 1960.
8. Frank Gabrielson and Bob Dwan, "Groucho Marx in the Magical Monarch of Mo," Monarch 2nd Script, Norman Lessing Papers 1943–1982, UCLA Library Special Collections.
9. Sidney Sheldon, "That's the Spirit," undated, Sidney Sheldon Papers, Wisconsin Center for Film and Theater Research, Wisconsin Historical Society.
10. Sidney Sheldon, "Just Call Me Julius," Revised Draft, September 29, 1964, Sidney Sheldon Papers, Wisconsin Center for Film and Theater Research, Wisconsin Historical Society.
11. *Ibid.*
12. Stefan Kanfer, *Groucho: The Life and Times of Julius Henry Marx* (New York: Vintage Books, 2000), 365.

Roddy McDowall

1. Norman Lear, private communication with author, February 1, 2016.
2. John Fink, private communication with author, October 12, 2015.

Ethel Merman

1. Erskine Johnson, "Hollywood," *Shamokin News-Dispatch*, December 16, 1961.
2. Quoted in Caryl Flinn, *Brass Diva: The Life and Legends of Ethel Merman* (Berkeley: University of California Press, 2007), 341–342.
3. Susan Watson, private communication with author, October 12, 2015.

Pat O'Brien

1. Hal Humphrey, "Pat O'Brien Refuses Crime Show Offers," *The Pittsburgh Press*, June 22, 1952.
2. "Pat O'Brien at 60 Is Too Young to Quit Acting," *The Daily Notes* (Canonsburg, PA), October 20, 1960.
3. Fred Remington, "No Laugh Track! Was Pat O'Brien's Condition for TV," *The Pittsburgh Press*, October 12, 1960.
4. "Pat O'Brien at 60," *The Daily Notes*.
5. Roger Perry, private communication with author, March 31, 2016.

Maureen O'Hara

1. Dave Kaufman, "On All Channels," *Variety*, August 30, 1957.
2. William Spier, *The Woman in the Case*, undated, William Spier and June Havoc Papers 1931–1963, Wisconsin Center for Film and Theater Research, Wisconsin Historical Society.
3. "Maureen O'Hara to Star in CBS-TV Series, 'Woman,'" *Variety*, August 26, 1958.
4. J.P. Miller, "*Woman in the Case*: Open Windows," undated, James Pinckney Miller Papers 1939–1999, University of Texas at Austin Library.
5. David P. Harmon, "*The Woman in the Case*: The Ninth Commandment," undated, Broadcasting Collection, American Radio Archives Collection, Thousand Oaks Library.

6. "Maureen O'Hara Nixes All Vidpix; Does Only Live TV," *Variety*, August 16, 1962.
7. Charles Andrews and John Hese, "*Daphne! The Skin Game*," September 27, 1965, Morton DaCosta Papers 1929–1978, Billy Rose Theatre Division, New York Public Library.

Anthony Perkins

1. Quoted in Bradford Evans, "The Lost Projects of 'Sledge Hammer!' Creator Alan Spencer," Splitsider.com, February 7, 2013, retrieved January 28, 2016.

Jane Powell

1. Dave Kaufman, "On All Channels," *Variety*, July 12, 1957.
2. Jack Tellander, "Calamity," undated, Jane Powell Papers 1911–1993, American Heritage Center, University of Wyoming.
3. Lynda Hirsch, "Daytime Dial: Jane Powell is 'Loving' Soap Role," *Reno-Gazette Journal*, August 29, 1985.

Basil Rathbone

1. Tex McCrary and Jinx Falkenburg, "Radioactivity," *Variety*, September 26, 1951.
2. "Basil Rathbone Plays Sherlock in Vidpix," *Variety*, December 14, 1951.
3. Walter Winchell, "On Broadway," *St. Louis Post-Dispatch*, July 22, 1952.
4. William Wellman, Jr., Private communication with author, December 4, 2015.
5. Vernon Scott, "Basil Rathbone to Start TV Series," *The Times* (San Mateo, CA), February 1, 1961.
6. Maurice Richlin, "*The Pirates of Flounder Bay*: Pilot Teleplay," Revised Second Draft, December 8, 1965, TV Script Collection, Popular Culture Library, Bowling Green State University.

Jane Russell

1. Hal Humphrey, "All Those TV Buckskin Heroes Did Wrong by Jane Russell," *Detroit Free Press*, January 25, 1959.
2. Bob Barbash, "Guns and Guitar," Final Revised Script, September 29, 1958, TV Script Collection, Popular Culture Library, Bowling Green State University.
3. Hal Humphrey, "All Those TV Buckskin Heroes."
4. Bob Thomas, "Jane Russell Happy with Supporting Role on 'The Yellow Rose,'" *Asbury Park Press*, December 27, 1983.

Randolph Scott

1. "Great Scott!" *Variety*, May 16, 1956.

Zachary Scott

1. Geoffrey Homes, "*Reno English*: 'The Lady with the Scales,'" February 1, 1954, Daniel Mainwaring Papers 1930–1970, UCLA Library Special Collections.

Ann Sheridan

1. Vincent Sherman, *Studio Affairs: My Life as a Film Director* (Lexington: University of Kentucky Press, 1996), 155.
2. Erskine Johnson, "Hollywood Today," *The Corpus Christi Caller-Times*, October 16, 1956.
3. Norman Lessing, "Pilot Script for Ann Sheridan," undated, Norman Lessing Papers 1943–1982, UCLA Library Special Collections.
4. Dave Kaufman, "Ann Sheridan Home Again—In TV; Shirley Booth Series?" *Variety*, July 26, 1966.
5. *Ibid*.
6. Carole Wells, private communication with author, April 24, 2016.

Alexis Smith

1. Pete Hamill, "*Nightside*: Revised Third Draft Script," January 29, 1973, Herbert Leonard Papers 1957–1977, UCLA Library Special Collections.
2. Jerry Krupnick, "Smith Back on 'Dallas' in Rich Role," *The Journal News* (White Plains, NY), April 6, 1984.

Barbara Stanwyck

1. Vernon Scott," 'No Soap!—I'm an Actress,' Says Barbara Stanwyck to TV," *The Brooklyn Daily Eagle*, November 30, 1953.
2. *Ibid*.
3. Charles Denton, "TV from Hollywood," *The Tipton Daily Tribune*, January 13, 1958.
4. Dave Kaufman, "On All Channels," *Variety*, February 17, 1959.
5. Jack Hellman, "Light and Airy," *Variety*, August 24, 1961.
6. Jackie Cooper with Dick Kleiner, *The*

Autobiography of Jackie Cooper: Please Don't Shoot My Dog (New York: William Morrow, 1981), 261.

7. Hal Humphrey, "A Two-Fisted Cowgirl," *The Akron Beacon Journal*, August 8, 1965.

8. Christopher Knopf, private communication with author, March 24, 2016.

9. Army Archerd, "Hollywood Cross-Cuts," *Variety*, July 16, 1969.

10. Richard DeRoy, "Until Proven Guilty, First Draft Script," November 6, 1969, William Dozier Collection, American Heritage Center, University of Wyoming.

11. Gay Talese, private communication with author, March 22, 2016.

12. Jerry Beck, "Miss Stanwyck Stars in Male Version of 'Charlie's Angels,'" *The Palm Beach Post*, April 2, 1980.

13. *Ibid.*

Gloria Swanson

1. Information about *The Gloria Swanson Show* obtained from the Gloria Swanson Papers, Harry Ransom Humanities Research Center, University of Texas at Austin.

2. Gloria Swanson, letter to Irving Salkow, March 20, 1952, Gloria Swanson Papers, Harry Ransom Humanities Research Center.

3. Gloria Swanson, letter to Thomas G. Sabin, October 24, 1952, Gloria Swanson Papers, Harry Ransom Humanities Research Center.

4. Stephen Michael Shearer, *Gloria Swanson: The Ultimate Star* (New York: St. Martin's Press, 2013), 283–284.

5. Larry Gelbart, "'Remember Mona Faye,' TV script," undated, Larry Gelbart Papers, UCLA Library Special Collections.

6. Jack Solomon, Jr., letter to Leo J. Shapiro, January 31, 1967, Gloria Swanson Papers, Harry Ransom Humanities Research Center.

Shirley Temple

1. Bill Hayes, private communication with author, November 21, 2015.

2. Dave Kaufman, "On All Channels," *Variety*, June 10, 1965.

Orson Welles

1. Desi Arnaz, *A Book* (New York: William Morrow, 1976), 305.

2. Quoted in Peter Prescott Tonguette, *Orson Welles Remembered: Interviews with His Actors, Editors, Cinematographers and Magicians* (Jefferson, NC: McFarland, 2007), 33.

3. Coyne Steven Sanders and Tom Gilbert, *Desilu: The Story of Lucille Ball and Desi Arnaz* (New York: William Morrow, 1993), 121.

4. *Ibid.*

5. Rick Jason, "Orson Welles and Feet of Clay," *Scrapbooks of My Mind*, retrieved August 7, 2015.

6. "Arnaz Prescription for Pushing Vidpix Sales: Make Pilots (Plural)," *Variety*, November 2, 1956.

7. Erskine Johnson, "In Hollywood," *Redlands Daily Facts*, April 29, 1957.

8. Orson Welles and Harry Ackerman, "*The Family Robinson*: A New Kind of Family Adventure Series," 1956, Papers of Harry Ackerman, Rauner Special Collections Library, Dartmouth Library.

9. Desi Arnaz, *A Book*, 306–307.

10. *Ibid.*

11. Oja Kodar was an actress and screenwriter as well as Welles' mistress during the final years of his life.

12. *Orson's Bag* (1968–1970) draft pages, Orson Welles-Oja Kodar Papers 1910–1998, University of Michigan. Other quotations relating to the content of *Orson's Bag* also come from these papers.

13. Tonguette, *Orson Welles Remembered*, 174.

14. TV Review, "The One Thousand Dozen," *Variety*, May 20, 1981.

15. Stephen Farber, "TV Show Lets Viewers Solve Crime," *New York Times*, September 24, 1984.

Mae West

1. "Dummy and Dame Arouse the Nation," *Broadcasting*, October 15, 1956.

2. "Mae West on TV Maybe," *The Plain Speaker* (Hazleton, PA), April 26, 1950.

3. Emily Wortis Leider, *Becoming Mae West* (New York: Farrar, Straus and Giroux, 1997), 140–141.

4. Mae West, "Diamond Lil: A Teleplay Treatment of her Internationally Famous Stage Play," undated, Mae West Collection, Margaret Herrick Library, Academy of Motion Picture Arts and Sciences.

5. Erskine Johnson, "Mae West Will Demonstrate Great Romances in History," *Long Beach Independent*, August 18, 1953.

6. "Catherine of Russia outline," undated, Mae West Collection, Margaret Herrick Library, Academy of Motion Picture Arts and Sciences.

7. Ibid.

8. "Untitled," circa 1956–59, Scripts Written for Mae West When She Was Thinking of Doing a TV Series, Mae West Collection, Margaret Herrick Library, Academy of Motion Picture Arts and Sciences. While there is no author listed for this treatment, the other treatments for the Glory Carter series were written by Dahl Lee Lyons, and so presumably was this one.

9. Dahl Lee Lyons, "Portrait of a Lady: An Original Story Written for Miss Mae West," September 16, 1958, Mae West Collection, Margaret Herrick Library, Academy of Motion Picture Arts and Sciences.

10. Dahl Lee Lyons, "The Lady and The Lawman: An Original Story Written for Miss Mae West," October 14, 1958, Mae West Collection, Margaret Herrick Library, Academy of Motion Picture Arts and Sciences.

11. "List of Material for Mae West TV Series," undated, Mae West Collection, Margaret Herrick Library, Academy of Motion Picture Arts and Sciences.

12. "Come Up and See Me Sometime: Outline for TV Series of 13 Half-Hour Films," undated, Mae West Collection, Margaret Herrick Library, Academy of Motion Picture Arts and Sciences.

13. Jack Kinney, *Walt Disney and Assorted Other Characters: An Unauthorized Account of the Early Years at Disney's* (New York: Harmony Books, 1988), 187.

14. Simon Louvish, *Mae West: It Ain't No Sin* (New York: St. Martin's Press, 2005), 414.

Esther Williams

1. Dave Kaufman, "On All Channels," *Variety*, March 18, 1958.

2. Eve Starr, "Inside TV," *The Oregon Statesman*, January 14, 1959.

3. Jack Hellman, "Light and Airy," *Variety*, March 2, 1959.

4. S.L. Remark, "Preparation for TV Series," undated, Shirley Jones Papers 1942–1980, UCLA Library Special Collections. Since the treatment for the *Esther Williams Show* was part of the Shirley Jones Papers, one can conclude that Ms. Jones was considered for a role on the proposed series probably as the sister-in-law.

Shelley Winters

1. Steve Pritzker, private communication with author, June 28, 2016.

2. Robert Kaufman and Steve Pritzker, "*The Shelley Winters Show* Pilot Script," November 29, 1973, Steve Pritzker Papers 1967–1986, UCLA Library Special Collections.

3. Dick Kleiner, "TV Series Possibility for Shelley Winters," *Journal Gazette* (Mattoon, IL), August 27, 1974.

4. Andy Lewis, private communication with author, September 21, 2015.

5. Barry Primus, private communication with author, September 11, 2015.

6. Peter Bonerz, private communication with author, July 29, 2015.

Bibliography

Andersen, Christopher P. *A Star Is a Star, IS A STAR!* Garden City, NY: Doubleday, 1980.

Archerd, Army, "Just for Variety," *Variety*, 1960, 1961, 1972.

Arnaz, Desi. *A Book*. New York: William Morrow, 1976.

Becker, Christine. *It's the Pictures That Got Small*. Middletown, CT: Wesleyan University Press, 2008.

Bruck, Connie. *When Hollywood Had a King: The Reign of Lew Wasserman, Who Leveraged Talent into Power and Influence*. New York: Random House, 2003.

Capua, Michelangelo. *Janet Leigh: A Biography*. Jefferson, NC: McFarland, 2013.

Cooper, Jackie, with Dick Kleiner. *The Autobiography of Jackie Cooper: Please Don't Shoot My Dog*. New York: William Morrow, 1981.

Cushman, Joe. *Stephen Boyd: From Belfast to Hollywood*. FeedaRead.com Publishing, 2013.

Everitt, David. *King of the Half Hour: Nat Hiken and the Golden Age of TV Comedy*. Syracuse: Syracuse University Press, 2001

Flinn, Caryl, *Brass Diva: The Life and Legends of Ethel Merman*. Berkeley: University of California Press, 2007.

Fraser, John. *Close Up: An Actor Telling Tales*. London: Oberon Books, 2004.

Hellman, Jack. "Light & Airy." *Variety*, 1959, 1961.

Humphrey, Hal. Various columns. *The Los Angeles Times* Syndicate, 1952, 1959, 1962, 1965.

Johnson, Erskine. "Hollywood Today." Newspaper Enterprise Association Syndicate, 1953, 1956, 1957, 1961.

Kanfer, Stefan. *Groucho: The Life and Times of Julius Henry Marx*. New York: Vintage Books, 2000.

Kaufman, Dave. "On All Channels." *Variety*, 1953–59, 1961–62, 1965–66, 1976.

Kinney, Jack. *Walt Disney and Assorted Other Characters: An Unauthorized Account of the Early Years at Disney's*. New York: Harmony Books, 1988.

Kennedy, Matthew. *Joan Blondell: A Life between Takes*. Jackson: University Press of Mississippi Press, 2007.

Leider, Emily Wortis. *Becoming Mae West*. New York: Farrar, Straus and Giroux, 1997.

Levinson, Peter J. *Puttin' on The Ritz: Fred Astaire and the Fine Art of Panache*. New York: St. Martin's Press, 2009.

Louvish, Simon. *Mae West: It Ain't No Sin*. New York: St. Martin's Press, 2005.

Miller, Merle, and Evan Rhodes. *Only You Dick Daring! Or How to Write One Television Script and Make $50,000,000*. New York: Berkley Publishing Corporation, 1964.

Rapp, Philip. *The Television Scripts of Philip Rapp: From the Marx Brothers to Joan Davis*. Albany, GA: Bear Manor Media, 2007.

Sanders, Coyne Steven, and Tom Gilbert. *Desilu: The Story of Lucille Ball and Desi Arnaz*. New York: William Morrow, 1993.

Scott, Vernon. Various columns. United Press International, 1953, 1958, 1961.

Shearer, Stephen Michael. *Beautiful: The Life of Hedy Lamarr*. New York: St. Martin's Press, 2010.

_____. *Gloria Swanson: The Ultimate Star*. New York: St. Martin's Press, 2013.

Sherman, Vincent. *Studio Affairs: My Life as a Film Director*. Lexington: University of Kentucky Press, 1996.

Shiach, Don. *Stewart Granger: The Last of the Swashbucklers*. London: Aurum Press Limited, 2005.

Stine, Whitney. *Mother Goddam: The Story of the Career of Bette Davis*. New York: Hawthorn Books, 1974.

Tonguette, Peter Prescott. *Orson Welles Remembered: Interviews with His Actors, Editors, Cinematographers, and Magicians*. Jefferson, NC: McFarland, 2007.

Turk, Edward Baron. *Hollywood Diva: A Biography of Jeanette MacDonald*. Berkeley: University of California Press, 1998.

Youngkin, Stephen D. *The Lost One: A Life of Peter Lorre*. Lexington: University Press of Kentucky, 2005.

Index

ABC 8, 14–15, 19–21, 28–29, 37, 39, 43, 53, 58–59, 61–62, 71, 77, 79, 84–87, 89–90, 94, 97, 100, 104, 109, 119, 127, 135–36, 139, 145–48, 152, 154, 157, 162, 165, 168, 170, 172, 176–77, 179–82, 184, 186–87, 194, 199
Ace of the Mounties 19
Ackerman, Harry 13, 46, 167, 192
The Adventures of Mr. Pastry 92–93
Alcoa-Goodyear Theatre 150–51
Alcoa Premiere 8, 10
American Eagle 180
And Baby Makes Three 19
Arnaz, Desi 2–3, 5, 84, 139, 143, 158–59, 190–92, 194
Around the World with Orson Welles 189, 195
Assignment Tokyo 138
Astaire, Fred 1, 7–12, 45, 56, 150
"At Your Service" 85
Attention for Invention 184–85

Ball, Lucille 1–3, 5, 18, 26, 94, 135
"Ballad for a Bad Man" 158–59
Banyon 16
Barbara Stanwyck Presents 174
The Barbara Stanwyck Show 175–76, 179
The Bette Davis Show 36, 38
The Betty Hutton Show 82
Big Rose: Double Trouble 211
The Big Valley 5–6, 177–80
Blondell, Joan 3, 15–21
Bobby Parker and Company 21
Box 13 97
Boyd, Stephen 22–24
Boyer, Charles 2–4, 64, 101, 150
Bridges to Cross 60, 131
Brolin, James 44
Bulldog Drummond 53
The Buster Keaton Show 92

Calamity 152
Calamity Jane 16
Calhoun 177
Call Her Mom 87–88
Call Me Ethel 134
Calling Terry Conway 166–67
Captain Kidd 54
Carnival 134
Cassidy Collins and Complexes 80
CBS 4, 12–14, 18, 26, 29, 33, 45–46, 57–62, 73–74, 77, 79–80, 82–87, 105, 107, 109–10, 112, 114, 116, 124, 132, 134, 136, 138, 141–44, 150–53, 156–57, 168, 177, 180, 185, 189, 191–95, 197, 205–6, 211–12
Chertock, Jack 4, 106, 166
The Chevy Show 13, 80, 123
The Claudette Colbert Show 26
A Closer Look 198
Colbert, Claudette 25–27, 31, 46, 64, 187
The Colbys 181
Collector's Item 111–12
The College Bowl 119
Columbia Pictures/Screen Gems 5, 25, 32–33, 46, 57, 69, 93, 115, 124–25, 134, 150–51, 160, 174, 195
Come Up and See Me Sometime 205
Conway and Company 148
Cooper, Gary 5, 28–29, 31
The Covenant 59–60
Crawford, Joan 3, 5, 7, 15, 30–35, 51, 57, 64, 151, 164
Crown Theatre 184
Cyn's for Me 152

Dallas 172
Daphne! 143
Dark Mansions 65–66
The Dark Side 195
Davis, Bette 1, 3, 5, 15, 30, 35–44, 61, 155, 166
DeMave, Jack 42
The Deputy Seraph 119–20, 122, 125
Desilu 2, 4–5, 17–18, 27, 68, 83–84, 116, 134–35, 139, 143, 152, 158, 175–76, 189–91, 194
Don't Blame Jane 158
Douglas Fairbanks, Jr. Presents 51, 53–56
The Dramatic Hour 173
Dunne, Irene 45–47, 162

Eddy, Nelson 48–49
Emma's First National Bank 68–69
Enigma 98
Everything Money Can't Buy 58–59

Fable Time 99
The Fabulous Oliver Chantry 160
Fairbanks, Douglas, Jr. 3–4, 12, 30, 51–55
Fairbanks, Douglas, Sr. 51, 55–56
Family Reunion 44
Famous Women of History 202

Index

Fantastic Journey 130
"Farewell to Kennedy" 95–96
Ferrer, Jose 57–60
Fitzgerald, Geraldine 61–63
Fitzgerald and Pride (aka *Heat of Anger*) 76–77, 180
Fontaine, Joan 26, 64–67, 160
For the Defense 155
For the First Time 12
Foreign Legion 53
Four Star Playhouse 2, 13, 26, 103, 150
Four Star Productions 2, 4–5, 15, 19, 26, 33, 38, 70, 85, 98, 150–52, 157, 175, 179
The Fred Astaire Show (situation comedy) 10–11
Furia, John, Jr. 44

Galaxy Beat 133
The Gaucho 55
Gaynor, Janet 68–69
General Electric Theater 4, 7, 17, 32, 47, 58, 85, 95–97, 115, 121–22
George Sanders Mystery Theatre 160
The Getter and the Holder 110–11
The Ghostwriter 145–46
The Ginger Rogers Show 13
Glitter 89–90
The Gloria Swanson Hour 182
Gloria Swanson Reminisces 184
The Gloria Swanson Show 182–84
Go Fight City Hall 47
Goodson-Todman 4, 33, 103, 105, 127, 185
Grandparents 147
Granger, Stewart 70–72
Grant, Cary 1, 45, 51, 64, 114, 162, 166, 170, 187, 200, 203
Grayson, Kathryn 73–75
Great American Short Stories 198
Great Loves 101
Greene, David 40

Hal Roach Studios 4–5, 36, 147, 160
Harrigan and Son 139
Hayward, Susan 38, 76–78, 180
Hello Mother, Goodbye 42
Here Come the Brides 16
Holiday 64
Hong Kong Express, 99
Hooray for Hollywood 18
Hotel 14, 44
Hothouse 172
The Hound of the Baskervilles 71–72
The House of Four Keys 70
The House of Riddle 195
Humor Around the World 99
Hutton, Betty 79–83

I Love Lucy 2, 4, 17, 81, 84, 119, 157, 189, 192
I Take Thee Susan 128
In the Land of Don Quixote 195
"The Incredible Jewel Robbery" 121–22

Inside Danny Baker 100
It Gives Me Great Pleasure 114, 165
It Takes a Thief 11
Ivy League 98

Jack London's Tales of the Klondike 199
The Jacksons 17–18
The Jane Powell Show 151–52
The Janet Leigh Show 106
The Joan Blondell Show 17
The Joan Crawford Show 33
Johnson, Van 3, 5, 84–91, 105
The Judge and Jake Wyler 41
Just Call Me Julius 126

The Kathryn Grayson Show 74
Keaton, Buster 91–94
Key West 22–24
Klondike Lil 202–3
Kona Coast 20

Ladd, Alan 3, 95–100
Lady Law 174
Lamarr, Hedy 3, 101–4
Leave It to Liz 25–26
Leigh, Janet 105–9
Life with Buster Keaton 92
London, Jerry 44
London and Davis in New York 130–31
Lone Woman 73
Lorre, Peter 110–13
Love Boat 44
Love Story 174
Love That Channel 13
Loy, Myrna 3, 57, 114–17, 165, 187, 212
Lupino, Ida 2, 64, 103, 150

Mabel and Max 62–63
MacCreedy's Woman 157
MacDonald, Jeanette 48–50
Madame Sin 40, 44
Madame's Place 37
Mae West Tells All About Love 205
Maggie Brown 134–35
The Magical Monarch of Mo 123
The Magnificent Montagues 116
The Man from the Pentagon 105
Man in the Middle 87
A Man's World 137
Mars, Kenneth 42
Marx, Chico 118–22, 124
Marx, Groucho 3, 5, 12, 104, 118–27
Marx, Harpo 118–24
MCA 4–5, 7, 31, 114, 134
McDowall, Roddy 128, 130–33
Medicine Man 93
Meet Maggie Mulligan 105
Merman, Ethel 134–36, 183
MGM Parade 147
Miner, Allen H. 36–37, 157
Mr. Kingston 148

Morgan and McBride 37
Morheim, Lou 40
Mother Is a Freshman 170
Mother Was a Swinger 83
Mrs. Thursday 20
My Wives Jane 106
The Myrna Loy Show (aka *Minerva*) 115

NBC 1, 8–10, 13, 16–17, 21, 24, 26, 32–33, 41–42, 51–52, 55, 57, 59, 65, 67–68, 70, 72, 79–80, 86, 88, 90, 116, 118, 124, 134, 143, 146–47, 149–50, 152, 159, 168, 173, 175–76, 178, 187, 192–93, 195, 198–99, 200, 208
Nelson Eddy's Back Yard! 48
Nero Wolfe 198–99
Nightside 170–71
Niven, David 2–4, 150

O'Brien, Pat 137–40
Officer Murphy 93
O'Hara, Maureen 141–44
On Our Way 108–9
Oringer, Barry 40, 44
Orson Welles and People 192
Orson Welles' Great Mysteries 199
The Orson Welles Show (anthology) 190–92
The Orson Welles Show (talk) 197–98
Orson Welles' Sketch Book 189
Orson's Bag 196–97
The Over-the-Hill Gang 140

Papa Romani 119
Parole Chief 137–38
The Pat O'Brien Show 137
Paula 36
Perkins, Anthony 145–46
Petal, Erica 42
Peter Lorre's Playhouse 112
Pidgeon, Walter 147–49
The Pirates of Flounder Bay 154
Pistols 'n' Petticoats 168–69
Planet of the Apes 130
Playhouse 90 73–74, 85, 193
Playhouse of the Stars 45
Police Boat 55
"Portrait of Gina" 193–94
Powell, Dick 1–4, 13, 15, 19, 20, 33 78, 85, 98, 150–51, 157, 162, 174–75, 209
Powell, Jane 7, 103, 150–52, 158
The President of Love 88, 90
Pretty Mae 206
Prima Donna 49
The Protectors 86

The Quinns 61

Randolph Scott's Theater of the West 162–63
Rathbone, Basil 153–54
Remember Mona Faye 185
Remo Williams 131–32
Reno English 164–65

The Return of Captain Nemo 59
Revue 4–5, 7, 10, 17, 32, 34, 47, 115
Rhubarb 127
The Ringmaster 160
Ringside 137, 173
Roach, Hal, Jr. 134, 138, 173
Robinson, Edward G. 3, 51, 155–56
Rogers, Ginger 7, 12–14, 45, 134, 150
Royal Bay 33
Royal Performance 57
Russell, Jane 157–59

Saddle Tramp 99
Safari 70
Sanders, George 160–61
Savage Is the Name 138
Say Goodbye, Maggie Cole 77
Scene of the Crime 199
School of Acting 92
Scott, Randolph 162–63, 203
Scott, Zachary 114, 164–65
The Seekers 176
Sellecca, Connie 44
Sharpe, Don 4, 18, 51, 53, 55
Shea, John 43
Shear, Barry 40
Shelley 212–13
The Shelley Winters Show 210
Sheridan, Ann 166–69
The Shirley Temple Show (comedy) 188
Shirley Temple's Storybook 123, 187
The Silent Man/Men 52
Sis 80
Sister Veronica 46
Six Star Playhouse 26, 33, 151, 175
Smile, Tiger 152
Smith, Alexis 170–72
Spelling, Aaron 5, 33, 38, 44, 65–66, 78, 90, 98–99, 140, 175, 181
Stanwyck, Barbara 5–6, 38, 76, 137, 151, 155, 173–81
Stewart, Jimmy 41–42
Swanson, Gloria 91, 182–85
Sweet Sixteen 68

Take Her, She's Mine 85
Take My Advice 104
Tales of the Gold Monkey 130
Tell It to Groucho 124–25
Temple, Shirley 3, 123, 187–88
Terry and the Pirates 51
That's My Mom 81
That's the Spirit 125
Third Platoon 99
This Family Robinson 192–93
Three Angel Way 47
The Three Marx Brothers 124
Three Wishes 55
Toni's Boys 181
Topper 128–30
Tramp Ship 55

Tuttle, Lurene 42
Twentieth Century-Fox 13, 22, 76, 86, 112, 129, 170, 187–88, 209, 212

The Unexplained 194
Universal 34, 41, 72, 86, 180, 212
Until Proven Guilty 180
The Untouchables 84, 176, 194

Van Ark, Joan 41
Van Johnson's Amazing Stories 85
Vanity and Mrs. Fair 46
Van Patten, Vincent 42
Vincent, E. Duke 44
The Virginian (aka *The Men from Shiloh*) 70–71

War Birds 153–54
Warner Brothers 22, 24, 37, 74, 109, 194
The Ways of Love 65

The Weaker Sex 141
Welles, Orson 3, 105, 189–99
West, Mae 1, 5, 15, 149, 162, 200–7
What Do You Want? 124–25
What's New 185
Williams, Esther 208–9
Winfield, Elizabeth 44
Winters, Shelley 210–13
The Woman in the Case 141–43
The World and I 31–32
Worlds Beyond 99

The Yellow Rose 159
You Bet Your Life 5, 12, 104, 118, 120, 124–26
Young, Loretta 1–2, 5, 65, 175–76, 178
Your Lucky Clue 153
Your Neighborhood 137
You're Gonna Love It Here 135

Zane Grey Theater 5, 162, 174–75, 209

www.ingramcontent.com/pod-product-compliance
Ingram Content Group UK Ltd.
Pitfield, Milton Keynes, MK11 3LW, UK
UKHW041948140426
5217IPUK00014B/698